DATE DUE			

AMERICAN WESTERN ART

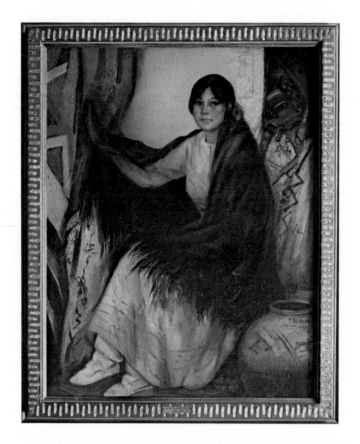

Taos Girl. 30 x 24 inches, oil. Julius Rolshoven.

WESTERN ART

A collection of

one hundred twenty-five

western paintings and sculpture

with biographies

of the artists

by Dorothy Harmsen

Foreword by Bill Harmsen

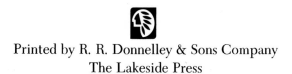

Printed by R. R. Donnelley & Sons Company
The Lakeside Press

F. C. Hilker, *Photographer*

Mildred Uhlig, *Editor*
Dick Hilker, *Assistant Editor*

ISBN 0-9601322-1-X
Library of Congress Number 77-080017

*To our grandchildren
William III, Amber, Lori, R. John Jr.,
Michael Jr., Patrick, Peter, and David*

State of Colorado

Executive Chambers

Denver

Publication of this second volume of western paintings from the collection of Bill and Dorothy Harmsen is a milestone. Because they recognized early that the significance of Western painting was being ignored, particularly in Colorado, the Harmsens began collecting with a mission. As this volume reveals, their efforts were foresightful because we have come to understand the value of western painting. We now know that such paintings reveal for us an authentic representation of the early West. Through them, we better understand our heritage.

Richard D. Lamm
Governor of Colorado

CONTENTS

FRONTISPIECE

THE VERY FIRST PAINTING we acquired was a nearly lifesize portrait of my husband Bill, Sr., as a young boy. It has held a prominent place in our home for thirty-eight years. The painting could be called a family portrait, as it reflects the countenance of so many members of this family . . . any one of our three sons and four of our six grandsons could have been the subject.

I saw a print of this painting hanging in Bill's home in 1937. The artist was Frances Cranmer Greenman, who lived in Minneapolis, Minnesota.

Mrs. Greenman first saw Bill and his mother on a streetcar in Minneapolis in 1919. She spoke to his mother, and then told young Bill, "Billy, you have the best brick-colored hair and the bluest eyes I have ever seen, I want to paint you." The sittings required many tedious hours.

After completion, the painting was sent to the 84th Annual Exhibition of American Artists in Chicago, called the "American Show" in the ateliers. More than 2,000 paintings were submitted by American artists—only 195 were exhibited. "The Boy" became the talk of the Chicago art world.

Eventually the Northwestern National Bank in Minneapolis reproduced the painting on a calendar in 1924. During the following years the canvas was sent to Europe for exhibition. The Harmsen family had lost contact with the now famous work of art.

In 1939, after we had been married for three months, I was walking down Nicollet Avenue in Minneapolis past French's Decorating Studio. As I was admiring the art objects in the window, time seemed to stop. There was the original version of the treasured calendar print. Still unbelieving, I entered the studio and inquired about it. Learning that the painting had just returned from Europe, I was told it was for sale at what seemed to me an incredibly high price. But the artist was again working in Minneapolis.

Bill and I called on Mrs. Greenman at precisely the right moment. She again saw the paintable, intangible something in my husband's face and stature. At that time she was attempting to paint a large portrait of Emil Oberhoffer, the man who was the first conductor of the Minneapolis Symphony Orchestra. Doing this from an old tintype had seemed to her a hopeless commission. Then, Bill Harmsen walked in with the same coloring, brow, and presence as the deceased man she was attempting to recapture.

Mrs. Greenman prevailed on "The Boy" to be a stand-in for her subject—which he agreed to do with cape and cane, seated in a wicker chair, while she measured, gyrated, and tore at her mop of blond-gray hair.

"The Boy" has hung in our home ever since. It was made available to us by the grateful artist of a very paintable subject. (See Page 80.)

Dorothy Harmsen

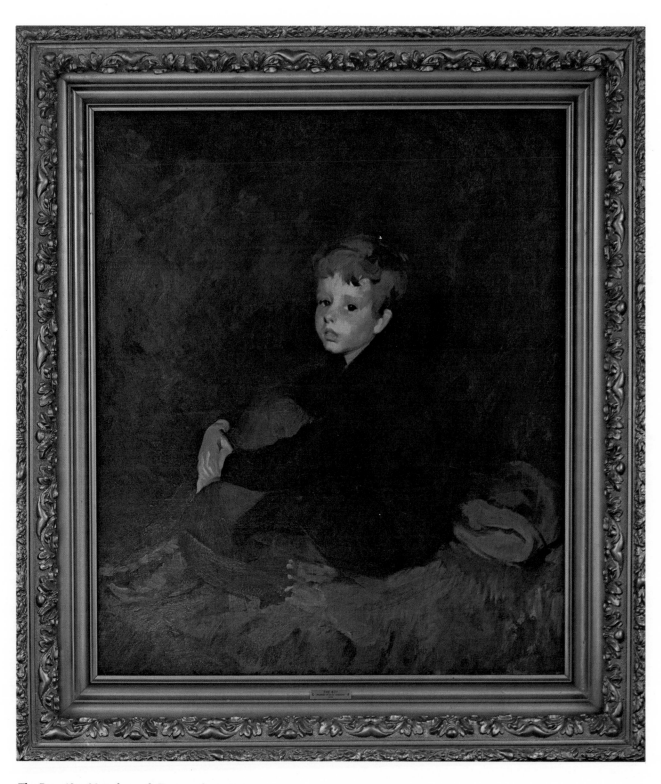

The Boy. 40 x 36 inches, oil. Frances Greenman.

FOREWORD

REVIEWING MY YEARS of acquiring western art gives me both pleasure and satisfaction—far greater than I had anticipated, considering the lack of knowledge and the financial risk involved when we first started putting this collection together in 1967.

Having had some exposure through previous years by visiting antique shops and galleries with my wife, Dorothy, it wasn't until I was taken by an interesting painting by a Colorado artist, John Howland, titled "In Ute Country," that I really became addicted. I was encouraged by a very astute remark made by our oldest son, Bill, Jr. "Dad," he said, "you can enjoy looking at that painting a lot more than at a stock certificate hanging on the wall." Eleven Raphael Lillywhites followed, then twenty-three Frank Hoffmans, and thirteen paintings by a young contemporary artist. Shortly after this, I found an A. D. M. Cooper, six by nine feet and in pretty sad shape, in a meat shop owned by a Japanese butcher in Golden, Colorado. After restoration and reframing, the problem arose—what to do with it?

By this time Dorothy was wondering what had happened to me—to be honest, I also wondered—and knew that I had to have a plan and an ultimate goal. Going too much in one direction is a common error of many inexperienced collectors.

Believing that it is important for both husband and wife to share a monumental interest such as this, I talked it over with Dorothy and she agreed to do the research, while I would do the buying. We bought every art reference book available, subscribed to art magazines, periodicals, and catalogs such as the *Kennedy Quarterly, American Art Review,* and the *Archives of American Art Journal.* Two books which became of particular interest were *Taos and Its Artists,* by Mabel Dodge Luhan, and *Taos and Santa Fe; The Artist's Environment,* by Van Deren Coke. On the back of each of the book jackets are listed the names of the more important artists of this Southwest area. Having purchased paintings by many of the artists listed, I checked them off on the covers. As the check marks increased, the ones unchecked became more important to find. No collector with six or seven of the famous "Taos Ten" would ever quit until he had them all. It was the same with "Los Cinco Pintores" in Santa Fe and other groups.

Once again we were carried away, but at least knew more or less what we were about. Our research made us more selective in our buying, because of the improvement and change in our art appreciation. We decided at this point to go all out and indulge in more major works of art, starting with John Mix Stanley, Alfred Jacob Miller, George Catlin, Albert Bierstadt, and Thomas Moran, gradually evolving into the John Marin, Marsden Hartley, Georgia O'Keeffe, Andrew Dasburg, and Robert Henri influences—still western in flavor, however.

Feeling we should become more aware of what was going on in the local art circles, we called on the director of a Colorado museum. During our conversation I was surprised to hear him say that "artists who had painted and were painting the western scene didn't know much about the West, it was doubtful if any of them had ever seen a buffalo, and most of them were Broadway cowboys." I replied that "Michelangelo had not seen the angels, but he managed a 'heck of a good job' painting them on the ceiling of the Sistine Chapel."

Shortly after this experience, Dean Krakel, a transplanted Coloradan, stopped by to see our collection. He is the director of the National Cowboy Hall of Fame and Western Heritage Center in Oklahoma City. Being concerned for the future of western art as I was, he asked me to serve on the Board of Trustees of the museum. This offer opened up many new channels for our interest in western art. It presented opportunities for both Dorothy and me to serve as judges for some of the Cowboy Artist and National Academy of Western Art shows. It was here we also learned to appreciate the magnificent medium of bronze sculpture.

In my younger days I was not interested in American history. Now it, in itself, has become a hobby through the development of our collection. Collecting also has created a sense of togetherness within our entire family, including our sons, Bill, Jr., Bob, and Mike and their families, as each member has developed a growing interest and appreciation of what Dorothy and I have tried to accomplish.

Acquiring some 700 paintings by about 300 artists is not only an art appreciation course, but a family venture, with an added bonus and something that cannot be measured in material values . . . the new friendships we have made—artists, dealers, collectors, and museum directors. This collecting has been very rewarding in every respect. I get a thrill when I walk into a museum, gallery, or art show and can recognize the artist of a particular painting from across the room, without first reading the signature . . . and I'm getting better at it. It is quite a challenge.

Bill Harmsen
1977   xi

INTRODUCTION

THE IMPORTANCE OF THIS COLLECTION of western art is inestimable. Besides visual enrichment, it offers educational opportunity for the serious student and collector of western art.

Each painting has a certain intrinsic value, which is determined by the art market of today, based on the quality of the painting, the prominence of the artist and his contribution to American art history, and, of course, the scarcity of his work in the event he is not a contemporary artist. The subject matter is also to be considered in the final analysis.

The Harmsen Collection of *American Western Art* is special because of its scope and variety. The student may use it as a visual aid for comparison or to follow the unwinding thread of adventure.

Russell and Remington will always go down in history as "the greats." They not only started the explosion in western art, they also liberated the much-maligned school of illustration. Being great illustrators themselves, they put western illustration into the field of art. My study revealed that most of the deceased artists represented in our collection were illustrators. It was their bread and butter until they could survive by pursuing their art careers in a less commercial manner. Many were the students of the great Howard Pyle, N. C. Wyeth, Harvey Dunn, and others. Of the contemporary artists in the collection, most of them started as illustrators or newspaper artists, and some still are.

We chose a timely period to start collecting western art—1967. This pre-dated by about three years the boom in western art collecting. However, the art market was sufficiently advanced so not all of the money invested was spent in one direction. Fortunately, our exposure was greatly diversified, and we ended up with more than 700 paintings by approximately 300 artists, a collection which encompasses many styles and periods in the western theme.

During our vigorous buying period, much research was required. The end result—we knew we had purchased major art: in some cases, unsung, forgotten, unappreciated artists, whose active periods came at a time when frontier America was more concerned with growth than the esthetics of our heritage. Research revealed the lives of many artists whose fame was "too little—too late" to rescue them from oblivion. In many instances their life stories seemed to die with them or were buried in the archives. There are many artists in this volume that fall into this category.

The Harmsen Collection includes many members and associates of the National Academy of Design, ethnologists, and topographical artists who accompanied the various expeditions into the new frontier, as well as painters who were employed by such engravers and printers as Peter Maverick, Louis Prang, and Currier and Ives. There are artists of the Hudson River School, the Ashcan School, the Taos and Santa Fe groups, including all members of Los Cinco Pintores, a few from the coterie of artists surrounding the Alfred Stieglitz Photo-Secession Gallery "291," and also the marvelous sculptors preserving the West in bronze.

There are many artists included who are classed as The Rocky Mountain School. The Rockies had a particular fascination for the eastern painters. Many were stricken with tuberculosis and came west looking for a cure. Others were suffering from wanderlust—they also found an answer to their physical and artistic needs. The WPA artists, who worked for the government projects during the depression years, decorating public buildings and civic areas, also are represented. There are members of the National Academy of Western Art at the National Cowboy Hall of Fame in Oklahoma City and also the Cowboy Artists of America Association. And last, but certainly among the forefront, the lesser-known contemporary artists into whose hands the future of western art will eventually fall.

There is a little bit of Sherlock Holmes in all of us and certainly a great deal of "whodunit" in art. The combination makes for great sport and at times a very exciting one. The discovery of a fine painting with an illegible signature and the deciphering of the name after months of research is reward in itself. The ultimate is to discover the elusive artist's name listed in the art reference books.

The paradox is that much of the fine western art purchased in the East is brought to the West. It also is true that much of the art from here in the West goes to the East, which proves there no longer are geographical boundaries in the arts. It all is American art—East or West.

Former *American Art Journal* founder Milton Esterow, editor and publisher of *ARTnews* magazine, has said: "Art is one of the most under-   xiii reported, mis-reported, and non-reported activities in modern life." He wants a more straightforward, clearer kind of writing, as "many art enthusiasts are turned off by the art jargon." This is the style in which this volume and our first book, *Harmsen's Western Americana,* published in 1971, are written. The facts about artists represented in this volume have been brought together from a thousand sources—checked, refined, condensed, and rewritten—to give the new and the experienced collector concise information, with a minimum of redundancy and superfluous adjectives, in a brief narrative style.

Many short stories on a given subject finally make one big story, and that is what these two volumes are—the story of *American Western Art.*

Dorothy Harmsen
1977

Editor's Note: The initials NA following an artist's name indicate National Academician. ANA refers to an associate of the academy, and AWS is the American Watercolor Society. Members of the Cowboy Artists of America are identified by CA.

INDEX

THE HARMSEN COLLECTION

Cassilly Adams

1843–1921

CASSILLY ADAMS PAINTED MANY western scenes. But he is best remembered for his epic work, "Custer's Last Fight," which he completed in 1885.

His rendering of that famous battle at the Big Horn River in Montana eventually was obtained by the Anheuser-Busch Brewing Company, which made thousands of reproductions for advertising and promotional purposes. Lithographs hung in taverns across the nation.

Born in Zanesville, Ohio, Adams was the son of William Apthorp Adams, a lawyer who traced his ancestry back to the John Adams family of Boston. The elder Adams was an amateur artist.

At an early age, young Adams was interested in art. He studied at the Boston Academy of Arts, under Thomas S. Noble, and later at the Cincinnati Art School.

He served in the army during the Civil War and was wounded while aboard the U.S.S. Osage at the Battle of Vicksburg.

Late in the 1870s, Adams moved to St. Louis where he found work as an artist and engraver.

"Custer's Last Fight" took one year to complete. As models he used actual Sioux Indians in battle dress and cavalrymen in uniforms of the period. The painting, which measured 9½ feet by 16 feet 5 inches, was produced for two members of the St. Louis Art Club, who exhibited the historical canvas around the country, charging a fifty-cent admission fee. The two promoters did not realize the profit they wanted from the venture, so they sold the painting to a St. Louis saloonkeeper who hung it in his barroom. When the saloon went bankrupt, the painting was acquired by one of the creditors— Anheuser-Busch Company. At that time it was valued at $10,000.

In 1895 the brewery gave the painting to the Seventh Cavalry. It was destroyed by fire at Fort Bliss, Texas, in 1946.

Adams is a relatively unknown artist, a victim of circumstance. Most of his illustrations were done for book publishers who did not credit him with the work. Therefore, many of his illustrations were borrowed for other books and were not attributed to him. Actually, he painted many scenes of frontier life, and it is known that he illustrated "Conquering the Wilderness" by Frank Triplett, published in 1883.

He died at Trader's Point near Indianapolis, Indiana.

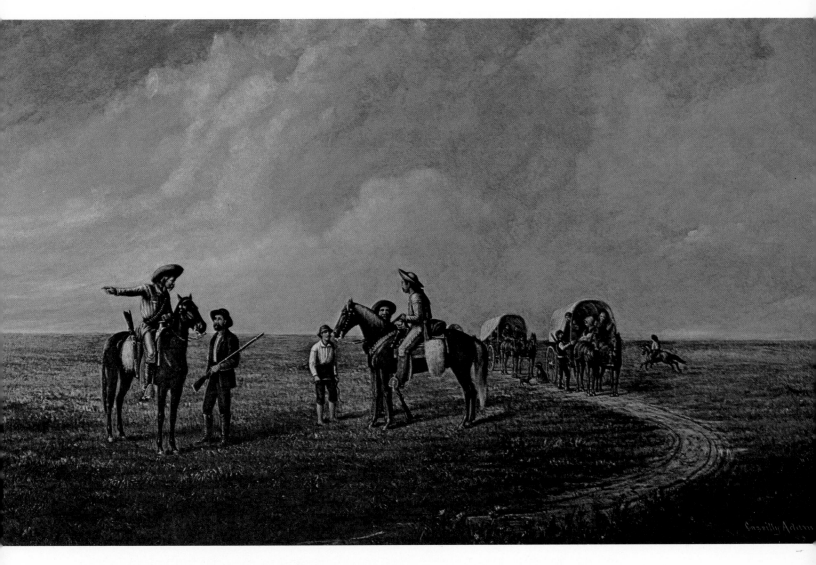

Warning the Wagon Train. Dated 1883. 30 x 50 inches, oil. Cassilly Adams.

Louis Akin

1868–1913

FROM PAINTING SIGNS in Portland, Oregon, Louis B. Akin became one of the foremost painters of western landscapes and Indian life. Before he died of pneumonia at age forty-five, Akin was known for his landscapes painted around Taos, New Mexico, and at the Grand Canyon in Arizona.

In 1903, he said of these places: "It is simply too good to leave. It's the best stuff in America and has scarcely been touched."

Akin also has been acknowledged for his work with the Hopi Indians in Arizona. On assignment from the Santa Fe Railway, in 1902, he spent over a year living in the Hopi village of Oraibi. Not only did he paint, he learned the Hopi language, became interested in preserving the tribe's traditions, and wrote several articles urging fair treatment and compassion for the Indians by the federal government.

This project gave him his first major opportunity for recognition in this field; his reputation brought him a commission from the Museum of Natural History in New York to decorate the room for the museum's southwestern Indian display.

Akin, the son of a western pioneer who crossed the Oregon Trail in the 1850s, was raised by an uncle after his parents died when he was a child. Sign painting was his first experience with art. He did not receive formal training until the age of twenty-eight, when he went from Portland to New York City to study at the New York Art School with William Merritt Chase and Frank Du Mond. He earned a living by working as a commercial artist and illustrator for outdoor magazines.

In 1905, he moved to Flagstaff, Arizona, to concentrate on painting the Grand Canyon area. Many of Akin's canyon paintings were commissioned by the Santa Fe Railway, and reproductions were widely circulated by restaurateur Fred Harvey. Akin's largest painting of the canyon is still on display at Verkamps at the South Rim. It measures six by nine feet.

Akin's paintings were exhibited by the National Academy of Design, the Pennsylvania Academy, and the Chicago Art Institute. Much of his work still can be seen in collections and museums throughout America specializing in early western paintings.

4

He was only briefly married and left no children. Akin died in Flagstaff.

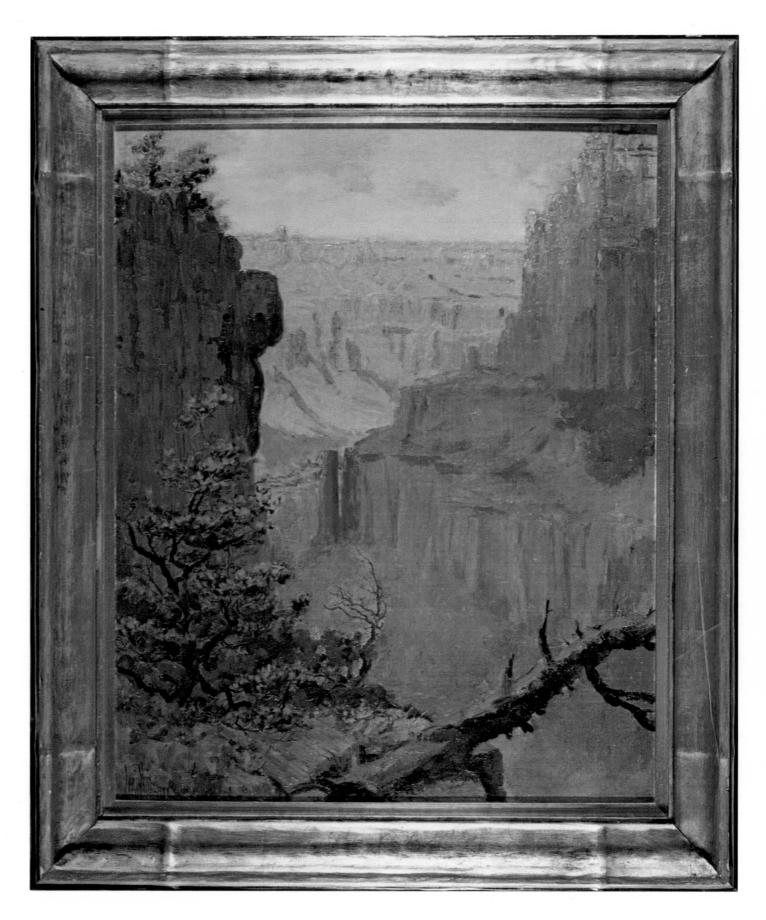

Grand Canyon. Dated 1908. 26 x 22 inches, oil. Louis Akin.

Stanley Arthurs

1877–1950

A NATIVE OF DELAWARE he is the state's artist laureate and the only artist ever commissioned by its General Assembly to paint murals. Arthurs produced a pictorial synthesis of America, from colonial times through the Civil War period, with scores of historically important paintings.

The colonial and Revolutionary periods had romantic appeal. Arthurs captured this aspect of the time, but also insisted on accuracy. His work is refreshingly factual, the result of a great deal of careful research. In fact, Arthurs became quite an authority on American history. In many instances he employed a seamstress to reconstruct authentic uniforms and costumes of the period to use as props for the historical concepts he incorporated in many of his paintings.

Arthurs was a student and associate of the famed illustrator, Howard Pyle, whose work appeared in many of the leading magazines of that day. Other students of Pyle at the Drexel Institute in Philadelphia and at his summer classes at Chadds Ford, Pennsylvania, included Maxfield Parrish, N.C. Wyeth, Frank Schoonover, and Harvey Dunn.

Editors from Harpers, Century, Scribners, Colliers, and Houghton, Mifflin and Company eagerly commissioned Pyle's better pupils to do book and magazine illustrations. The first published work of Arthurs appeared in *Harper's Weekly*, December 2, 1899. The work was widely acclaimed; thus, Arthurs became one of the featured young artists in Pyle's studio in Wilmington, Delaware. Following Pyle's death in 1912, Arthurs purchased the studio. It was the heyday of American illustration on the eastern seaboard and the western frontier, and Arthurs was very much a part of it.

Blanche Swain of Wilmington and Arthurs were engaged for forty-two years, but circumstances did not permit their marriage.

In his final years, although suffering from cancer, Arthurs continued to work. After his death, Miss Swain experienced considerable anguish when his paintings were sold at a Philadelphia auction house at extremely low prices; also, many of his notes and sketches were destroyed.

Miss Swain generously presented hundreds of his prints to the Brandywine River Museum at Chadds Ford. His murals, including one of Revolutionary War troops leaving Dover Green to join General Washington in 1776, appear in the Delaware State Capitol.

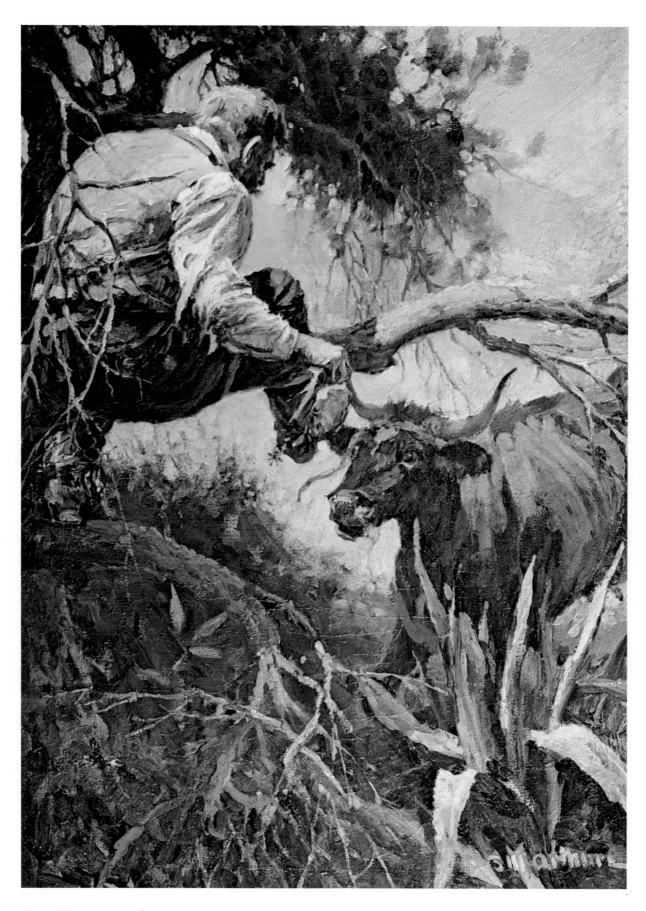

Through the Long Afternoon and Evening the Colonel Roasted. 36 x 26 inches, oil. Stanley Arthurs.

Jozef Bakos

1891–1977

A MEMBER OF THE NOW FAMOUS Los Cinco Pintores group of Sante Fe, New Mexico, Jozef G. Bakos lived to see the paintings from this legendary circle become widely known and collected. This little band of avant-garde painters, often referred to as "The five nuts in adobe huts," worked and exhibited together for only three years in the early 1920s.

Jozef Bakos was born of Polish parentage in Buffalo, New York. To support himself he worked in a glass factory. He received his early art training under an Albright Art School scholarship in Buffalo, and he studied privately with John E. Thompson. In 1918 he followed John Thompson to Denver, Colorado, where Bakos taught art at the Denver University. Later he became the first art instructor at the University of Colorado in Boulder.

In 1921 Bakos and his artist wife Teresa homesteaded in the pinon-covered hills northwest of Santa Fe. His love for the people and the land made him a very emotional and dramatic painter. He called himself an expressionist landscape painter. He was a close friend of Andrew Dasburg.

To supplement his income in the early days, Bakos worked for the Forest Service. He made hand-carved furniture and doors in his spare time. He also taught painting at the Santa Fe High School.

Bakos said that the most productive, yet carefree, period in his life was during the time he and the other "nuts" were building their adobe "huts" on the Camino del Monte Sol. Besides a desire for a good time, they had another common bond—to take art to the people. They believed in the universality of art and thought that it should "sing to the peasant as well as the connoisseur."

Jozef Bakos has been recognized by critics for half a century. His paintings currently hang in the permanent collections of important museums, including the Brooklyn and Whitney in New York City, the University of Oklahoma Art Museum, the Ford Foundation, and in Denver and Santa Fe museums. A number of paintings hang in the Gallery of the American Hereford Association in Kansas City, Missouri.

He exhibited at the Carnegie Institute, Pittsburgh, Pennsylvania; the Chicago Art Institute, Chicago, Illinois; and the Pasadena Art Institute, Pasadena, California. Bakos is also listed in *Who's Who In American Art*.

He died April 25, 1977, in Santa Fe.

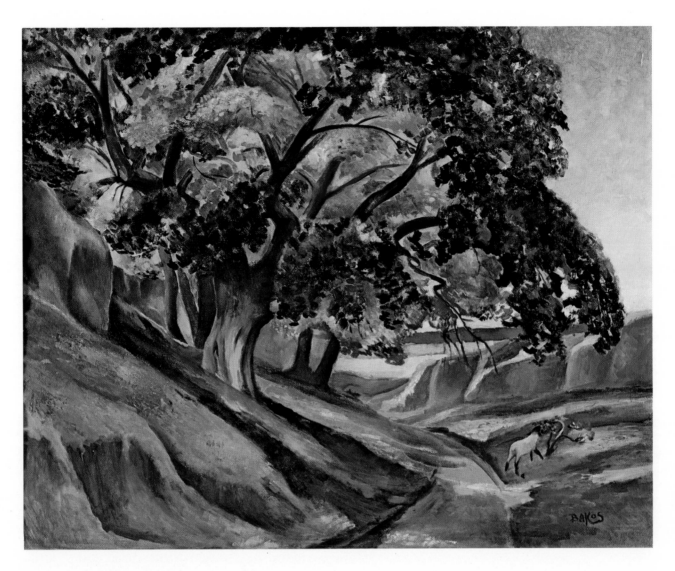

Cottonwood Fall. 26½ x 32½ inches, oil. Jozef Bakos.

Henry Balink

1882–1963

HENDRICUS BALINK WAS BORN in Amsterdam, Holland, where he earned his early art training by working as a bicycle racer and ice skater. His parents were very opposed to his artistic ambitions.

As a recipient of a Queen Wilhelmina merit scholarship, he took his advanced art training at the Royal Academie of Amsterdam. It was with this discipline that he interpreted the totally new world to which he moved.

In 1914, after emigrating to New York City where he was employed by the Metropolitan Museum, he became Henry Balink. In 1917 Balink and his wife were lured to the Southwest by a travel poster in a railway station. They lived in Taos, New Mexico, for two years and, after a short visit to their homeland, returned to New Mexico to settle in Santa Fe permanently.

At this time, a great transformation came over his paintings; he found the subject which was to be the central theme of his work for the rest of his life —the American Indian. With his new surroundings, his style of painting also changed. The tones and technique were transformed into bright colors and bold brush strokes. Yet he also painted with meticulous detail when reproducing Indian pottery and weavings in his paintings. He was keenly interested in both the crafts and the ceremonial dances of the Indians of the area. He painted members of sixty-three tribes and, in 1927, was commissioned to paint portraits of Oklahoma's Indian chiefs. In addition to his painting, Balink carved fine furniture, as well as intricately beautiful frames which are part of most Balink paintings.

As it was with many of his contemporaries of that era, times were not always good. "An artist's life is a funny life," he once said, "You eat chicken today and the guts and feathers tomorrow."

He lived on the Camino del Monte Sol in the growing artist's colony before building his permanent home and studio in 1924 on the Old Pecos Road.

Many of his works hang in museums of the Southwest, including the Museum of New Mexico in Santa Fe, The Gilcrease Institute of Art in Tulsa, Oklahoma, and in many private collections.

He is survived by a son, Henry B. Balink, and a daughter, Margaret Balink Finkhousen.

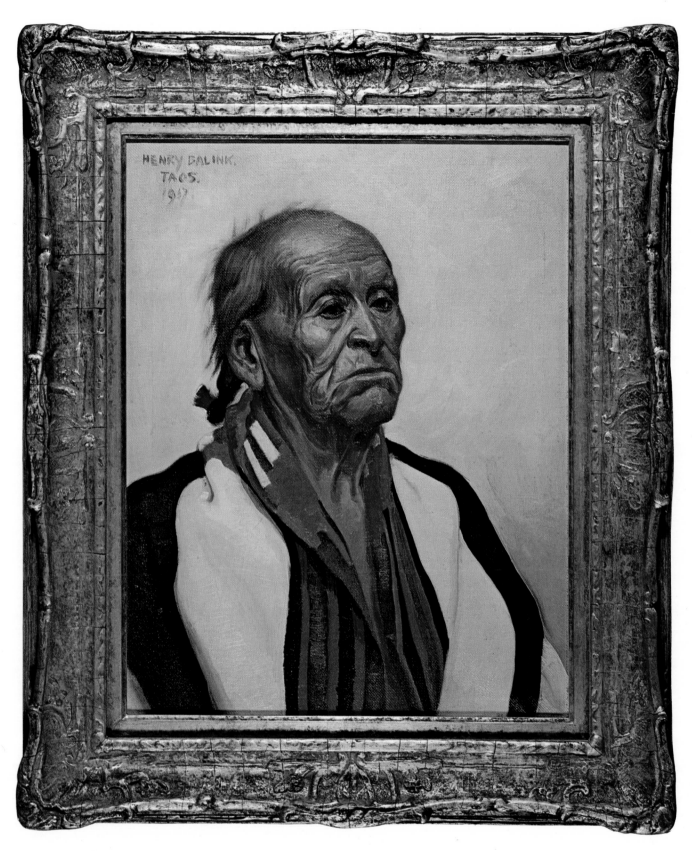

Ta-quee-quala (Soaring Eagle). Dated 1917. 20 x 16 inches, oil. Henry Balink.

Gray Bartlett
1885–1951

GRAY BARTLETT WAS fifty-two years old in 1937 and still in the engraving business. He had not worked with a sketchpad and canvas for three decades. But in the next fourteen years, until his death, he achieved a lifelong goal and became a foremost western artist.

He grew up with a love for art and a love for the West. Born in Rochester, Minnesota, his parents moved to Colorado when he was a youth. By the time he was sixteen he was working as a cowhand on the open range, sketching western scenes in a battered sketchbook he carried in his saddlebags. These sketches were later transferred to canvas.

At first his ambition was to be a rancher, for the wide-open life in the West seemed to suit him so well. Then he began to realize how strongly he felt about his sketches and paintings of the West, and he soon became aware that his true ambition was not ranching, but to be an artist. He left the cattle country to study at the Greeley Art School in Greeley, Colorado, and on a scholarship at the Chicago Art Institute.

The death of his mother forced a decided change in the course of his life. He gave up his art training and went to work as a commercial artist, employed by various photo-engraving companies, to help support the family. He had many such jobs in Denver and other western and midwestern cities. After marrying, he borrowed $1,800 and bought an interest in an engraving firm. The business prospered and, in 1937, Bartlett retired and moved to California where he returned to his first love—art.

His desire to paint came back stronger than ever. Despite being neglected for so many years, his skill with a brush and his eye for color did not fail him, and his early sketches refreshed his memory.

With camera and notebook he traveled extensively in Colorado, Utah, Texas, Arizona, and New Mexico, capturing the West he remembered so well as a boy. At times he lived among the Indians, while maintaining studios in Los Angeles and in Moab, Utah.

His paintings of the Southwest are in many western collections, including the Santa Fe Railway Collection, Arizona State University, and the California State Library.

Bartlett died of a heart attack suffered while in his studio in Los Angeles.

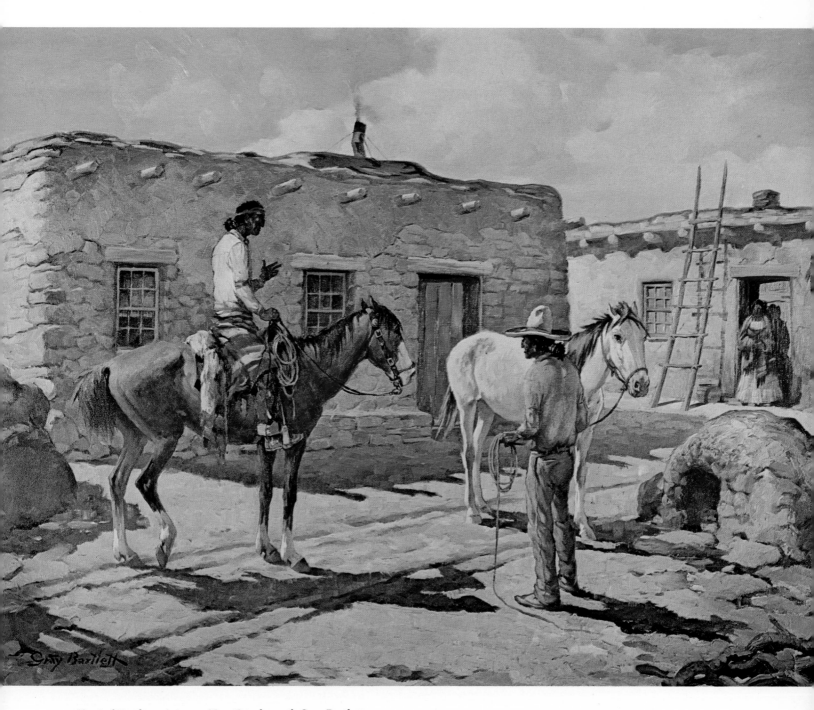

Hopi of Northern Arizona. 30 x 40 inches, oil. Gray Bartlett.

Gustave Baumann
1881–1971

PRINTMAKING WAS HIS OUTSTANDING artistic expression, and in that medium Gustave Baumann was a master. He worked in oils as well, but his woodblock prints overshadowed all else.

Born in Magdeburg, Germany, he grew up in Chicago, and he attended the Chicago Art Institute at night while working as a commercial artist during the day. He joined the Palette and Chisel Club where he met Walter Ufer, Victor Higgins, and E. Martin Hennings. All were members of the Taos Society of Artists. From these men he first learned of the flourishing artist colonies in Taos and Santa Fe, New Mexico.

Saving enough money for a year of study in Europe, Baumann decided to go to Germany, settling in Munich where he attended the Kunstgewerbe Schule. He concentrated on the art of cutting woodblocks to attain a full range of colors in the final relief blockprint. This method is known in Germany as jugendstil. When Baumann had decided to specialize in this exacting technique, he was surprised to find that it was not as simple as he had envisioned. With diligence, he mastered the art that was to be a great part of his life's work. He employed the true Japanese manner of cutting a separate block for each color, sometimes eight or nine for a single print.

By 1915 he was exhibiting in Paris, and he won the printmaking award at the San Francisco Exposition.

Returning to the commercial art world in Chicago, he still had not found the right artistic climate or subject matter for his work. "Art is a kind of tyrant," Baumann once said, "It pushes you around." It seemed to push him in the right direction, however, as it sent him to Santa Fe, via Taos, New Mexico, in 1918 where he found what he had been looking for.

In 1919 he visited Frijoles Canyon near Santa Fe. Here he made drawings and rubbings of the pictographs inscribed on the cave walls by the Anasazi. A decade later he published a book, *Frijoles Canyon Pictographs*, for which he won the "50 Books of the Year Award."

Baumann's work is emerging as one of the important art forms that transcends the boundaries of conventionalism and is limitless in subject matter, ranging from objective to abstract in style.

14

He is well represented in many museums and private collections. He lived in Santa Fe with his wife, Jane, and a daughter, Ann, until his death.

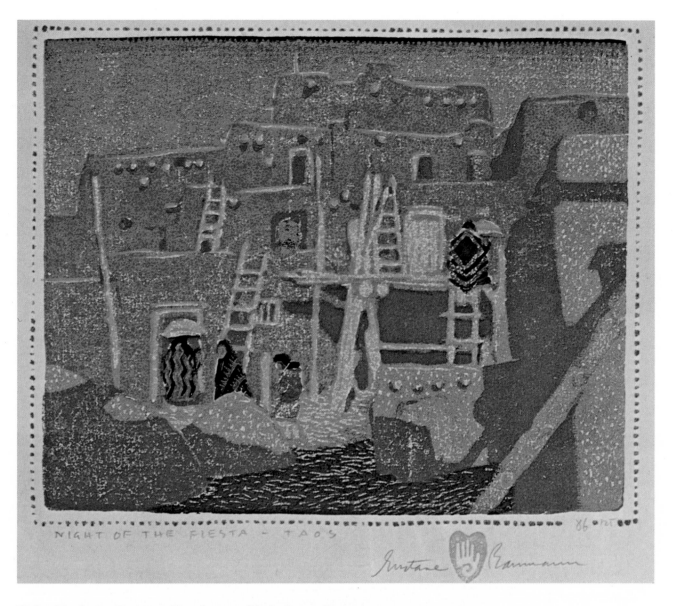

Night of the Fiesta, Taos. 5½ x 7½ inches, woodblock. Gustave Baumann.

Theodore Baur

1835–unknown

FOR THE WORLD'S FAIRS of the nineteenth century, it was the custom of silversmiths to create monumental objects of art to advertise their skills. The display pieces served as the focal point of the shows. To Theodore Baur, the most significant fair was the Philadelphia Centennial, of 1876.

Baur, a modeler-sculptor, was born in Wurttemberg, Germany. He had come to America when he was fifteen, gaining recognition here and in Canada for his architectural sculpture.

When the Meriden Britannia Company, forerunner of The International Silver Company, contracted for a large exhibit at the Centennial Exposition, they engaged the services of Baur.

The surging interest in the new western frontier influenced the Meriden Britannia Company to commission Baur to create a piece symbolizing this phase of the American scene. Baur opened a studio in New York City's Washington Square. He spent many hours studying the buffalo in the New York Zoo and the American Indian in museums.

His finished sculpture was an epic piece called "The Buffalo Hunt." The original casting was in bronze, but the exhibit model, weighing seventy-five pounds, was produced in heavy silverplate on white metal. After the Philadelphia Centennial, "The Buffalo Hunt" was shown at international expositions; subsequent castings were offered as a standard catalog item, priced at $315, in "old silver" finish.

The artist and his incredible display model then dropped from prominence. Baur worked in relative obscurity while continuing his realistic renderings of the American Indian. But 100 years later, the story of the famous display sculpture and the artist again came to light in International Silver Company's 1976 Christmas catalog. A picture of the magnificent piece appeared, and the history of "The Buffalo Hunt" revealed the fact that in 1877 it had been sold to the famous Field family and engraved with their name and the date.

Shortly after the turn of the century, International Silver Company reacquired the sculpture and kept it in its heirloom collection for display only in their showrooms at Meriden, Connecticut. To commemorate the 1976 Bicentennial year, the Company once again offered the classic "Buffalo Hunt," now at the price of $87,500. Theodore Baur remains a mystery.

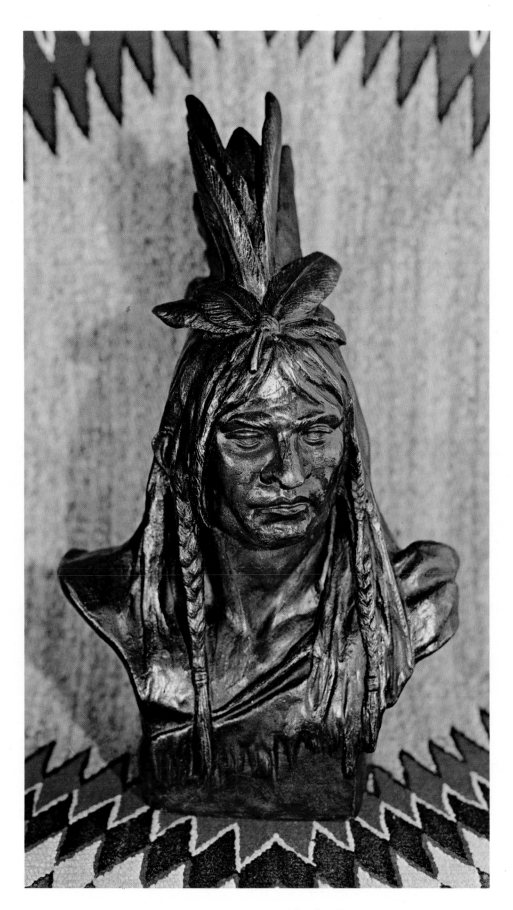

Chief Crazy Horse. Dated 1885. H. 14 inches, bronze. Theodore Baur.

Donald Beauregard

1884–1914

WHEN HE DIED AT the age of thirty, Donald Beauregard had produced a wealth of art and achieved a lasting reputation. He painted extensively in Europe, in New Mexico, Arizona, and his native Utah. He and Carlos Vierra were two of the earliest painters in Santa Fe, New Mexico, and today Beauregard's work is prized by serious collectors.

The son of Mormon pioneers, he grew up on a ranch in Fillmore, Utah, and it is here he returned to die of cancer. As a small boy, he painted the scenes around his home. He entered Brigham Young University at the age of sixteen, and two years later transferred to the University of Utah, where he took a serious interest in art. Beauregard became an assistant in the Art Department in his second year. Deciding on a career in art, he worked two years as a manual laborer to earn enough money to study abroad.

He studied for two years at the Academie Julien in Paris and painted throughout Europe. His work took on definite characteristics of French impressionism and cubism.

Returning to Utah in 1908, he became the director of art for the Ogden Public Schools. Then his interest in archeology led him to join an expedition that explored the relics of the Franciscan Monks in Arizona and New Mexico. He worked under Professor Byron Cummings at Frijoles Canyon near Santa Fe.

In New Mexico, he met lawyer Frank Springer, a patron of the arts, who was impressed by Beauregard's painting and his intellect. Springer commissioned him to do murals of the life of St. Francis de Assisi, patron saint of the Southwest, for the 1915 Panama-California Exposition in San Diego, and for permanent installation at the Museum of New Mexico in Santa Fe.

Beauregard researched the assignment extensively in Washington, D.C., and in Europe. But while there, in 1912, he experienced the first symptoms of his terminal illness. He returned to Santa Fe to work on the large panels, but completed only about half of the painting before his death. Carlos Vierra and Kenneth M. Chapman completed the murals from drawings which Beauregard had left.

He was known as a "deep thinker, keen observer, and thorough investigator." The most extensive collection of his work, including thirty-two watercolors, is owned by the Museum of New Mexico at Santa Fe.

18

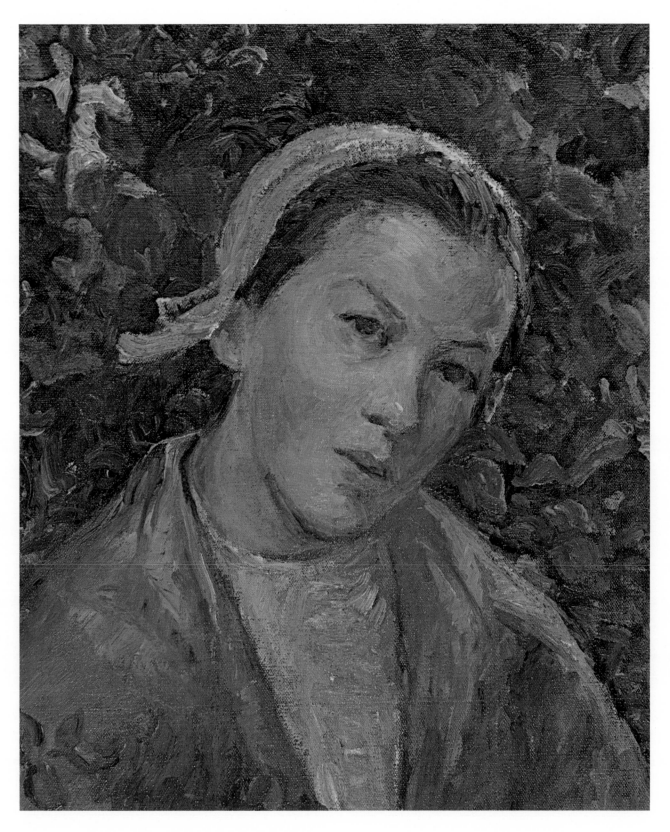

Portrait of a Maiden. 16 x 13 inches, oil. Donald Beauregard.

August Becker

1840–1903

AUGUST H. BECKER WAS KNOWN primarily for his Indian paintings and decorative art. He was among the leading artists of his period, but he never attained the fame of his half brother, Charles Wimar, who was twelve years older.

Born in Bonn, Germany, Becker moved with his parents to St. Louis, Missouri, when he was three years of age. His interest in the West was furthered by the Indians who lived near the family home. At the age of ten, he showed a fondness for art, which both he and Wimar inherited from their artistic mother.

Unlike Wimar, Becker never left the St. Louis area, where he studied under Leon Pomarade, the noted European artist. The two young artists had difficulties in the early St. Louis days. During the Civil War, there was little demand for their paintings, and Becker left his palette to drive a horse-drawn streetcar on Market Street.

Becker was a muralist and frescoer, as well as an easel artist. His work decorated many noted buildings and historic old homes in St. Louis. The ceiling of the dome of the old Court House was one which he started with Wimar, who became ill and was barely able to complete the project. Becker later restored the paintings in the dome that Wimar had executed, saving them from total obliteration at the ruthless hands of a foreign frescoer who had been employed to do restoration work.

Becker completed many of Wimar's charcoal sketches, some after his brother's death from consumption in 1862 at the age of thirty-four. Becker himself died of paralysis at sixty-three, leaving two children.

For the last five years of his life, he devoted himself to perpetuating the memory of his brother. As his paralysis worsened, he knew that time was of the essence. He said, "I am just about ready now to do the best of my work. You know, it takes a man more than a lifetime to learn how to see things. The painter, like the poet, must reach the heart with a ring of truth."

Because of the difference in life-span, Wimar left far less work than Becker. Ironically, Wimar's fame has overshadowed his brother's reputation. But the new interest in western art will place August Becker with the very best of western painters. His works are in the Montana and Missouri Historical Societies. A major canvas he painted was a portrait of his half-brother Charles Wimar.

Buffaloes Drinking at the Yellowstone. 16 x 12 inches, oil. August Becker.

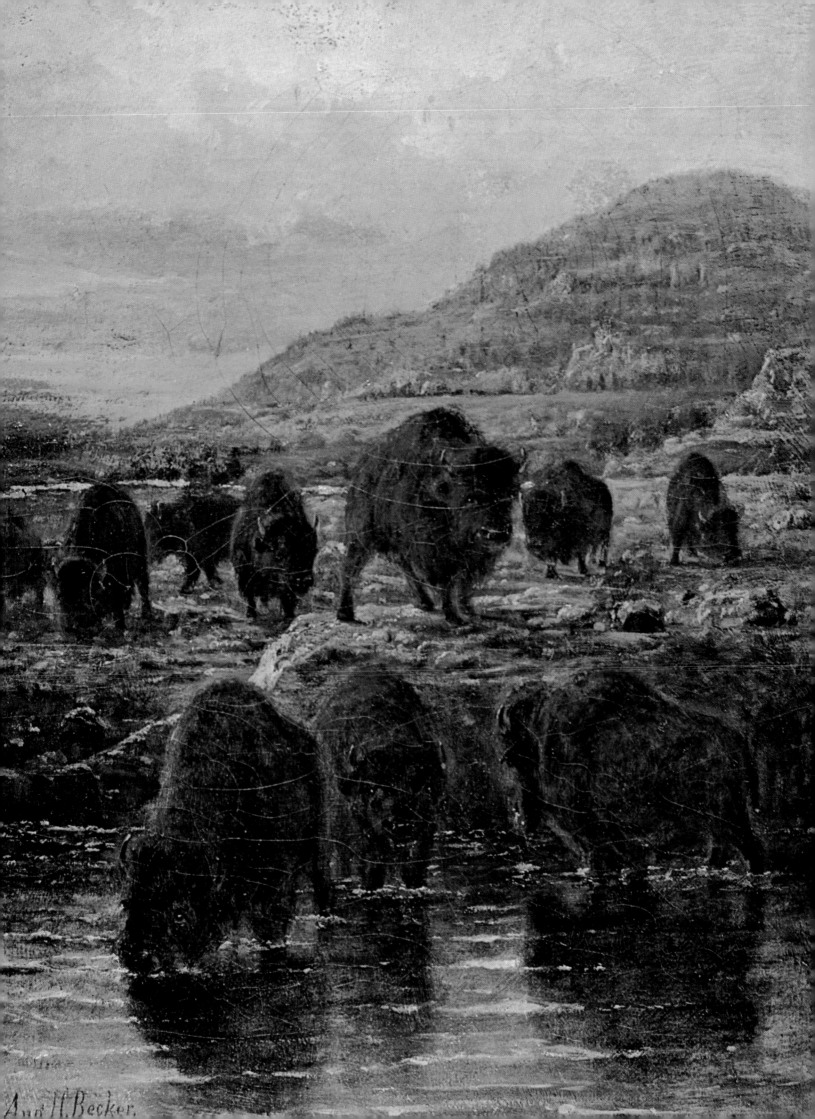

Tom Benrimo

1887–1958

NOT MANY WESTERN PAINTERS have specialized in surrealist or abstract art. One was Tom Benrimo. After moving from New York to New Mexico in 1939, Benrimo slowly won a national and international reputation.

Born in San Francisco, his formal education ended in the fourth grade when he went to work to help support his family. He studied on his own and was deeply interested in many subjects, including physics, engineering, history, music, literature, and philosophy.

Most of his early drawings, models, and notebooks were ruined in the San Francisco earthquake of 1906, when he was nineteen. Soon after, Benrimo moved to New York City with his family. On the trip east he first saw the great southwestern desert to which he later returned.

Wretched tenement living in New York City brought on tuberculosis, which plagued him until he was forty. In spite of his illness he struggled to support his tubercular mother and a brother, Harvey.

He worked hard doing illustrations for magazines and advertising, becoming a very successful commercial artist. He also taught at the Pratt Institute of New York City. At the Armory Show in 1913, he first saw the possibilities of modern art. For Benrimo, it was a decisive experience.

In 1917 he married his first wife, Helen; they had one daughter, Rita, who was born in 1926.

Interested in surrealism and cubism and influenced by Dali, Benrimo began easel painting seriously. Much of his early work he either destroyed or abandoned in order to have a fresh start when he and his second wife, Dorothy, a talented jewelry designer, moved to Taos, New Mexico. They made their home in a tiny restored adobe ruin, lighted by kerosene lamps, where he could devote all his energies to painting.

Gradually he evolved from surrealism to a more abstract and personal style during the last eight years of his life. "Abstract art departs from reality and nature only to draw far-reaching conclusions about reality," Benrimo once said.

His most important exhibitions were at the Guggenheim Museum in 1954 and at the Museum of Modern Art in 1955. He is represented in many private collections and museums.

22

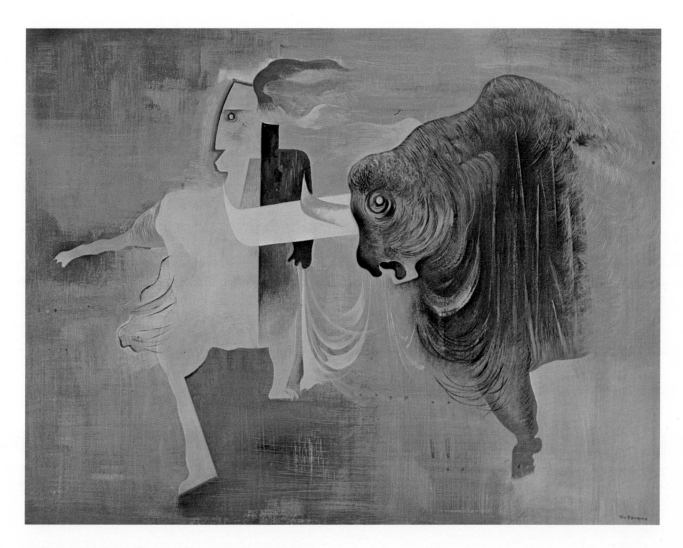

Buffalo Indian Hunt. 15 x 21 inches, casein. Tom Benrimo.

Emil Bisttram

1895–1976

EMIL JAMES BISTTRAM lived in Taos, New Mexico, and was one of the Southwest's leading artists and teachers. His murals decorate major public buildings. His paintings and watercolors have won national acclaim.

As a poor Hungarian immigrant growing up on New York City's East Side, Emil Bisttram had only one goal in life—to be an artist. He worked at many jobs from cabinetmaking to prizefighting before he entered art school. He made many sacrifices to pursue his career.

Once into art, success came quickly. After studying at the National Academy of Design, Parsons School of Art and Design, and the Art Students League in New York with Howard Giles, Bisttram established his own advertising art agency at the age of twenty. Working at the Parsons School, he also displayed an unusual talent for teaching art.

A milestone in his career came in 1931 when he received a Guggenheim Fellowship to study abroad. Because of the threat of war in Europe, Bisttram went to Mexico City to work with Diego Rivera on the National Palace murals. He was deeply impressed with Rivera and Jose Orozco. He was influenced by the strong realism and sculptured surfaces, later turning to non-objective art.

He and the great Mexican artist Rivera had many common interests, especially the concept of dynamic symmetry in art. Upon completing work in Mexico, he returned to Taos, which he had first visited in 1930. Mayrion, his wife, awaited him there. He toured the Navajo country and made countless sketches of Indian life and the landscape.

In Taos he was a leader in the art and civic communities. He organized the Taos School of Art, later named the Bisttram School of Fine Art. He was one of the founders of the Taos Art Association and was its president from 1956 to 1958. Bisttram taught in Phoenix and Los Angeles in the winter.

His work has won major awards in Philadelphia, New York, and Los Angeles, and he is well represented in many fine collections.

Bisttram murals appear in the lobby of the Department of Justice Building in Washington, D.C., and in the courthouses in Taos and Roswell, New Mexico, and in Ranger, Texas.

He died February 26, 1976, at Holy Cross Hospital in Taos, New Mexico.

The Breadmakers. 48 x 36 inches, oil. Emil Bisttram.

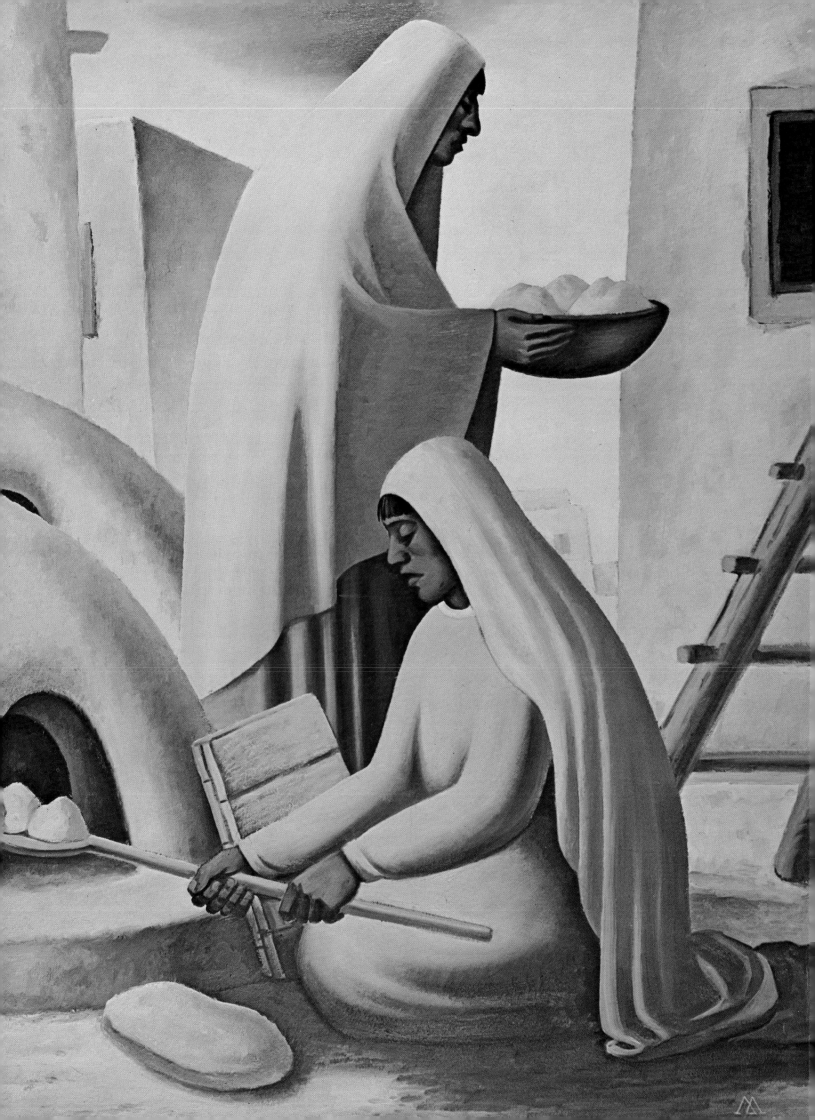

Homer Boss

1882–1956

BEFORE HIS FIRST TRIP to the Southwest in 1925, Homer Boss had been acclaimed in New York City for nearly a quarter of a century for his beautiful masterly full-length portraits. He was elected a life member of the National Arts Club.

Boss broke away from tradition when he moved to New York City in the early 1900s from Blanford, Massachusetts, where he was born. He became one of the rebel artists who ignored the nineteenth-century standards.

During this important period in American art, he studied with Robert Henri, William Merritt Chase, and Thomas Anshutz, other leaders in the revolt. In 1910 Boss was represented in the first Independent Show in New York, organized by Henri and others in rebellion against the traditional Academy exhibitions. Boss helped form the Independent Society and served on its board.

He gradually changed his approach to art, and his work became more colorful and simplified, eventually taking on a direct and brilliant style. He exhibited two paintings in the famous Armory Show of 1913. This show left its impact on many American artists.

His long teaching career began when Robert Henri went to Europe and turned his Henri School over to Boss. Upon Henri's return, the two artists disagreed over school policies. Boss renamed it the Independent School and continued to teach there. He also taught at the Art Students League, the Parsons School of Fine Art, and the New York School of Design for Women. His lectures on anatomy at the Art Students League were attended by many well-known artists. He illustrated the fundamentals and techniques of structural values by building muscles of plasticine on a full human skeleton, while a nude model demonstrated the muscle action.

After several trips to New Mexico, he and his wife moved there permanently in 1933. With a canvas strapped to his saddle, he would ride horseback into the desert to do landscapes of the clay hills and the Sangre de Cristo Mountains.

After his death in Santa Cruz, New Mexico, the Art Museum of New Mexico gave Boss a memorial exhibition and sent a select number of paintings from the exhibition as a traveling show throughout the state.

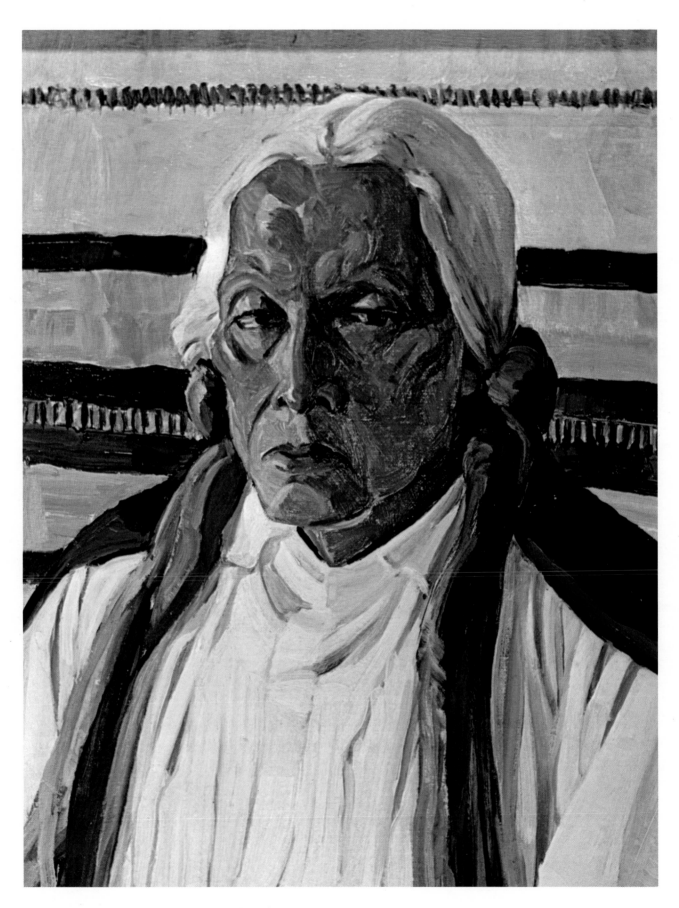

Kotseh (Yellow Buffalo). 32 x 26 inches, oil (detail). Homer Boss.

Harold Bryant

1894–1950

HE WAS CALLED COLORADO'S "maverick with a paint brush," by his friend Al Look of Grand Junction, Colorado, who wrote Harold Bryant's biography, published in 1962. With the cooperation of Bryant's wife and sister, Look was able to piece together Bryant's life story, a story that almost died with the artist.

Born in Pickrell, Nebraska, Bryant drew pictures from the time he could hold a pencil and practiced regularly by sketching the outbuildings. He was an only son with eight sisters. The family moved near Grand Junction, Colorado, in 1902.

In 1914 Bryant enrolled at the Chicago Art Institute to study the surrealists and abstractionists; but before long he decided he "liked pictures you could tell the bottom of." He served in the Army for two years, then returned to Chicago in 1919 to work for an advertising agency illustrating magazine stories. Again, he soon discovered that all he wanted to do was paint cows in cow country.

Bryant purchased forty acres and a cabin on Pinon Mesa in Colorado in 1926. His commercial art business flourished, and he rented a studio in New York. He was tops in his field of modern western art.

After losing his savings in the stock market crash, New York lost its glamour for Bryant. Poverty or riches, he decided, made little difference to his happiness. He returned to his cabin in Colorado and, after two years of near starvation and loneliness, he married his wife, Ruth, in 1940. She took over the selling of his paintings with the help of his sister, Dorothy, who was living in Denver. This gave them a meager living, but little else.

His big break came in 1941 when the jury at the Grand Central Art Gallery in New York City approved his work, and he became a contributing artist member. His paintings also were being used on calendars, which did more to establish him than any other factor.

He died of cancer just when he was beginning to make a living at painting his West. He had executed only eighty-five easel paintings, but hundreds of magazine and advertising illustrations.

Ruth Bryant gave the bulk of his private collection to the Museum of Texas Tech University at Lubbock. He was buried with military honors at Grand Junction, Colorado.

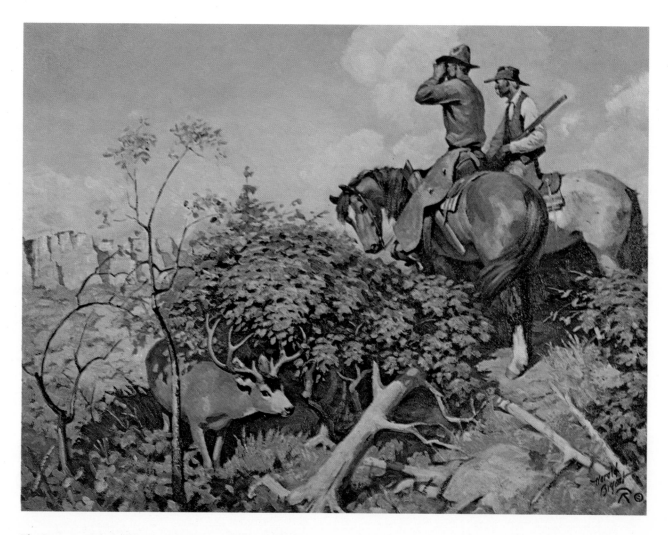

The Strategy of the Wild. 24 x 32 inches, oil. Harold Bryant.

Conrad Buff

1886–1975

WHEN CONRAD BUFF ARRIVED in the United States from Switzerland in 1905, there was little to suggest that he would become a successful artist.

At nineteen years of age he had no formal training in art, no friends, no money, and knew only a few words of English. But he had a driving ambition to succeed in art, and, after almost two decades of hard work, he achieved his goal.

Buff was born in Speicher, Switzerland, where his father was a storekeeper and farmer. At fourteen, after failing to convince his parents that he should become an artist, he was given a job as an apprentice baker. They later compromised and sent him to Munich, Germany, to study lacemaking.

Unhappy with the meticulous work, Buff emigrated to the United States. Because of his language problems, he set out to find other people of Swiss descent; he settled in Wisconsin, where he obtained a job in a dairy.

Then, for ten years while moving west across the continent, he engaged in a series of rigorous outdoor jobs—cowboy, railroader, muleskinner, and sheepherder—and mentally painted the life he saw.

Buff finally arrived in Los Angeles. He worked as a house painter and, in his spare time, prepared to be a "real artist." He painted scenes around Southern California and the deserts of Utah, Arizona, and New Mexico, using a pointillist technique, a carry-over from his lacemaking days.

An unusual project headed by Los Angeles artist Edgar Payne proved to be a turning point in Buff's career. Commissioned by a Chicago hotel to decorate its hallways with paintings of outdoor scenes, Payne rounded up a group of local artists, including Buff, and they turned out 1,000 feet of landscapes on muslin strips that were installed in the Chicago hotel.

The second turning point came in 1922 when he married Mary Marsh, a young artist and assistant curator of the Los Angeles County Museum of Art. She gave up her painting to write children's books, which Buff illustrated. The first, and among the most famous, was *Dancing Cloud*, the story of a little Navajo girl.

The Buffs enjoyed a lifelong friendship with artist Maynard Dixon, who greatly admired the landscapes Buff created—landscapes that were said to radiate sunshine and light. Conrad Buff attracted a large following before his death in Laguna Hills, California.

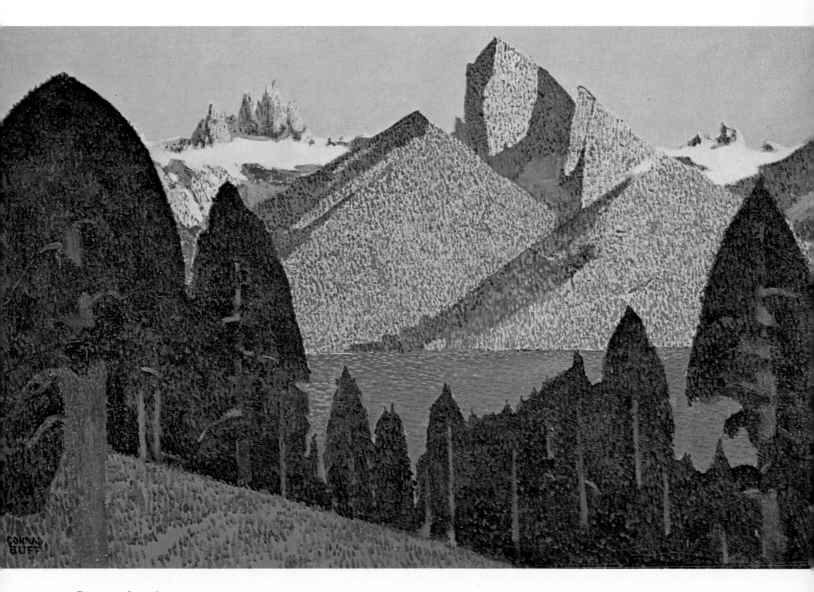

Giants in the Lake. 24 x 40 inches, oil. Conrad Buff.

Paul Burlin

1886–1969

ONCE CONSIDERED THE MOST MODERN ARTIST in the Taos-Santa Fe art colony, Paul Burlin might best be described as "ahead of his time." Born in New York City, he received his training there and in England.

The International Exhibition of Modern Art in 1913 in New York City, known as The Armory Show, had a great influence on his career. It was here that he was first overwhelmed by Matisse's personal expression of color and Picasso's leanings toward cubism. Burlin was the first artist among the exhibitors in that show to go to New Mexico.

He became an avid student of the Southwest. From 1913 to 1920 he spent part of each year painting in New Mexico and researching the life and lore of the Indians. His wife, the former Natalie Curtis, who he met in Santa Fe, specialized in Indian music. "In truth," Burlin said, "the American Southwest was practically the beginning of my interest in painting. I was ignorant of the Indians and knew nothing of their lifestyle." His study of the abstract elements in Indian art influenced his early semi-abstract technique. But it was years later before his work—noted for its daring color and distortion of form—received recognition.

The other southwestern artists of that day, such as Carlos Vierra and Gerald Cassidy, did not grasp the significance of Burlin's expressionism. Guy Pene Du Bois said Burlin's canvases were "executed with a strait-arm motion, which does away with sensitiveness." A news story printed in the *Santa Fe New Mexican* in 1916 reported: "While not a futurist or even a post-impressionist, his technique and treatment of themes were the most advanced of any." Burlin was a "loner," detaching himself from the realities of his physical environment. He was known for his teaching at Washington University (in St. Louis), the University of Minnesota, and the University of Southern California.

His series of Indian portraits and landscapes assimilated the concepts suggested by the Armory Show. He also did murals and figure paintings. In 1919 he was chosen one of a committee of fifteen New Mexico artists to select works by Americans to be shown at the United States Exhibition in Paris. A year later, Burlin himself moved to Paris, where his increasingly expressionistic style was more quickly accepted.

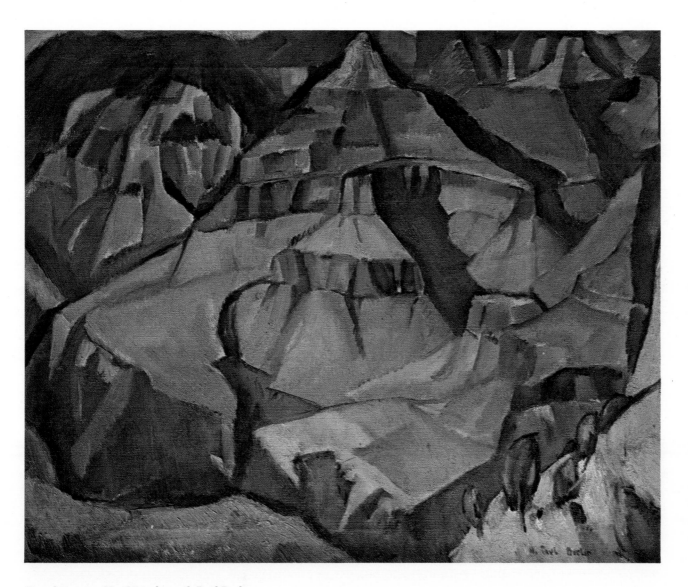

Grand Canyon. 20 x 25 inches, oil. Paul Burlin.

Pruett Carter

1891–1955

PRUETT A. CARTER'S ROOTS in western art go back to his childhood. Born in Lexington, Missouri, he was reared on an Indian reservation in Wyoming where his father ran a trading-post and his mother taught school. Memories of his childhood on the frontier supplied him with much of the authentic subject matter he later painted.

After his family moved to California, a noted cartoonist of the day, James Swinnerton, creator of "Little Jimmy," recognized Carter's artistic talents and encouraged his career.

Carter studied at the Los Angeles Art School, then headed east for jobs as a newspaper artist with the *New York American* and the *Atlanta Georgian.*

His desire to become a magazine illustrator led to the art editorship of *Good Housekeeping* magazine. For the next forty years he was regarded as one of the nation's leading magazine illustrators, and his work was in wide demand. His illustrations were used by *Woman's Home Companion, McCall's,* and *Ladies' Home Journal.*

In 1930, he returned to his studio in Los Angeles and air mailed his paintings to magazine editors in New York. He also engaged in art work for the leading movie studios.

He was noted for having the ability to make his subjects live, breathe, and react to each other as the author intended. He had a special talent for portraying women with delicate beauty and compassion, and his heroines were recognized for their loveliness. Thoroughly researching the subject matter to be painted, he was meticulous in rendering every detail. This was true of his western paintings showing costumes of a particular period and gear used on horses.

Carter also found time to teach, and many of today's top illustrators were schooled under his direction. He taught at the Grand Central School of Art in New York and at the Chouinard Art Institute in Los Angeles where he headed the illustration department for several years. A great storyteller, Carter was well liked by his fellow artists and his students.

In 1955, he met a bizarre death. Faced with the pressures of caring for a twenty-six-year-old retarded son, whom he loved intensely, and the desire of his wife to return back east to live, Carter shot them both in a fit of despair. Brooding over the bodies for two days, he then ended his own life.

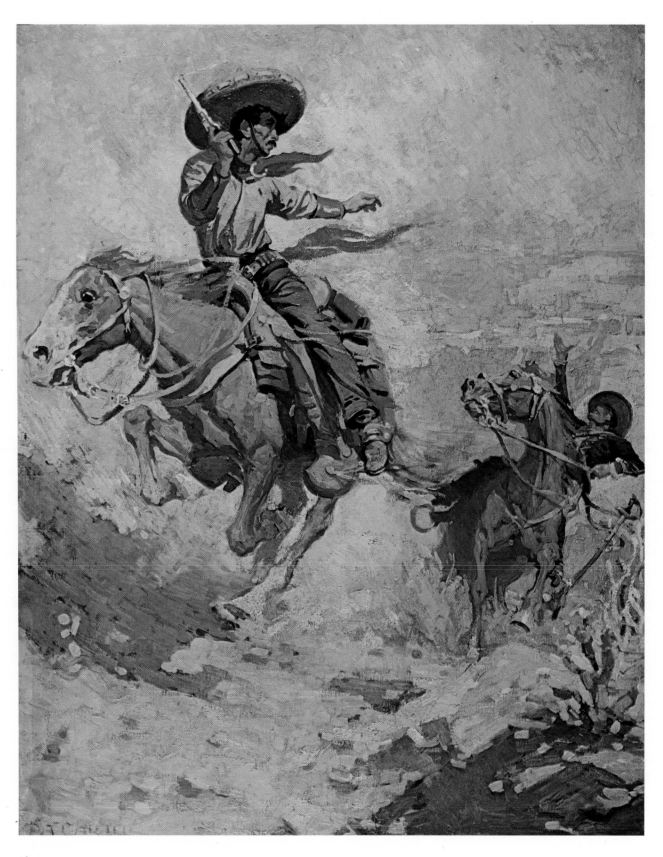

The Escape. 36 x 29 inches, oil. Pruett Carter.

John Casilear NA

1811-1893

AS ONE OF AMERICA'S great landscape painters, John William Casilear was active with the group known as painters of the Hudson River School. The term referred to similarity in thought and style, since many of the artists actually painted landscapes west of the Mississippi River.

Casilear was the sole support of his widowed mother, brothers, and sisters. His early career was that of a bank note engraver. He was an apprentice at the age of sixteen, learning the demanding trade under Peter Maverick, one of America's leading early engravers and lithographers. Eventually, he worked with, and was part of, one of New York's most respected engraving firms—Tappan, Carpenter, Casilear and Company. In 1847–48 he worked with his brother, George W. Casilear.

Casilear started painting as an avocation; his instructors were two of the best landscape artists of the day—Asher B. Durand and Thomas Cole. He made two trips to Europe to study. When twenty-nine years old, he went to Europe for three years with Durand and John F. Kensett. Upon his return to New York, Casilear worked another ten years at engraving before he felt financially secure enough to devote himself entirely to painting.

Along with John Kensett, he was among the leaders of a group called "luminists," who sought to reproduce special effects of atmosphere, air, light, and weather. Casilear's "luminism" can be seen effectively in his "Upper Hudson River Landscape."

New York City was Casilear's lifetime home, but his summers were spent in upstate New York and Vermont, where he painted its varied landscapes. In 1879 he went west as far as the Rocky Mountains in Colorado. He found a wealth of beauty to be captured. These paintings were exhibited at the National Academy, Apollo Association, American Art-Union, and the Pennsylvania Academy.

Casilear was elected an Associate of the National Academy in 1835 and became a full Academician in 1851.

His work is represented in many major collections in the United States, including the Metropolitan Museum of Art in New York and the Corcoran Gallery of Art in Washington, D.C. His granddaughter, Mrs. Charles P. Rogers, owned many of his sketches and papers.

He died in Saratoga, New York.

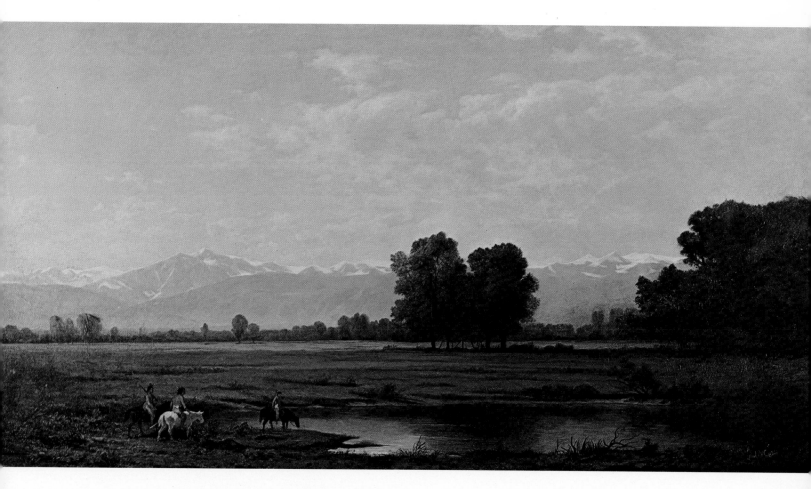

Near Greeley, Colorado. Dated 1882. 24 x 47 inches, oil. John Casilear.

George Catlin

1796–1872

TRAGEDY, POVERTY, AND FAILURE best describe the life of George Catlin. The son of a lawyer, Catlin was born in Wilkes-Barre, Pennsylvania. As a boy, he heard tales of the Indians from settlers, hunters, and soldiers who returned from the frontier.

Catlin's skills as an artist were self-taught. After attending law school in Litchfield, Connecticut, and practicing law for five years, he moved to Philadelphia to pursue his art as a portrait painter. Here he enjoyed a blossoming career and in 1824 was elected to the Academy of Fine Arts. But the competition among portrait artists was keen, and he sought a new challenge and a completely different way of life as a painter.

The inspiration came when Catlin saw a delegation of Plains Indians who were passing through Philadelphia enroute to Washington to discuss treaty affairs and fair treatment of their tribes.

Newly married, Catlin headed west alone in 1830 with an invitation from General Clark, Superintendent of Indian Affairs, to attend Indian councils at Fort Crawford in Wisconsin. This experience formed the nucleus from which his Indian Gallery started and the material for the books and articles he later published.

He traveled extensively throughout the Great Plains and visited many tribes, painting portraits and sketching in the field. He developed a deep compassion for the Indians and their civilization.

In 1837, he returned east and established his highly successful Catlin's Indian Gallery in New York City, an exhibit of paintings, artifacts, costumes, and implements. It also was shown in several other large eastern cities.

In 1839, Catlin took his family, now a son and three daughters, and his Indian Gallery to London, Paris, and Brussels. Although crowds were large, expenses were high, and he fell deeply in debt.

Illness claimed the lives of both his wife and son, and at the age of fifty-seven, deaf and penniless, he mortgaged his collection to an American friend, Joseph Harrison. He had made several attempts to sell his collection to the United States government with no success.

After Catlin's death in 1879, Harrison's widow gave the paintings to the Smithsonian, where more than 80 per cent of the paintings from the original London exhibition have been preserved.

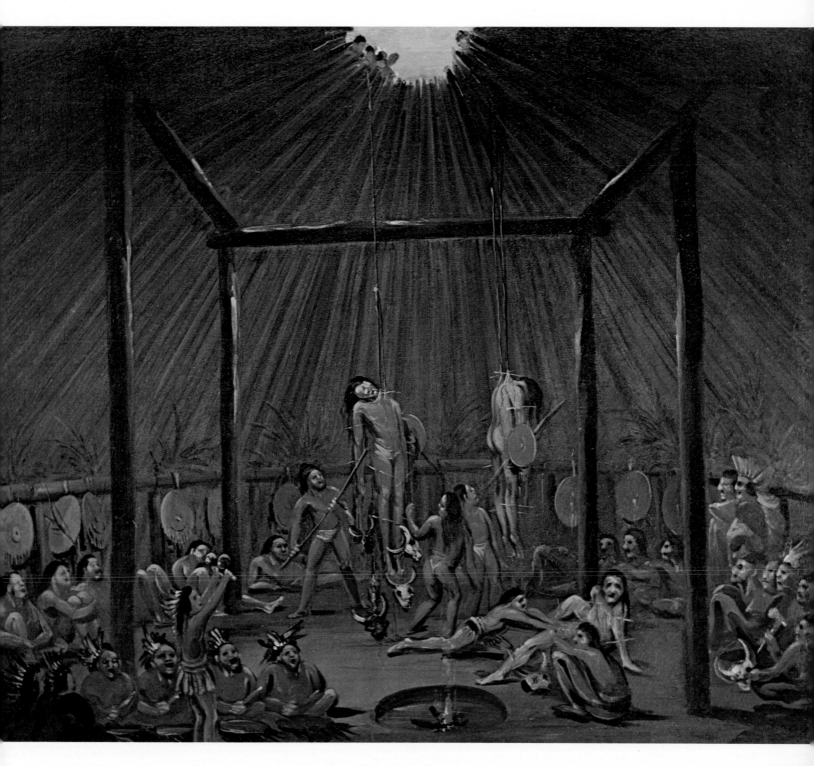

Self Torture in Mandan Okipa Ceremony. 22 x 27 inches, oil. George Catlin.

Charles S. Chapman NA

1879–1962

THE INFLUENCE OF the famed western artist Frederic Remington did much to shape the life and career of Charles Shepard Chapman. Born in Morristown, New York, Chapman studied at the Ogdensburg, New York, Free Academy, and at the Pratt Institute in Brooklyn, where he received his first formal art training. He then attended the Chase School of Art and the Art Students League, where he was both a student and a teacher.

In 1901 Chapman met Remington, also a native of northern New York, and spent several weeks with him in Bermuda. Remington instructed Chapman in the bolder use of color and encouraged him to paint the outdoors. At Remington's urging, he endured a year of rugged living and work in a Canadian lumber camp at Notre Dame de Laus. The spartan conditions intensified Chapman's love for the outdoors and his desire to paint it.

After the year in the camp north of Ottawa, in 1902, Chapman settled in the art colony of Leonia, New Jersey, where he conducted a school of illustration with Harvey Dunn. He also shared a studio with artist Howard McCormick.

He married Ada, his wife of more than fifty years, in 1911. She wrote the heartwarming biography of his life in 1964. Although Chapman spent most of his life in the East, he was very familiar with the West. In the 1930s the Museum of Natural History in New York commissioned him to paint a thirty-by-thirty-foot mural of the Grand Canyon as a background for the Puma group exhibit. The Chapmans camped at the Canyon rim for several weeks to gather material.

In 1941 he spent the summer teaching at the University of Wyoming and painting several landscapes of neighboring ranches. After World War II he and his wife rented a cottage at Jackson, Wyoming, where Chapman painted the massive Tetons with his friend and former student, Conrad Schwiering.

He was a member of the Salmagundi Club and won all its major art prizes. During his career, Chapman won the Saltus Gold Medal, the Altman Prize, and the Carnegie Prize twice each, and the President's Prize at the National Arts Club. His famous painting, "In The Deep Woods," was purchased by the Metropolitan Museum of Art. He was elected to the National Academy of Design in 1926. Charles Chapman died in Leonia, New Jersey.

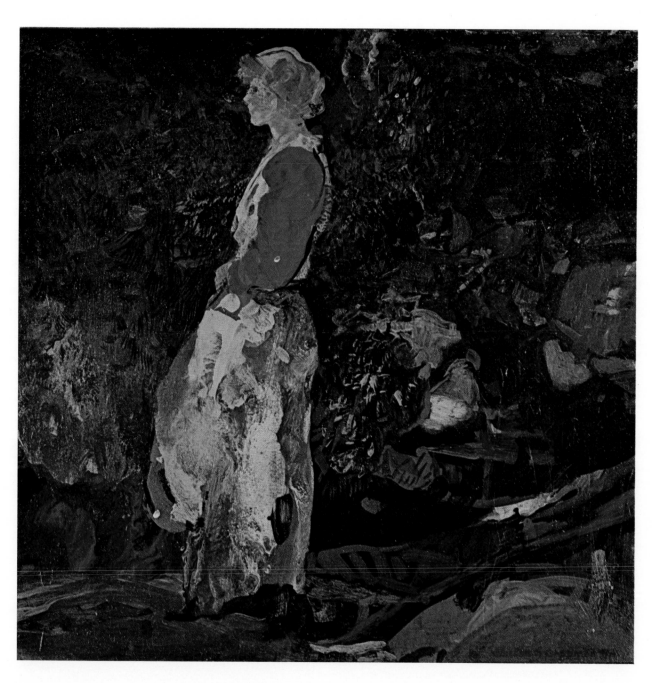

Western Girl. 10 x 11 inches, oil. Charles S. Chapman.

Samuel Colman NA

1832–1920

ONE OF AMERICA'S MOST DISTINGUISHED ARTISTS, Samuel Colman made several trips west to paint in Colorado, Wyoming, and the Yosemite Valley. In 1870 he followed Albert Bierstadt to the Western Frontier, where he made "on the spot" watercolor studies. The movement of immigrant trains on the prairies into the mountains became his special interest. He painted several versions, which became prototypes for many larger paintings.

Born in Portland, Maine, Colman moved to New York City at an early age. His father, Samuel Colman, Sr., a publisher and fine arts book dealer, encouraged young Colman's artistic studies. Through his father's influence he came into contact with many of the leading authors and artists of the day, giving him great exposure to the culture of the period.

He became a student of the noted Asher B. Durand, one of the leaders of the Hudson River School. By the time Colman reached the age of eighteen, he was exhibiting his work at the National Academy of Design. At the age of twenty-two he was elected an associate of the National Academy.

Scenes along the Hudson River and in the White Mountains were his main concern; but he went to Europe in 1860 to study in Paris and Spain and to find new subjects to paint. Returning to the United States in 1862, he was elected a full Academician of the National Academy of Design.

He helped found the American Society of Watercolor and was its first president, serving five consecutive terms. Colman was among those who recognized the potential and durability of watercolor painting, which heretofore had been a medium considered inferior to oils. The main objective of the Society was to promote exhibitions for introducing the beauty of watercolor to the public.

As it was with many artists, his talents spilled over into other means of expression. Colman authored two books on art, *Nature's Harmonic Unity* and *Proportional Form*. He became an etcher, a collector, and an authority on oriental art and porcelains. He also achieved fame as an interior designer; in the 1880s, he worked with Louis Comfort Tiffany and John La-Farge, catering to the whims of the "wealthiest of society." In 1881, he was one of the Associated Artists of New York who decorated the library in the Mark Twain house in Hartford, Connecticut. He died in New York City.

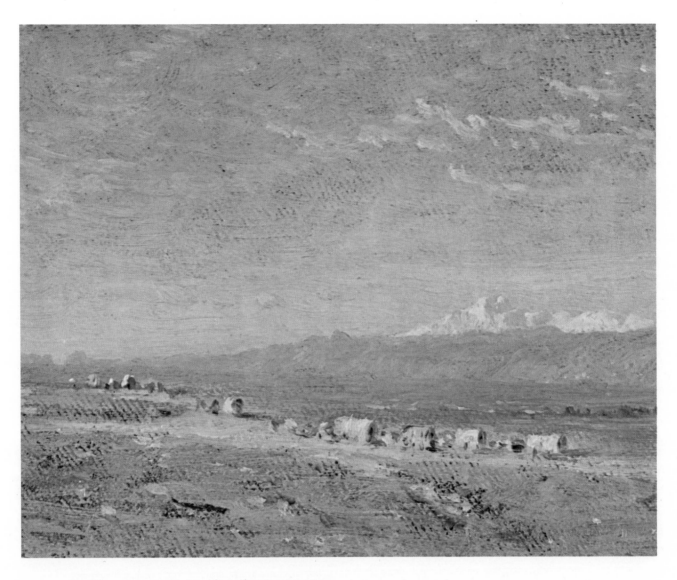

Crossing the Plains. 7¼ x 18 inches, oil (detail). Samuel Colman.

Dean Cornwell NA

1892–1960

ILLUSTRATOR DEAN CORNWELL painted in the tradition of the "old school," using sound craftsmanship and the awareness that the field of illustration was an important art form. He made a significant contribution to the history of art in America. He used models constantly, the camera rarely. Cornwell felt that the measure of an illustrator was his ability to take a subject in which he may have neither interest nor information and tackle it with everything he had.

He was born in Louisville, Kentucky, the son of a civil engineer. The drawing board, pens and india ink were easily accessible to him; but as a boy, he had little hope of becoming an artist, since he suffered headaches for many years from improperly fitted glasses. As he grew older, he gave up all hope of an artistic career because of his eyes and joined a union as a musician. When a young doctor arrived in his town and properly fitted him with glasses, he turned back to art.

At Harvey Dunn's School at Leonia, New Jersey, Cornwell was imbued with the teachings of Howard Pyle through Harvey Dunn, his instructor. He also was a pupil of Charles S. Chapman. Later he went to England to study under the British muralist, Frank Brangwyn.

Cornwell was not only a dominant illustrator of books and magazines, but perhaps also one of the greatest muralists. He created a style of his own in producing massive works portraying both colonial and western history, and the evolution of industrial America. An untiring worker, the left-handed artist made many preliminary studies before developing his final painting.

In 1927 he was commissioned to do a mural for the Los Angeles Public Library. It took five years to complete and was his largest work. Other major murals were for the Eastern Airlines offices and the Raleigh Room at the Warwick Hotel in New York City, and the "Story of Steel" for the Bethlehem Steel Company. His honors and awards are numerous. He was elected to the National Academy of Design in 1941, and he was a fellow of the Royal Society of the Arts. He also was president of the National Society of Mural Painters from 1952 until 1956.

Cornwell was married to his wife Mildred in 1918, and they had two children, Kirkham and Patricia. He died in New York City.

44

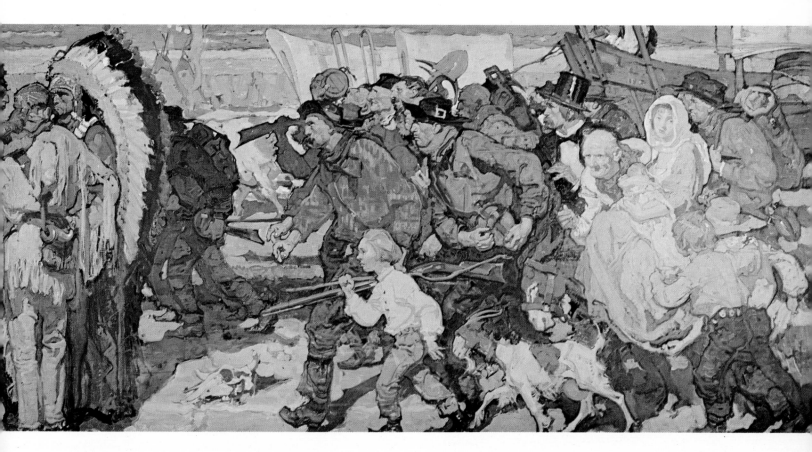

Gold Rush. 32 x 68 inches, oil. Dean Cornwell.

Elliott Daingerfield NA

1859–1932

THE CAREER OF Elliott Daingerfield encompassed many artistic techniques and subjects. But he is most famous for his paintings of the Grand Canyon. Daingerfield first visited there in 1911 and declared it "The Beautiful." Within a year he completed what he called his chief work, the brilliantly executed oil painting entitled "The Grand Canyon."

From his studio in Carmel, California, he frequently traveled to Arizona to reinterpret the area in more subtle tones; he was called the "genius of the canyon."

Daingerfield was born in Harper's Ferry, West Virginia, and grew up in Fayetteville, North Carolina. His aptitude for art was stimulated when as a child he received a box of watercolors for Christmas; he began to paint seriously as a teenager. At twenty-one he left the South for New York City to study at the Art Students League. His work was soon exhibited at the National Academy of Design.

A major break in his career came in 1884 when he met George Inness, the master of American landscape painting. Inness eagerly promoted Daingerfield's work. Eventually, Daingerfield moved into the Holbein Studios, which was home at one time or another to such artists as J. Alden Weir, Homer Martin, Childe Hassam, George deForest Brush, John Singer Sargent, Frank Duveneck, and Winslow Homer, and to Inness as well.

From landscapes, Daingerfield turned, in the 1890s, to painting religious themes. He painted a series of large murals for the Lady Chapel of the Church of St. Mary the Virgin, in New York City. "Art is the principle flowing out of God through certain men and women, by which they perceive and understand the beautiful," he said. "Sculpture, architecture, pictures, and music are the language of the spirit." In 1906, he was elected to the National Academy of Design, and his work was later described as "American decorative impressionism."

Daingerfield was married to Roberta French in 1884; she died during childbirth in 1891. Four years later he married Anna Grainger of Louisville, Kentucky, with whom he had two daughters, Marjorie and Gwendoline.

Following a physical breakdown in 1925, he moved his studio from Blowing Rock to Gainsborough, North Carolina, where he died.

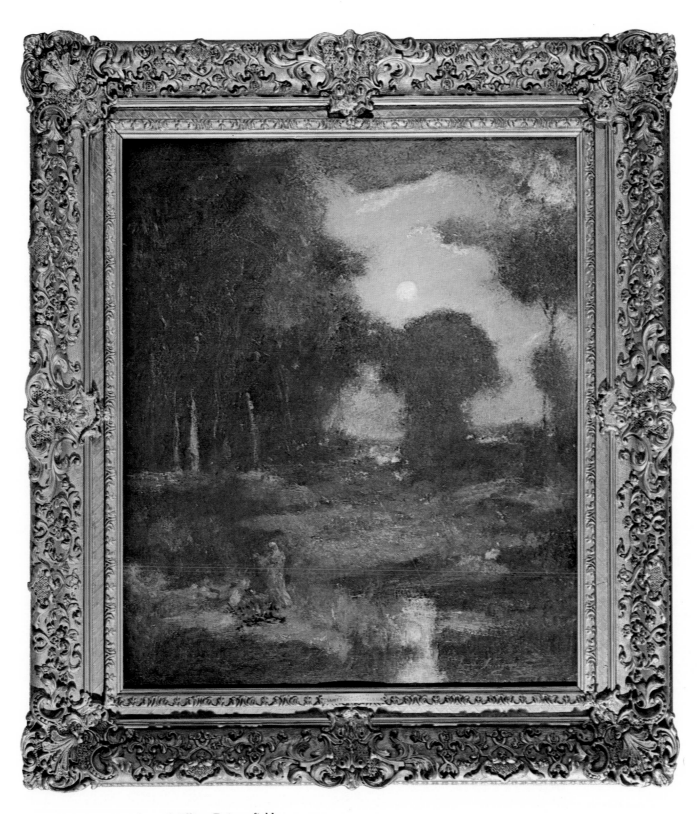

Moonlight. 28 x 24 inches, oil. Elliott Daingerfield.

Cyrus Dallin NA

1861–1944

ONE OF NINE CHILDREN, Cyrus Edwin Dallin was born in the frontier settlement of Springville, Utah. His first attempts at art were figures made from white clay taken from local mines. When he was a young man, he worked with his father in the silver mines and sculpted as a hobby. He created two small busts, which were exhibited at the Utah State Fair. Two wealthy mine owners recognized the young artist's potential and sent him east for study. In Boston, Dallin became an apprentice to Truman Bartlett, and later he opened his own studio. His first Indian head sculpture was completed in 1884.

In 1888 Dallin went to Paris to study at the Academie Julien under Henri Michel Chapu and Jean Dampt. In Paris for two years, he often visited Buffalo Bill's Wild West Show, where the Indians posed for his clay models.

In 1930 Dallin was elected to the National Academy in New York City. He also was invited to become a member of the Institute of Arts and Letters and of the Royal Society of Arts in London. He taught modeling for two years at the Drexel Institute in Philadelphia and at the Massachusetts Normal School of Art for forty years. He retired in 1940, four years before his death in Arlington, Massachusetts.

Dallin's five famous equestrian sculptures on Indian themes were "The Signal of Peace," "The Medicine Man," "The Protest," "The Appeal to the Great Spirit," and "The Scout." Modeled in 1914–15, "The Scout" was dedicated in 1922. The life-size version is in Penn Valley Park, Kansas City, Missouri. A monumental collection of Dallin bronzes is in the Springville Museum of Art at Springville, Utah.

Many of his other works commemorated the Utah pioneers. His sculpture of the Angel Moroni stands atop the Mormon Temple in Salt Lake City. His mother posed for the sculpture, "Pioneer Women of Utah."

Dallin possessed an almost supernatural fascination for the Springville, Utah, mountains. He firmly believed that the plains produced the painters, but the mountains produced the sculptors.

In 1891 he married Vittoria Murray. They had three sons—Edwin, Arthur, and Lawrence. Arthur was one of the first Americans killed in World War II, on June 12, 1940, the same day Dallin learned his Paul Revere statue had been completed in bronze.

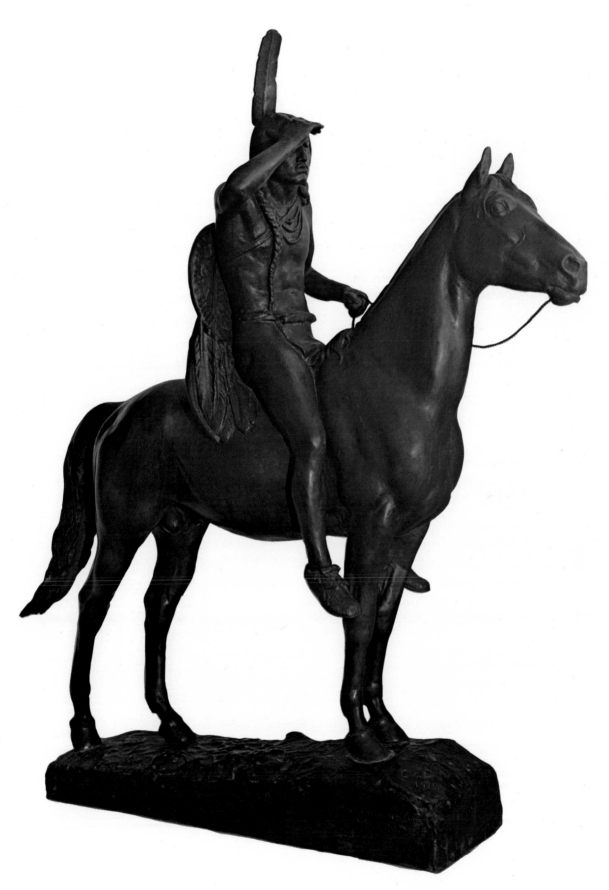

The Scout. H. 39 inches, bronze. Cyrus Dallin.

Felix Darley NA

1822–1888

FEW AMERICAN ARTISTS have been more prolific than Felix Octavius Carr Darley. To collectors of nineteenth-century currency, bank notes, and bonds, he is famous for his vignettes on the various kinds of tender.

Darley illustrated some of the classic books of his day, including Washington Irving's *Rip Van Winkle, The Legend of Sleepy Hollow,* and the novels of J. Fenimore Cooper, Harriet Beecher Stowe, Charles Dickens, and Henry Wadsworth Longfellow.

Western art collectors covet his illustrations depicting the settling of the West, the early life on the plains, the Indians, white settlers, trappers, and hunters. He was especially adept at portraying the dramatic action of the Indian buffalo hunt. Critics marvel at Darley's creative ability and the authenticity of his reproductions. He was a superb draftsman, and he had a thorough knowledge of his characters and the costumes of the period.

Darley was born in Philadelphia of English parents, both of whom had professional stage careers. His parents did not encourage his early talents in art. When he was fourteen, young Darley went to work as an apprentice in the counting room of a mercantile firm.

He developed his artistic skills in his spare time, and at the age of twenty, he said goodbye to the counting house and began his long career as a professional illustrator. Darley soon outmatched all of his contemporaries. When the publishing house of Carey and Hart launched its *Library of Humorous American Works* in 1846, the series carried the credit line, "Illustrated by Darley." In the early years, the illustrator's name was rarely mentioned, but Darley's popularity had forced the publishers to acknowledge the value of a name illustrator.

In 1848 Darley moved his studio from Philadelphia to New York City, where he became more involved in book illustrations. In 1852 he was elected a Professional Honorary Member of the National Academy of Design, and two years later he was elected a National Academician in the Graphic Arts.

When he was thirty-seven, besieged with commissions and at the height of his career, he decided to live a less demanding way of life. After his marriage, he left New York to settle in Claymont, Delaware, where he continued to paint at a slower pace until his death.

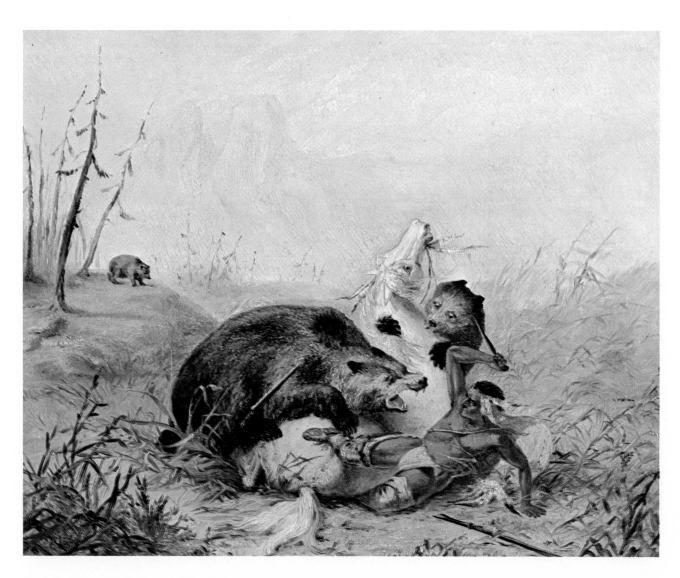

Bear Attack. 11 x 14 inches, oil. Felix Darley.

Herndon Davis

1901–1962

MANY OF HERNDON DAVIS' western paintings hang in prestigious locations—art galleries, museums, industrial firms, business offices, hotels, and the Smithsonian Institution. But his best-known creation was painted on the hardwood floor of a tavern as a prank.

The world-famous "Face On The Barroom Floor" was done in 1936 in the Teller House in Central City, Colorado. Each year more than 150,000 people visit the hotel bar to see the oil painting, which is surrounded by a wood and brass rail and illuminated by fluorescent lights. The beautiful Victorian girl was painted late one evening while Davis sipped rum and Coke. He was working in Central City, painting scenery in the nearby Central City Opera House, and had just had an argument with his employer.

"Why don't we do something to make them remember you?" said a friend. "You are sure to get fired." With a brick, they sanded a spot on the floor in the barroom, and Davis painted the face. The work immortalized the old heartbreaking ballad, "Face On The Barroom Floor," written in 1877 by Hugh Antoine D'Arcy. The final two verses of the poem are:

Say boys, if you give me just another whiskey, I'll be glad,
And I'll draw right here a picture of the face that drove me mad.
Give me that piece of chalk with which you mark the baseball score—
And you will see the lovely Madelaine upon the barroom floor.

Another drink, and with chalk in hand, the vagabond began
To sketch a face that well might buy the soul of any man;
Then, as he placed another lock upon the shapely head,
With a fearful shriek he leaped and fell across the picture—dead.

Davis was born in the Choctaw Nation in what is now Oklahoma. To pay for art lessons, he worked as a bootblack, engraver's apprentice, commercial artist, farm hand, drug clerk, and hotel cashier.

He studied at William Jewell College, Corcoran School of Fine Arts, Art Students League, the National Academy, and Yale University. Although appointed to West Point, he failed the mathematics entrance examination. "My only interest is in human figures," he explained.

He worked for several newspapers and magazines, including the *Denver Post* in Denver, Colorado. Davis died while painting a massive mural for the Smithsonian Institution in Washington, D.C.

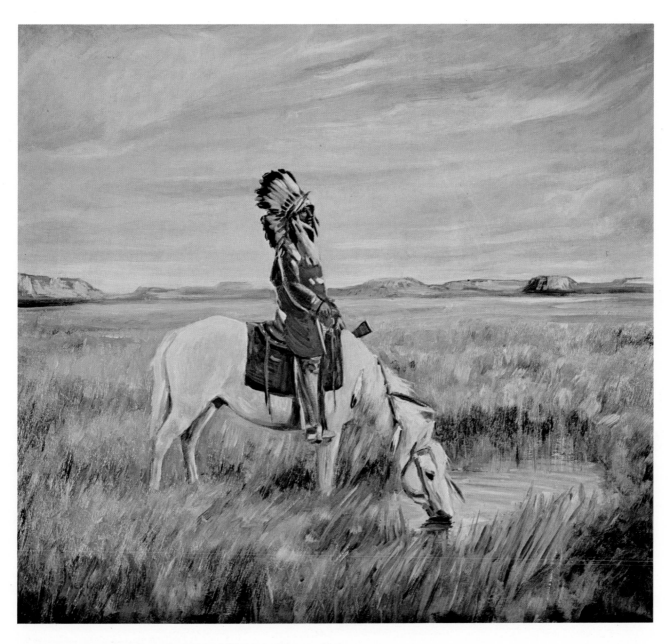

Red Hawk in Dakota Bad Lands. 38 x 34 inches, oil. Herndon Davis.

Edwin Deming

1860–1942

FROM A STANDPOINT OF IMAGINATION, there were few better western artist historians than Edwin Willard Deming. No painter knew more about the American Indian—his life, culture, and religion. The adventuring, robust little man spent most of thirty-one years living with the Indians, using oils and watercolors to reproduce their way of life and ceremonials in murals, book illustrations, and sculpture.

He once wrote of his work: "The white man owes the red man a greater debt than he can ever repay, and is honor-bound to record as true a history of the oldtime Indian as possible. There has never been in literature or art a more splendid subject to treat." He dedicated his life to a pictorial preservation of this culture.

Born in Ashland, Ohio, Deming grew up in western Illinois when the area still was populated by the Sac, Fox, and Winnebago.

His first paintings were done with housepaint scraped from old containers and with clay he dug from riverbanks for use in molding likenesses of animals that roamed the area.

As a teenager, Deming traveled west by train and stagecoach to make sketches in the Indian territory. At the age of twenty, his parents sent him to Chicago to study business law. But he was set on being an artist; he soon sold most of his possessions to get enough money to go to New York City for serious training. He studied there at the Art Students League and at the Ecole des Beaux Arts in Paris.

In 1887 he returned to the southwestern United States to begin three decades with the Indians. He made periodic trips back to his New York studio to complete his field sketches; and while there, in 1892, he married Therese Osterheld. They raised six children in the West. The Blackfoot Indians adopted the entire family and gave Deming the name "Eight Bears."

After returning to New York in 1916, the family's unique home and studio in Greenwich Village was dubbed "The Lodge of the Eight Bears." Here Deming continued to paint Indians and to assist in the creation of displays at the American Museum of Natural History. Teddy Roosevelt had advised him "to paint Indians, as you know them, leave the white man to Remington who knows his cowboys and plainsmen."

54

Osage Warrior. 24 x 20 inches, oil. Edwin Deming.

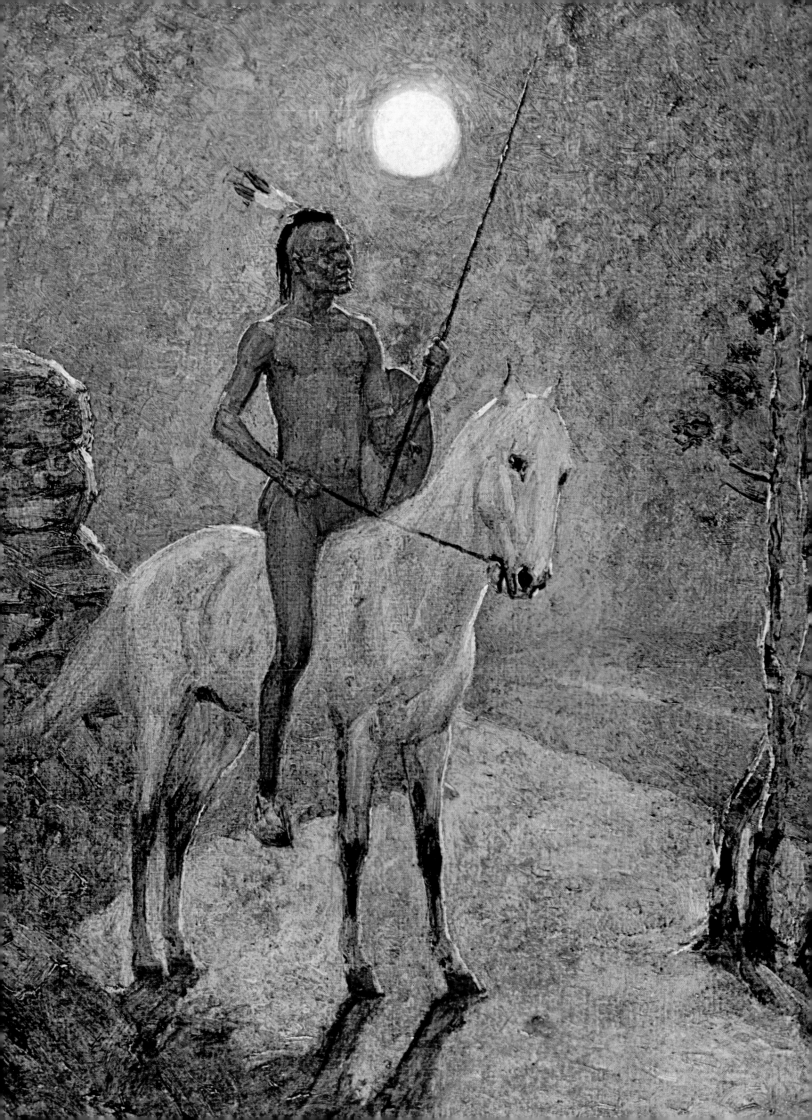

Charles du Tant

b. 1908

HIS YOUNG YEARS were lived in the big pasture country of the Southwest. Charles du Tant was born in Eschiti, Oklahoma, where he enjoyed the early tutelage of Herman Lehmann, famed boy-captive of the Texas Apaches.

Another teacher was a bluest-of-blood Nashville lady pioneering in the Southwest with her school superintendent husband. Twice a week, up in the schoolhouse belfry, du Tant received private art lessons from her. Conte crayon was used; du Tant learned through interminable sessions of mixing and matching colors—plus cleaning, polishing, and shining the palette—and then by copying from worn Leonardo prints, followed by the ritualistic soaping of the brushes.

He soon developed a facility for what today would pass for advanced pop art. He earned expenses during summer holidays by converting many square feet of park fencing (mainly around baseball fields) into illustrated calligraphy. With his stepladder tied to the running-board of his Model T, he worked his way to California and back.

After his marriage, du Tant and his wife settled on a 200-year-old ruins at Talpa Plaza, six miles southeast of Taos, New Mexico. He bought the intriguing pile of adobe, which had an unhindered view of Wheeler Peak to the north and of Abiquiu Peak seventy miles on the south. The couple added a large studio tower, several more rooms, and modern plumbing.

In addition to exploring every stream and trail in northern New Mexico, sketching and fishing along the way, he became editor and co-owner of the *Taos Star*, a newspaper that won numerous gold cup awards in National Editorial Association competitions.

After disposing of the newspaper, the du Tants moved to New York and then back again to New Mexico, this time to Santa Fe. Here he designed and built one of the first solar residences in the Southwest, became administrative assistant to the governor of New Mexico, and successfully directed a statewide campaign for President Eisenhower's second term.

Mabel Dodge Luhan wrote of du Tant, "He belongs to this group that is revitalizing the galleries in Taos. . . . He does not hesitate to attack the enormous mountains . . . nor does the deep canyon stretching ponderously upward dismay his heart." He is still living and painting in Santa Fe.

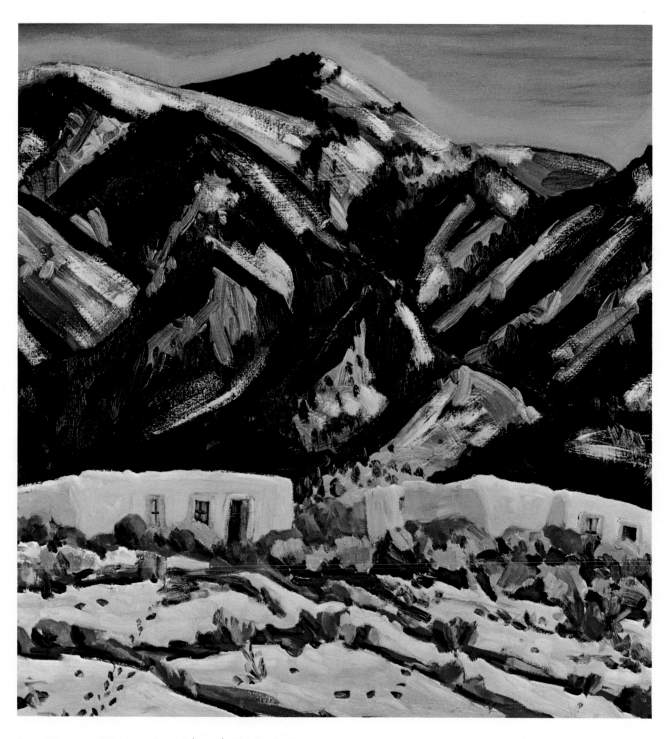

Snow Mountain. 28 x 34 inches, oil (detail). Charles du Tant.

Henry Elkins

1847–1884

ALTHOUGH HENRY ARTHUR ELKINS was born in Vershire, Vermont, he became known in the Middle West for his paintings of Colorado and California and spent most of his short life traveling and painting in the West.

Elkins was one of the artists who crossed the plains to the Rocky Mountains after the Civil War. In the summer of 1866, H. C. Ford, J. F. Gookins, and Elkins, all living in Chicago, formed a party and started out from the Missouri River. On an adventurous trip to Denver, Colorado, they joined an emigrant train for protection through Indian country. Denver was then a city of 7,000. One of their harrowing experiences occurred when a tornado near Cottonwood Springs, Nebraska, toppled their wagons and collapsed their tents.

Elkins was greatly influenced by the great Albert Bierstadt, under whom he studied. While visiting Chicago Lakes near Georgetown, Colorado, Elkins was with a party that included Bierstadt, when a storm arose. Bierstadt asked the group to wait while he made a sketch for his masterpiece, "A Storm in the Rocky Mountains."

Elkins' landscapes were acclaimed by the early settlers of Denver. For some years the Denver newspapers reported on Elkins' work and the receptions held in his honor by Denver society. Many times the Denver papers also reprinted accounts from the Chicago newspapers of Elkins' artistic endeavors in that city.

In 1872 Elkins completed his monumental painting, "Mt. Shasta," which took three years to accomplish. The picture was on exhibition in Vienna, when he leased a studio in Chicago to paint a companion piece, entitled "Sierra Madre." After being exhibited the world over, "Mt. Shasta" was sold for $15,000, an unheard of price at that time; it was later destroyed in the Illinois Club fire.

Shortly after Elkins' death in Georgetown, Colorado, his most valuable works were stolen from his studio in Chicago. The search for the missing paintings was continued by his son, H. A. Elkins. "Sierra Madre" was discovered in a Chicago Loop saloon. The find rated headline coverage in Chicago newspapers. Many of the other paintings were found in the Y.M.C.A. and in an old people's home in Elgin, Illinois, where they were donated by a purchaser who hadn't known they were stolen.

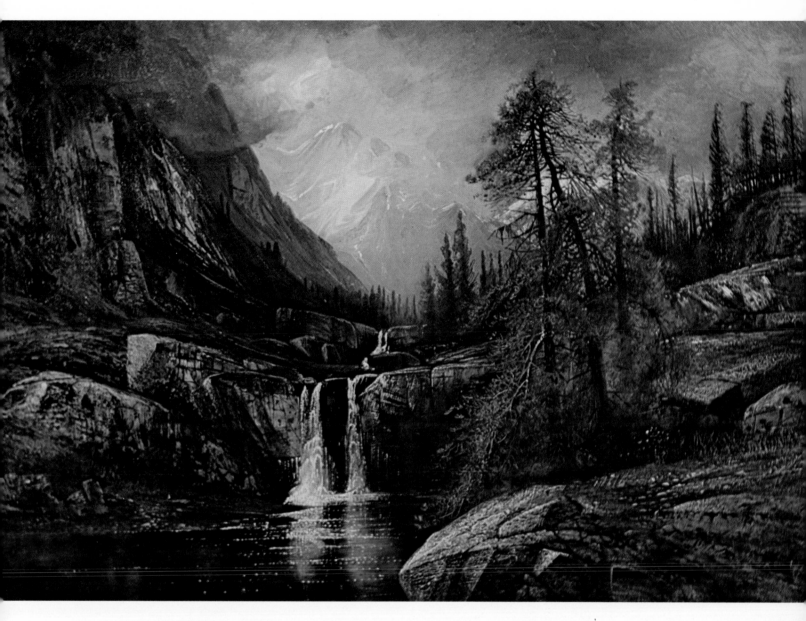

After the Storm. Dated 1882. 24 x 36 inches, oil. Henry Elkins.

Fremont Ellis

b. 1897

BACK IN GOLD RUSH DAYS, vigilantes in the boom town of Virginia City, Montana, hung their former sheriff and his gang of gold thieves. They were hung from a beam extending from the unfinished structure of the house where Fremont Ellis was later born. He was the son of a traveling dentist.

The family did not linger long in Montana; their travels took them to New York City, where young Ellis was able to spend hours at the Metropolitan Museum "memorizing" the paintings to be copied in the privacy of his home. Exercising his memory in that manner contributed much to his artistic success. Ellis' talents are largely self-taught. He attended the Art Students League for a short time, but he believed "you learn by painting."

Starting his career as a painter in El Paso, Texas, he moved to Santa Fe, New Mexico, in 1919. Here he quickly became part of the artist colony. Ellis built an adobe house on the Camino del Monte Sol. Willard Nash, Walter Mruk, Jozef Bakos, and Will Shuster were also building there; they formed the group, "Los Cinco Pintores." All five artists developed in different directions, but exhibited together for a few years. Ellis was the loner and soon went his own way. He married and moved to San Sebastian, ten miles north of Santa Fe, where he transplanted an old Spanish house from Galisteo. It became one of the most beautiful houses in that area.

He loved the old way of life—the people, the manners, the customs. This emotional and romantic quality shows in his art. He is a man distinguished in appearance, and the twinkle in his eye is a clue to his ready wit.

Ellis has become a painter primarily of impressionistic landscapes, also completing a few seascapes, portraits, architectural studies, and still life. He doesn't copy what nature has already done for his subject matter. "Leave that to the photographer," he says. "I want my finished product to be a good painting. The subject is merely a means to an end." He has a rare gift of being able to paint not merely what he sees before his eyes, but also what he feels from within. His awards are many, and he is represented in major museums and collections throughout the country.

For the past twenty years, he has been living alone on Canyon Road in Santa Fe, making his home and studio in the unique house built by artist William Penhallow Henderson.

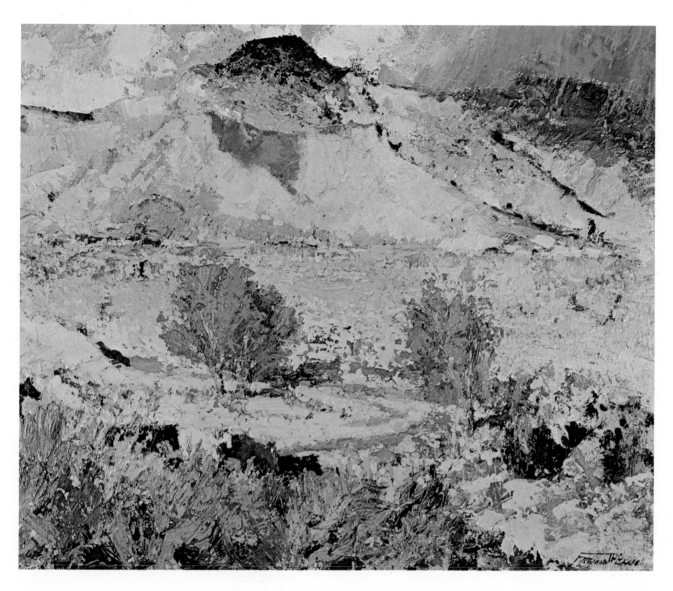

Ghost Ranch Country. 25 x 30 inches, oil. Fremont Ellis.

Clarence Ellsworth

1885–1961

HIS PAINTINGS PORTRAYED THE WEST with great skill and detail. Yet Clarence Arthur Ellsworth sought neither fame nor fortune, and his work was not fully appreciated during his lifetime. His research was meticulous. He studied the position of every feather in an Indian headdress, every strap and buckle on a set of harness, every muscle in the human and animal anatomy.

While his hundreds of portraits and historical scenes now are proudly possessed by museums and private collectors, they originally were sold or traded for groceries and rent money.

Ellsworth was born in Holdredge, Nebraska, in a one-room apartment behind his father's drugstore. By the time he was four years old, he was sketching animals on wrapping paper from the store. At the age of seven, he saw Indians for the first time when a group passed through Holdredge. Three years later he paid his first visit to the Pine Ridge Reservation—a journey he was to repeat many times.

As a youth, he was a loner, traveling through the West and adding to his knowledge of the Indian. He used his self-taught art skills to earn a meager living. He fell in love with an Indian girl, but she died before they could be married, and Ellsworth remained a bachelor the rest of his life.

His most permanent and gainful employment in his early years came as a newspaper artist. He worked for both the *Denver Post* and the *Rocky Mountain News* in Denver, Colorado. During employment at the Baker Engraving Company in Omaha, Nebraska, he came in contact with the work of contemporary artist A. B. Frost. It was the example of Frost's work that gradually led him away from the field of illustration. During vacations or between steady jobs, he always returned to visit the Sioux, Blackfeet, and Shoshone Indians.

In 1929 Ellsworth and his widowed mother went to Hollywood, where he became a title artist and set designer for the young motion picture industry. Yet he continued to paint and his interest in the Indian remained.

Ellsworth's biography was written by Otha Donner Wearin and published in 1967. Twenty of Ellsworth's paintings of the Blackfeet Indians hang in the Southwest Museum in Los Angeles.

62

He died in Hollywood after a long illness.

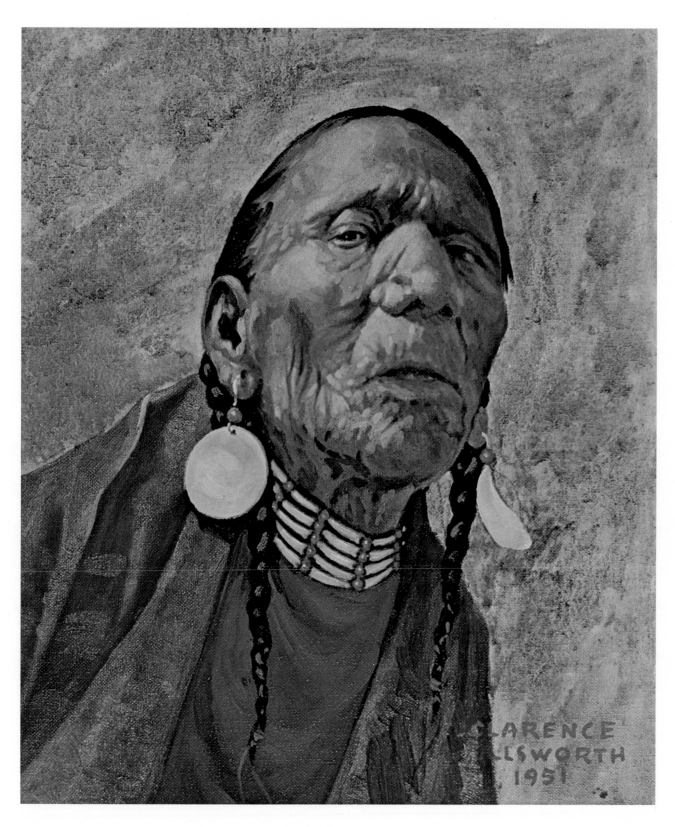

Black Track. Dated 1951. 10 x 8 inches, oil. Clarence Ellsworth.

Henry Farny

1847–1916

UNLIKE THE WORK OF MANY early western artists, Henry Francois Farny's paintings met with almost instant acclaim and quick sale. His repeated trips to Indian encampments resulted in the storytelling type of art that was so typical of the times. Although his paintings were done with restraint, their implications were clear and impressive. Farny's miniature-like technique was void of the sensationalism which generally was the tool of the less accomplished artists of the day. Paintings by Henry Farny are "blue chip" in the art market; they have appreciated more in value per square inch than those of any other artist.

Farny was born in Alsace, France. His parents fled to America, as political refugees, after the Napoleonic party came to power. The family first settled in Pennsylvania at the headwaters of the Allegheny River. Their home was near a Seneca Indian camp, and the artist's early encounters with the Seneca led to a lifelong interest in the Indian.

The family eventually migrated down the Allegheny and Ohio Rivers to Cincinnati, where the boy found work as an apprentice lithographer. By the age of eighteen, he had work published in *Harper's Weekly*.

The following year Farny went to Europe for three and a half years of study in Rome, Dusseldorf, and Vienna. Returning to America, he worked as a book illustrator, revolutionizing the schoolbook industry when he salvaged the declining McGuffey Reader series with his illustrations. His book pictures showed his realistic technique, portraying everything that would delight a child.

Farny made numerous trips to the West, including a thousand-mile canoe trip down the Missouri River, in 1878, and an 1893 journey to Montana to attend ceremonies marking completion of the Northern Pacific transcontinental railroad. He was adopted by a tribe of Sioux Indians and named "Long Boots."

A noted gourmet cook and after-dinner speaker, he also could speak French, German, Italian, and Indian.

When Farny was fifty-nine years old, he married his eighteen-year-old ward, Ann Ray. They had one son, Daniel. Farny predeceased his wife by twenty-five years. Upon Ann Farny's death, their ashes were mingled and buried in Spring Grove Cemetery in Cincinnati.

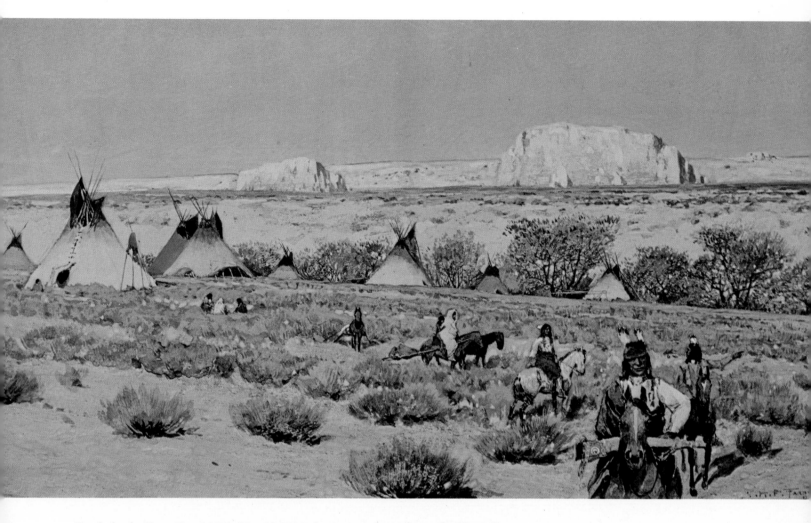

Ready for the Hunt. Dated 1892. 9½ x 16-3/4 inches, watercolor and gouache. Henry Farny.

Harrison Fisher

1875–1934

AN ARTIST OF diverse talent, Harrison Fisher is remembered for creating an American feminine society symbol. His "Harrison Fisher Girl" was the vogue of its day, and his drawings of beautiful girls became known throughout the world. Along with Charles Dana Gibson and Howard Chandler Christy, Fisher was part of the "Girl Triumvirate" of American art. He also was recognized by Christy as the "king of magazine cover illustrators."

Fisher was born in Brooklyn, New York. Both his father, Hugo A. Fisher, and his grandfather were artists of note. His career in art was influenced by his father, who was his first teacher.

After attending art schools in San Francisco, England, and France, he held jobs as a newpaper artist with the *San Francisco Call* and the *Examiner*. In 1898, Fisher moved to New York City to begin a thirty-six-year career as a magazine and book illustrator. A prolific worker, he used ink, charcoal, pastels, and watercolors.

Fisher illustrations appeared in most of the leading magazines of the day, such as *Cosmopolitan, Saturday Evening Post, McClure's, Puck,* and *Ladies' Home Journal.*

While in France, he made a sketch of a French girl who had lost most of her hair because of typhoid fever and had swathed her head in a ribbon tied with a large bow. Fisher admired the headdress and painted a large ribbon and bow on a typical American girl. The style became immediately popular for a generation of women.

Fisher sought to draw other subjects, but his editors demanded more and more "Fisher Girls;" they told him his other efforts would never sell. Girls flocked to his studio, hoping to be chosen as models, as well as besieging him with letters.

The artist never married, claiming he had seen so much female beauty that it was no longer a mystery to him.

Fisher was a retiring person throughout his life. He avoided publicity, and he had few personal friends. His favorite club was the Bohemian Club of San Francisco; he also belonged to the Friars of New York and the Society of Illustrators.

He died in New York City following an emergency operation.

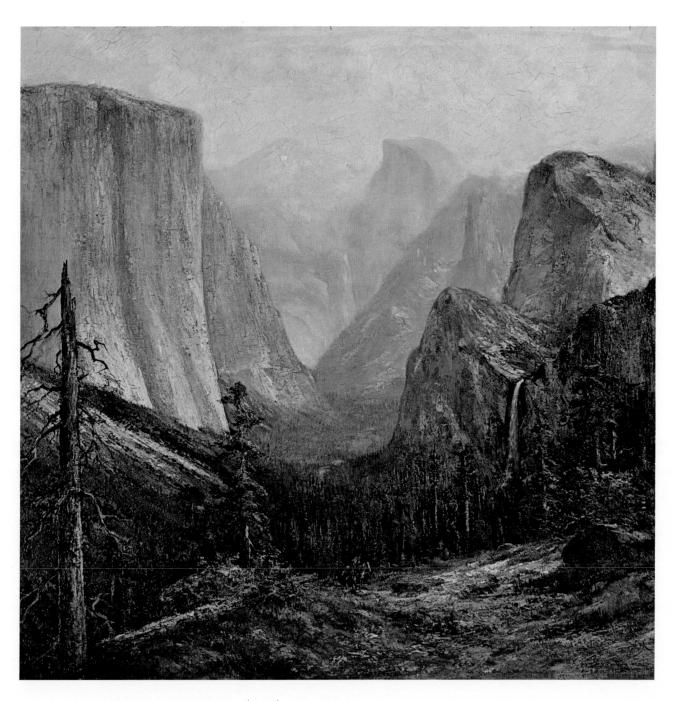

Yosemite, Near Half Dome. 30 x 36 inches, oil (detail). Harrison Fisher.

Joseph Fleck

b. 1893

AFTER VIEWING A TRAVELING exhibition of paintings sponsored by the Taos Society of Artists, the career of Joseph Fleck changed.

That was in Kansas City, Missouri, in 1924, and in a very short time the native Austrian moved to Taos, New Mexico, to begin painting portraits, landscapes, and murals of the Southwest. Like so many artists before him, he became thoroughly absorbed in his new surroundings.

From his studio at Ranchos de Taos, he depicts the colorful region and its people in a simple straight-forward style; his European training gave way to a freer style of paint application and use of color.

Born in Vienna, he attended the Royal Academy of Fine Arts and the Institute of Graphic Art. Following graduation, he immigrated to the United States and settled in Kansas City.

From 1934 through 1941, Fleck was artist-in-residence and Dean of Fine Arts at the University of Kansas City, where he fell under the influence of Thomas Hart Benton.

During his seven years there, his style developed into broad impressionism. While his earlier work was without the flourish of technique or decorative color, his later landscapes were marked by strong emphasis on swirling smudges of bright pigment. He felt the need for a new style, which allowed more room for improvisation.

Fleck's work is exhibited throughout the world; his murals at the University of Kansas City, and at the Raton, New Mexico, and Hugo, Oklahoma, post offices have become famous.

Through the years, Fleck has won numerous awards and medals. The Federal Ministry of Education in Austria requested one of his works for that country's collection of modern paintings and sculpture.

Paintings by Joseph Fleck are in the collections of the Breckenridge Museum in San Antonia; the Fort Worth, Texas, Art Center; the William Rockhill Nelson Gallery of Art; the Kansas City Library; the War Museum, Richmond, Virginia; the Museum of New Mexico in Santa Fe; the University of New Mexico Art Gallery in Albuquerque; and the Harwood Foundation in Taos.

Fleck and his wife, who are still living in Taos, have one son, a laser physicist for the University of California, Dr. Joseph A. Fleck.

68

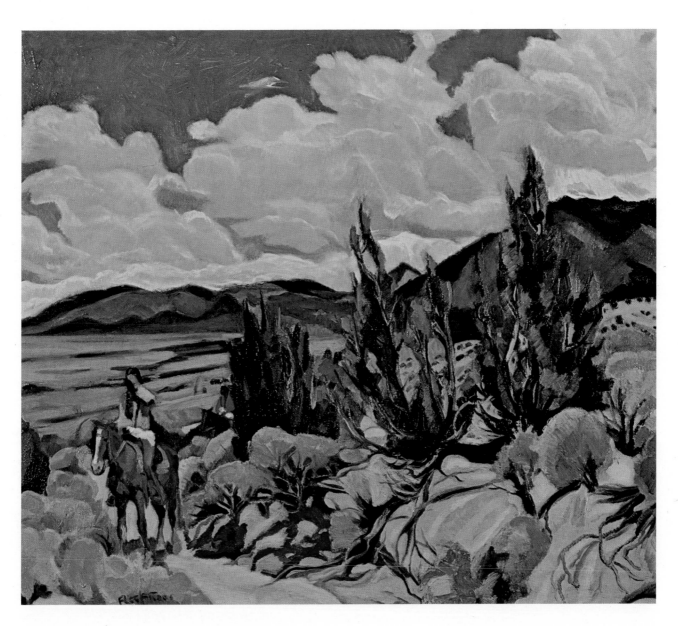

Peaceful Hunt. 25 x 30 inches, oil. Joseph Fleck.

Charles Fries

1854–1940

A NATIVE OF THE MIDWEST, Charles Arthur Fries became known as the dean of San Diego artists after he settled in that California city in 1897. His first home in Southern California was at the unrestored mission of San Juan Capistrano in 1896. It was here, at the suggestion of Charles Lummis, editor of *Sunset Magazine,* that he began a series of pictures that completely identified the art of Charles Fries with the spirit of California.

His paintings traced the robust history of the young state and the majestic beauty of its deserts. He also devoted his canvases to painting landscapes, mountains, and eucalyptus trees. His work was noted for its truth and beauty and for the pure use of color, sound craftsmanship, and bright atmospheric light.

He was described as "a gentle, compassionate man, whose bright blue eyes twinkled. His build was slight. He had a Van Dyke beard and customarily wore gray and a flowing black bow tie. He pedaled around town on a bicycle," becoming known as an aristocratic character.

Born in Hillsborough, Ohio, Fries was raised in Cincinnati and attended the McMiccan Art Academy when it was among the most prestigious schools. Other students there at the time included J. H. Twachtman, Robert Blum, Kenyon Cox, Joe DeCamp, and Frank Duveneck.

At age seventeen Fries went to New York to work in a lithographer's shop, learning the art of printing through use of lithographic stones. Five years later he went to Europe to continue his art studies. He gained a wide reputation on the continent and received many glowing reviews in the Paris art journals. Fries returned to the United States, living in Vermont before moving across the country to California. He married in 1888.

He did many illustrations for periodicals and school textbooks, which included *Leslie's Magazine, Harper's Weekly, Puck, McGuffey Readers,* and the *Illustrated School History of the United States.*

Fries' works have hung in exhibitions from coast to coast. His painting "Rugged Grandeur" was purchased by the American College Club of San Diego and presented to the Fine Arts Society for its permanent collection.

The California desert is decidedly better known and appreciated because of his many paintings.

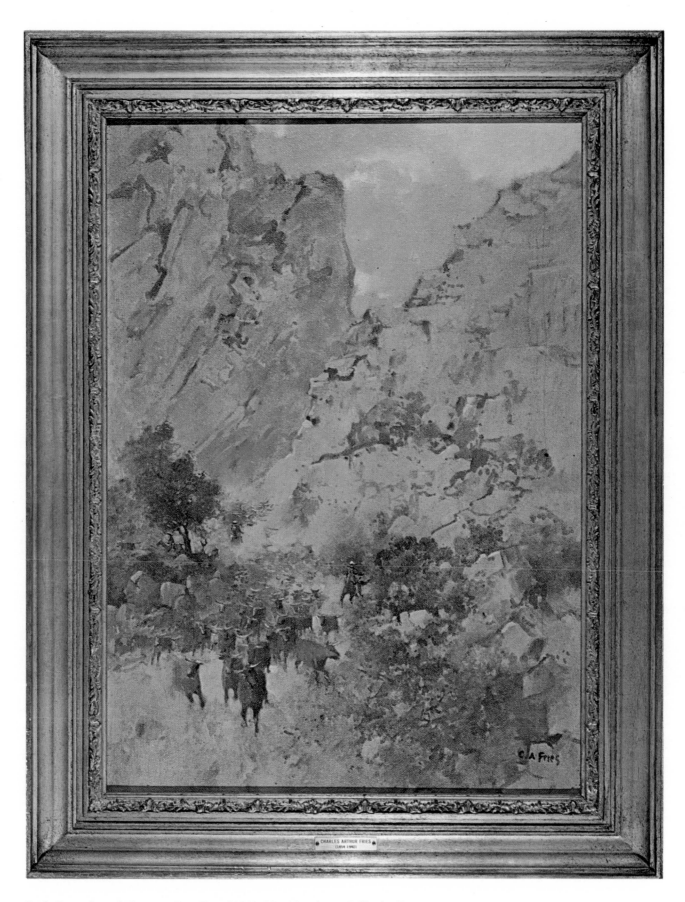

Cattle Drive through Gaviotta Pass. Dated 1901. 30 x 22 inches, oil. Charles Fries.

Gilbert Gaul NA
1855–1919

WILLIAM GILBERT GAUL'S PAINTINGS of Union and Confederate Army subjects, rendered in the last quarter of the nineteenth century, earned him the reputation of being an outstanding Civil War artist. He inherited a farm in Van Buren County, Tennessee, and while residing there for four years, he painted the remnants of the Civil War. Of equal fame are his renderings of the American cowboy and Indian.

He was born in Jersey City, New Jersey, attending the public schools in Newark and the Claverack Military Academy. Ill health forced him to give up his dream of a career in the Navy, so he turned to the study of art.

During the 1870s, Gaul studied under L. W. Wilmarth at the National Academy of Design and with John J. Brown at the Art Students League in New York City. He was elected a member of the National Academy of Design in 1882.

He saw the West for the first time in 1876, and on subsequent trips went as far as California. He lived with the Indians and at army posts for months at a time, recording the various lifestyles with his camera and brush and later transferring them onto canvas at his studio in New York City and in Nashville, Tennessee, where he also maintained a home.

In 1890, along with Peter Moran, Henry Poore, Julian Scott, and Walter Shirlaw, he was assigned by the United States Census Bureau to conduct the eleventh census of Indians living throughout the country. He not only illustrated the life of the red man, but also wrote about his observations of their conditions for a 683-page document entitled *Report on Indians Taxed and Indians Not Taxed,* now a very rare volume.

His illustrations appeared in the leading periodicals of the day. In Nashville he made arrangements for the publication of a print portfolio of some of his paintings. The originals are presently in the collection of the Birmingham, Alabama, Museum of Art. An illustrated account of his travels in Mexico, the West Indies, Panama, and Nicaragua was exhibited at the World's Columbian Exposition in Chicago in 1893.

Gilbert Gaul was married twice; his family included four children—two from his first marriage and two from his second wife's previous marriage. He died in New York City following a long illness.

72

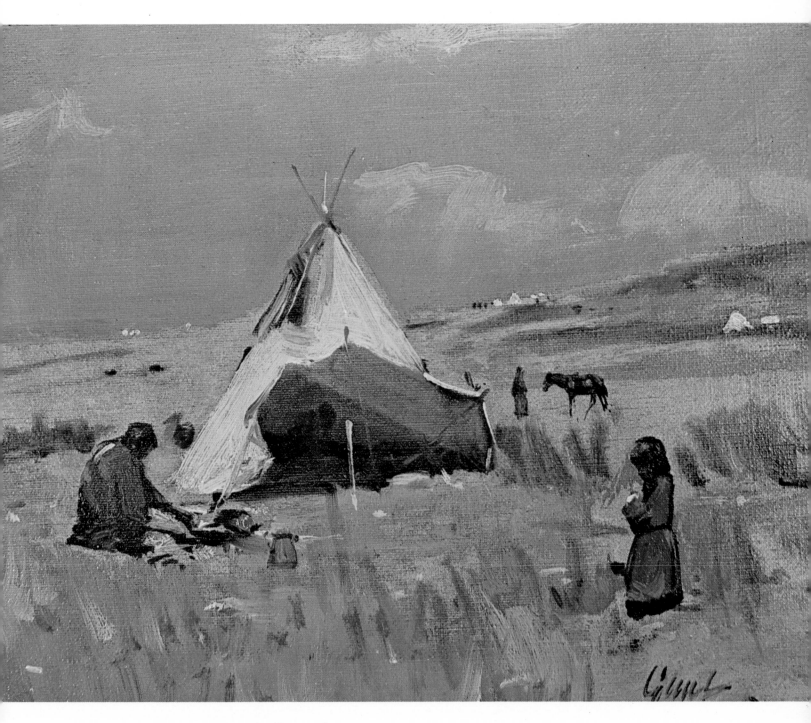

Plains Indian Family. 7 x 9 inches, oil. Gilbert Gaul.

Glenna Goodacre

b. 1939

AWARDS FOR ACHIEVEMENT in various fields of art from the National Cowboy Hall of Fame and Western Heritage Center in Oklahoma City, Oklahoma, have become some of the most coveted in this day of extreme competition in the arts. Glenna Goodacre is one of the fortunate few who has received one of these much sought-after medals of merit for her polychrome, feminine sculpture, "The Waterbearer." She also won recognition at the 1975 invitational Solon Borglum Memorial Sculpture Exhibition, competing with twenty-nine other artists.

In 1974 and 1975, Mrs. Goodacre was given the Allied Arts of America award for her bronze bust, "Winona," and a bas-relief, "Buffalo Dance." She exhibited at the National Academy of Design in New York in 1975 and her bronze, "Warrior," was shown with the National Sculpture Society in 1977 in New York. The 1970s are banner years for Mrs. Goodacre.

The Winter 1975 issue of *Artists of the Rockies* and the December 1976 *Southwest Art* magazine printed articles on Mrs. Goodacre. She also is included in the 1976 issue of *Who's Who in American Art*.

"Charming, witty, and an achiever" are the words that would best describe Glenna Goodacre. Her wise, indulgent parents recognized her talent and guided her footsteps in the right direction.

She presently lives in Boulder, Colorado, with her husband, Bill, and their two children, Tim and Jill. She was born and grew up in Lubbock, Texas.

After graduating from Colorado College in Colorado Springs, Colorado, she studied art at the Art Students League in New York. Her early work was in oils, painting landscapes and still life. Her best work embodies the human figure and head studies.

Alternating easily from sculpturing to painting, she feels that this change is necessary to keep her work interesting and exciting. She incorporates a variety of oil techniques from traditional underpainting to direct application. Water media techniques range from dry brush to washes, combined with pastel. She quickly grasps the subject and admits that she works best under pressure.

Collectors of western art are giving Glenna Goodacre's paintings and sculptures a second look and are buying all of the sensitive work she is able to create.

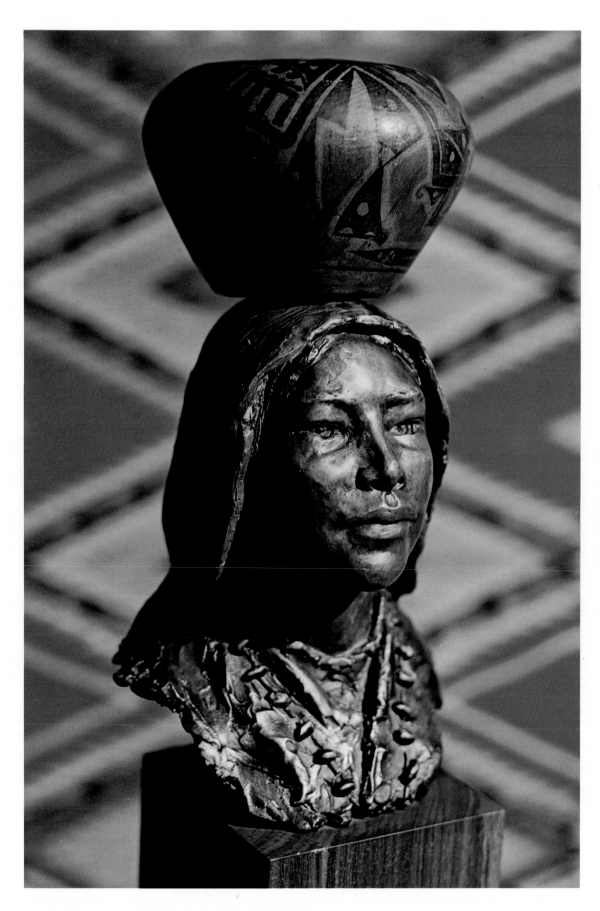

The Waterbearer. H. 13½ inches, bronze. Glenna Goodacre.

Philip Goodwin

1881–1935

SPORTSMEN REMEMBER PHILIP RUSSELL GOODWIN'S large calendar prints, usually "predicament" paintings, which hung in mercantile establishments across the country during the twenties and thirties. There were also covers for *Outdoor Life* and *Saturday Evening Post* and advertising posters for Remington Arms and Winchester Arms. A very special painting, "Horse and Rider," became the trademark of the Winchester Company.

Philip Goodwin was born in Norwich, Connecticut. Sketching was a consuming childhood pastime. He was eleven when he sold his first illustrated story to *Collier's* magazine. At seventeen he was a promising student of Howard Pyle at the Brandywine School at Chadds Ford, Pennsylvania, and a classmate of N. C. Wyeth and Frank Schoonover; he later attended the Rhode Island School of Design. Goodwin was also a member of the Art Students League in New York.

While still in his twenties, he became friends with Carl Rungius and Charles Russell, when all three artists maintained studios in close proximity in New York City. Thereafter, whenever financially possible, Goodwin spent his summers in the West. Many of his adventures with Russell are recorded in the book, *Charles M. Russell,* by Adams and Britzman.

Probably influenced by Russell, Goodwin became adept at sculpting. In a letter to his mother from the Russell ranch in Kalispell, Montana, Goodwin wrote that on rainy days, when he and Charlie were unable to be out sketching, they worked on models. After Russell's death, Goodwin helped Nancy Russell assemble the book of his letters, *Good Medicine,* which contains three of Russell's illustrated letters to him.

Goodwin never married; his lifelong commitment was to the field of illustration. In addition to commercial advertising commissions, he painted for a goodly number of leading authors. Notable among the many books that he illustrated were *Call of the Wild* by Jack London and *African Game Trails* by Theodore Roosevelt.

There was a peculiar irony in his untimely death at the age of fifty-four. While attempting to complete commitments in preparation for a move to Death Valley, California, Goodwin was found dead of pneumonia in his Mamaroneck, New York, studio.

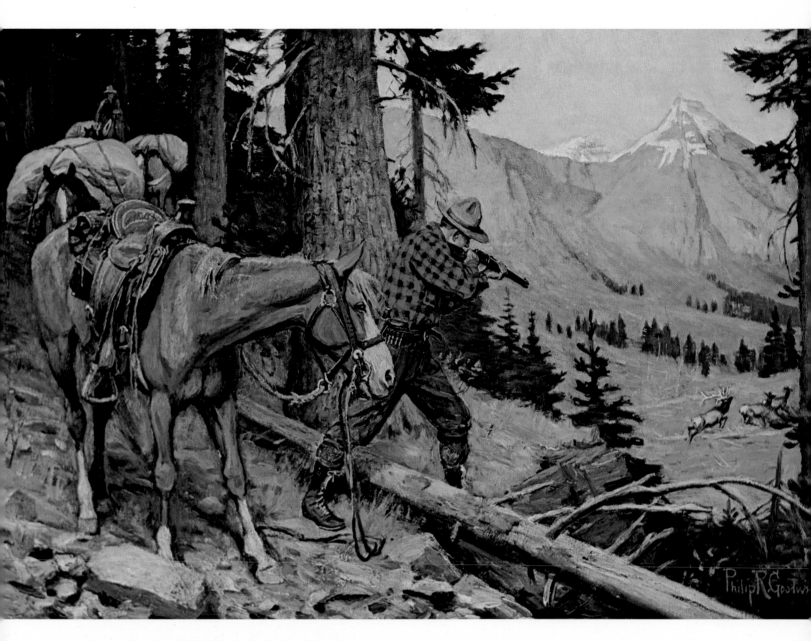

A Chance Shot. 24 x 36 inches, oil. Philip Goodwin.

Olaf Grafstrom

1855–1933

DURING HIS FORTY YEARS in the United States, Olaf Grafstrom not only reproduced majestic landscapes and scenes of Indian life, but also, quite democratically, painted nudes for barrooms, as well as many altar pieces for Lutheran churches.

His work—done in pastels, watercolors, pencil, pen and ink, and oil—reflected painstaking accuracy in every detail. He developed an interesting technique for landscape studies, which included a rather subdued portrayal of nature. Scenes from his native Sweden were an exception, as they reflected the lighter approach of his earlier training. Grafstrom won quick acclaim for his landscapes of the Swedish mountains, and one of his works was purchased for the private collection of King Oscar II.

Born in Attmar Medelpad in northern Sweden, he was the son of a farmer. Grafstrom showed a talent for art at an early age. He enrolled at the Academie of Arts in Stockholm, where he was a contemporary of Anders Zorn, Bruno Liljefors, and Richard Bergh, the country's leading artists.

In 1886 he immigrated to the United States and settled in Portland, Oregon. His landscapes of the Pacific Northwest were eagerly purchased by western collectors and for display in public buildings. He also painted many Indians and was acquainted with the northern tribes.

From Portland he moved to Spokane, Washington. He was well represented at the expositions in both cities the next few years. A landscape, "A Scene From Lapland," won the grand silver medal in Portland. A painting, "View of Portland, Oregon," is in the M. H. de Young Museum's collection in San Francisco. In 1893 Grafstrom accepted a position of art instructor at Bethany College in Lindsborg, Kansas. From 1897 until 1926 he was on the faculty of the Rock Island Art School at Augustana College in Illinois. In these two positions he exerted a marked influence on behalf of art among the Swedish-Americans.

His portrait of Martin Luther is owned by the Museum of History in Des Moines, Iowa. The Birger Sandzen Memorial Art Gallery at Bethany College in Lindsborg, Kansas, has a number of Grafstrom's paintings.

Grafstrom was married in 1904, and he and his wife had two daughters. He died in Stockholm, after spending the last five years of his life there.

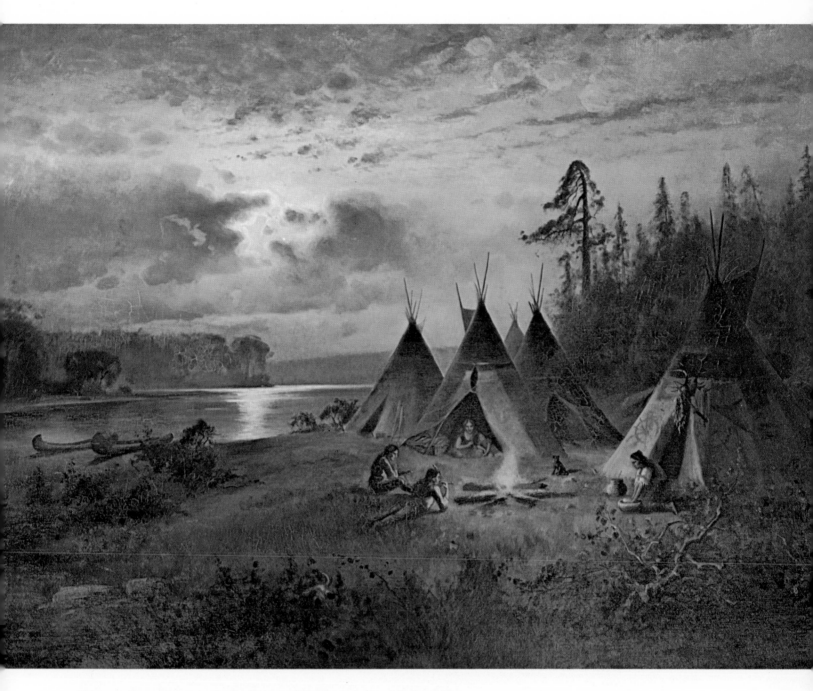

Chippewa Encampment at the Confluence of the Mississippi and St. Croix Rivers.
Dated 1904. 40 x 66 inches, oil (detail). Olaf Grafstrom.

Frances Greenman

b. 1890

I'VE PAINTED A THOUSAND portraits in almost every state in the Union. I've painted men and women drunk and sober, children, bankers, governors, movie stars, and pretty ladies who cried into their real pearl necklaces. I love work. I love people."

The preceding is the opening paragraph in the autobiography titled *Higher Than The Sky*, written by Frances Cranmer Greenman in 1954. The book reveals not only the life of a great artist, but a woman with great sensitivity and a talent for relating endless humorous anecdotes.

The beginning was in Aberdeen, South Dakota, where the Cranmers lived when Mrs. Greenman was a child. At the age of five years, she was entranced by the aromatic talent of a neighbor who painted china. The smell and clutter of it all enchanted her to the point of influencing her into a creative career of her own. When the artist was eleven years old, she joined the art class of another china painter. Her first commission was to paint twenty-five place cards for a party, placing two large sweet peas on each card.

Before completing high school she went to Madison, South Dakota, where she finished her academic training at the Madison Academy. The Corcoran School of Art in Washington, D.C., was next, then came study at the Art Students League under William M. Chase and Robert Henri. Henri became her lifelong friend and greatest influence. Her final formal art education was at the Academie de la Grande Chaumiere in Paris.

With her marriage to John Greenman, a second career was added, and subsequent motherhood with the birth of her two daughters, Patty and Coventry. The lives of her family were filled with excitement and travel, as they were usually included in the artist's glamorous lifestyle in New York City. The marriage, however, ended in divorce.

Mrs. Greenman is a painter of portraits; in her work she combines the fearless vigor of a man with a woman's sympathy for her subject. In 1924 she won first prize in the exhibit of Twin City artists conducted by the Minneapolis Art Institute for her painting, "The Pioneer Woman." Her honors are many, with numerous shows and exhibitions to her credit. She is also represented in many of the major museums throughout the world.

Frances Greenman is currently living back in Minneapolis, Minnesota, in the apartment and studio she has called home all through the years.

The Boy. 40 x 36 inches, oil. Frances Greenman.

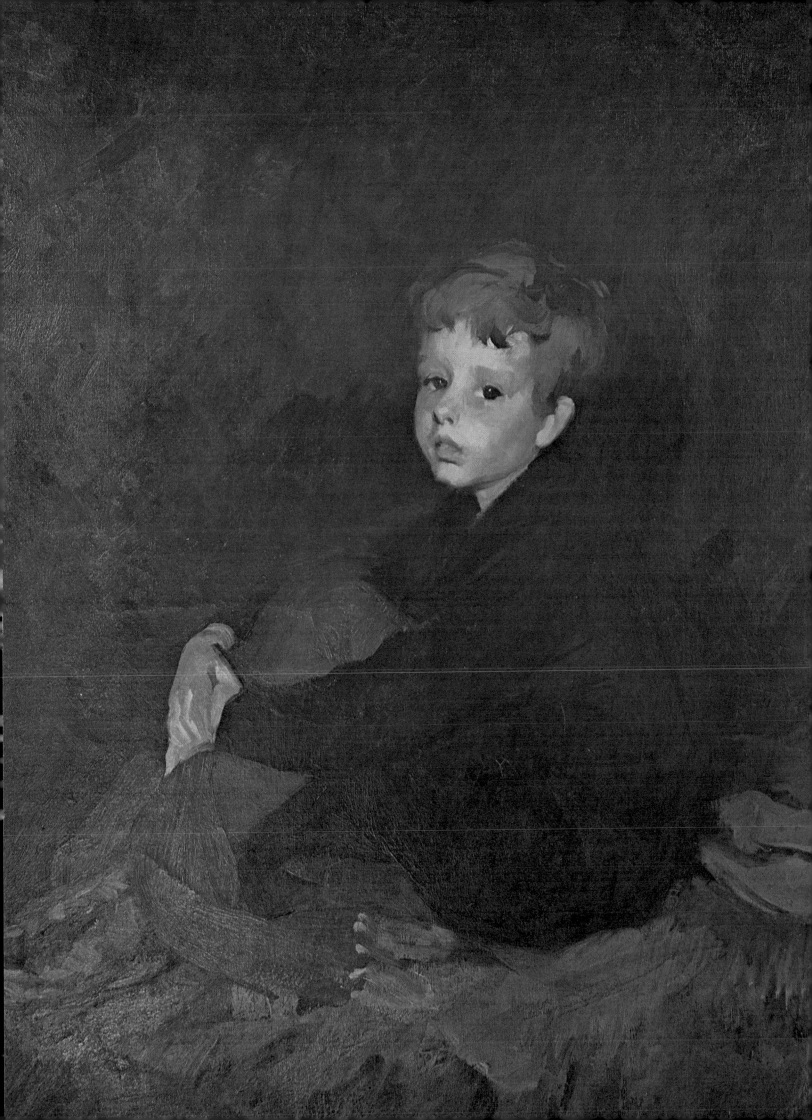

Paul Gregg

1876-1949

HISTORICALLY IMPORTANT to the state of Colorado, Paul Gregg's artistic endeavors are like windows framing the events of times past. Six hundred and four of his paintings remain in the archives of the *Denver Post* in Denver, Colorado, as silent reminders of the struggles that developed this territory.

Gregg was born in Baxter Springs, Kansas, where his pioneer parents had settled after coming west by oxcart. He saw firsthand the ways of the Indian and observed that a cow gets up rear-end first, the horse front-end first, the buffalo is immune to disease, and the front and rear wheels of a stagecoach do not have the same number of spokes. When he painted a covered wagon, it was not a copied scene from a history book, but was an exciting picture from his earliest memory.

At the age of seventeen Gregg left Kansas to spend a year at the St. Louis Museum of Fine Arts. He then was employed by the *St. Louis Republic,* at a salary of twelve dollars a week. Gregg returned to Baxter Springs each summer to sketch and study nature. While on a vacation in Denver, in 1902, he met H. H. Tammen and Frederick G. Bonfils, who persuaded him to join the *Denver Post* staff. As news photography was still in its infancy, newspaper artists not only drew cartoons and painted decorative scenes, but were also called upon to illustrate news events—sometimes from sketches on the spot, sometimes from descriptions, and sometimes from a photographic memory and imagination.

Out of his ability to produce lifelike illustrations for western stories, Gregg developed his oil paintings for the Sunday *Denver Post* magazine section. For forty years he produced western scenes—one a week, totalling well over 2,000 in all—he also did countless cartoons and sketches. He developed his oil painting from a scant sketch, working nonstop until completed.

In the last twenty years of his career, Gregg enlisted the talent of his poet friend, Gene Lindberg, to add verses to his works. The joint effort became a full-page weekly color feature in the *Post.* Each feature developed from short notes jotted down by Paul or his wife, Marian, as they traveled. Lindberg wrote of his friend, "He was above all a storyteller in oils, and the stories were as varied as the West itself—old as the fur trade, new as the streamlining of planes."

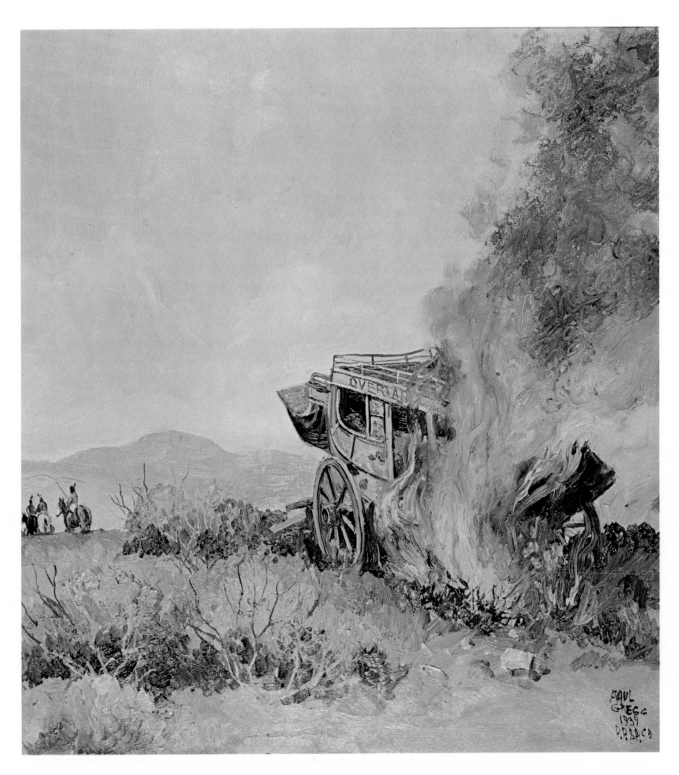

No Mail. Dated March 19, 1939. 24 x 24 inches, oil. Paul Gregg.

Albert Groll NA

1866–1952

REFERRED TO AS "America's sky painter," Albert Lory Groll was said to have been one of the first artists to capture the grandeur of the western plains.

Groll was born in New York City, but most of his student years were spent in London, England, and Munich, Germany. He studied under Nickolaus Gysis and Ludwig Von Loefftz.

Figure painting was his preference; but as he could not afford models for anatomy studies, he found his models in the trees, rivers, hills, and fields. Before going west, he painted the atmospheric effects along the Atlantic Coast—Cape Cod, Sandy Hook, and New York City.

Groll accompanied Professor Stuart Culin of the Brooklyn Museum of Arts and Sciences on an exploration trip to the Southwest. The sketches he made of the desert furnished material for two of his characteristic landscapes that were shown at an exhibition of the Society of American Artists. He won a gold medal at the Pennsylvania Academy with his canvas, "Arizona." He was elected to the National Academy of Design in 1910.

Despite his success in the East, he returned to the desert again and again. His cloud renderings of the desert are his most popular paintings. Not until Groll began to picture Arizona under the varying conditions of wind and weather, did Americans realize the artistic possibilities that existed in the desert land of that area. This sagebrush and cactus country, laying broad and low with arid yellow soil, stretching away to a sky full of clouds, makes an unforgettable picture.

Much of Groll's work in New Mexico was done around Laguna Pueblo, Taos, and Santa Fe. His Pueblo Indian friends who admired his ability to depict their land with beauty and truthfulness, named him "Chief Bald Head-Eagle Eye."

Although his paintings reveal the rugged character of the Southwest, they still maintain a delicate symphonic charm, the appeal of which has been recognized by many leading musicians. A Groll painting, which was inspired by a moonlight symphony by McDowell, hung on the wall above the great composer's bed. Among Groll's friends were men of the highest standing in the world of music.

84

He died in New York City, where he had always maintained a home.

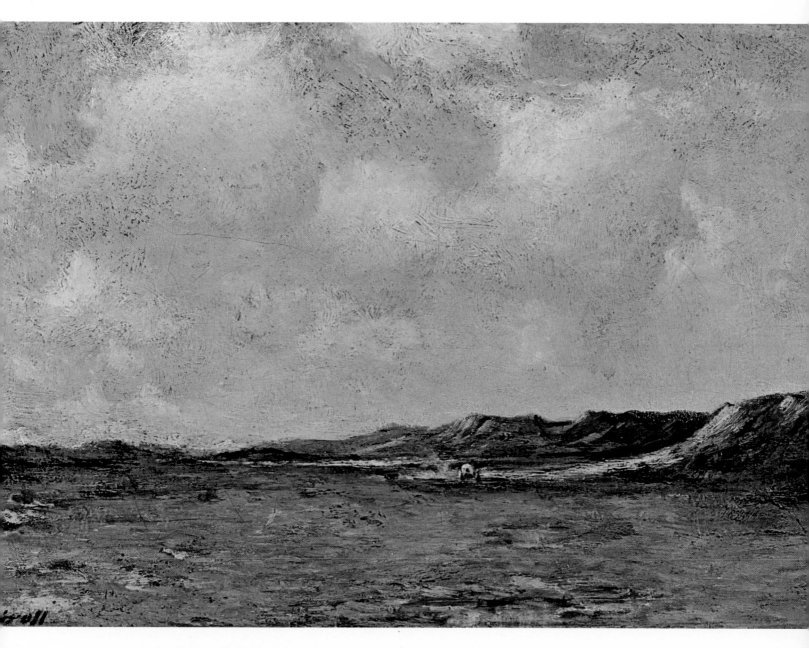

Mesa # 2. 9½ x 16½ inches, oil. Albert Groll.

Fred Harman CA

b. 1902

FRED HARMAN IS WIDELY KNOWN for his comic strip "Red Ryder and Little Beaver." But in his second career of painting scenes of the American West, he also has achieved remarkable success. Born in St. Joseph, Missouri, he moved with his family to Pagosa Springs, Colorado, when he was two months old. Harman and his younger brothers, Hugh and Walker, grew up on the ranch and became familiar with the Ute, Apache, Navajo, and Paiute Indians who lived nearby. As a child, he liked to draw, spending long winter evenings at the kitchen table making sketches.

In 1916 the family moved to Kansas City where the elder Harman opened a law practice. During World War I young Harman joined the National Guard, returning to Colorado after the war to work as a ranch-hand.

For twenty years he worked as a cowboy and as an artist, with little recognition. In Kansas City he made slides for silent movie houses, and eventually he formed his own company with another local artist, Walt Disney. The firm went broke and Disney headed for California. In 1924 Harman was employed by The Artcraft Engraving Company in St. Joseph, Missouri, where he illustrated catalogs for western rigs and cowboy boots. Two years later he married Lola Andrews.

In 1938 Fred Harman started his syndicated cartoon of "Red Ryder" and his young Indian sidekick "Little Beaver." For twenty-four years it was published in 750 daily newspapers and was the subject of over forty motion pictures, weekly radio shows, and numerous commercial endorsements.

When he completed his last strip in 1962, Harman began to paint western canvases, which were eagerly bought by collectors. Presently he is living and painting at his ranch near Pagosa Springs, Colorado, and making occasional rodeo show appearances. He says, "With my hair showing many winters, each morning before sun-up finds me hurriedly returning to my easel."

A book about his art, *The Great West in Paintings*, was published by Swallow Press in 1969. It reproduced eighty-nine of his paintings. Fred Harman was one of the first members of the board of directors of the Cowboy Artists of America Association. He is a member of the National Cartoonist Society and the Society of Illustrators. Fred Harman has a special place in the field of art for his great contribution to the education of all generations of Americans.

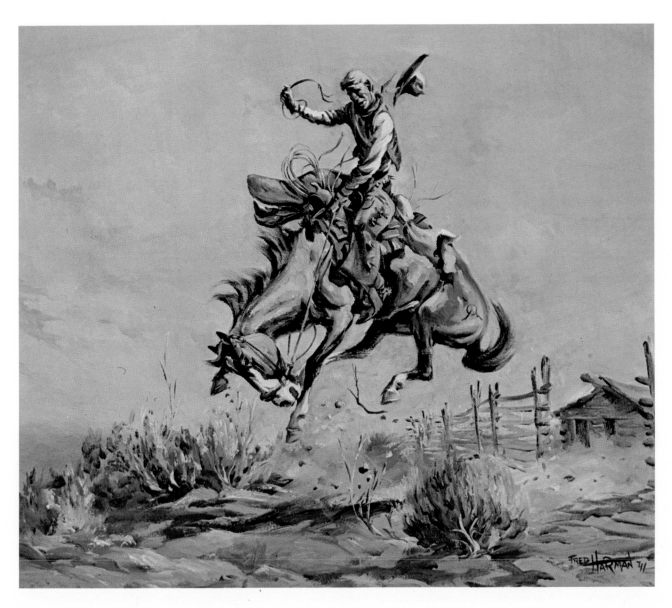

Rainbowin'. 20 x 24 inches, oil. Fred Harman.

Marsden Hartley

1877–1943

THE WORDS "PIONEER" AND "EXPERIMENTALIST" are often used to describe the churning and changing development of artist Marsden Hartley. Caught between European tradition and American adventure, and between the desire to paint and the desire to write, Hartley spent much of his career trying to find himself and a style. Many critics believe his work did not become a unified whole until the final decade of his life.

Born in Lewiston, Maine, of English parents, Hartley spent his boyhood in Ohio and won a scholarship to the Cleveland School of Art. In New York City he studied under F. Luis Mora, F. V. Du Mond, and William M. Chase, and in 1909 he had his first exhibition at photographer Alfred Stieglitz' Photo Secession Gallery "291."

Three years later, Stieglitz and Arthur B. Davies, one of the artists of the Ashcan School and Armory Show fame, helped send Hartley to Europe. A highly successful auction of Hartley's paintings in 1921 also was promoted by Stieglitz, the husband of Georgia O'Keeffe.

In Paris, Hartley experimented with cubism and other abstract compositions. In 1922, his first book of verse was published in Paris. Through the years, his work was influenced by many of the leading artists of the period, including Albert Pinkham Ryder, Segantini, Cezanne, and Picasso.

A major point in his development came with a trip to New Mexico in 1919 and 1920. In Taos and Santa Fe, he produced a series of expressionist mountain landscapes, which seemed to bring a new definition to his work. During an extended stay in Berlin, Germany, he produced a series of nine canvases on the theme, "Recollections of New Mexico," which were reminiscences of his life in the Southwest.

As a painter, writer, and poet, he traveled almost continually in search of style and subject matter. Although New England perhaps became "home," Hartley went to Paris, Berlin, Munich, Mexico, Bermuda, and Nova Scotia, as well as New Mexico to paint still life and landscapes.

Hartley once wrote, "I can hardly bear the sound of the words 'expressionism,' 'emotionalism,' 'personality,' and such, because they wish to express personal life, and I prefer to have no personal life. Personal art is for me a matter of spiritual indelicacy. Persons of refined feeling should keep themselves out of their painting." He died in Ellsworth, Maine.

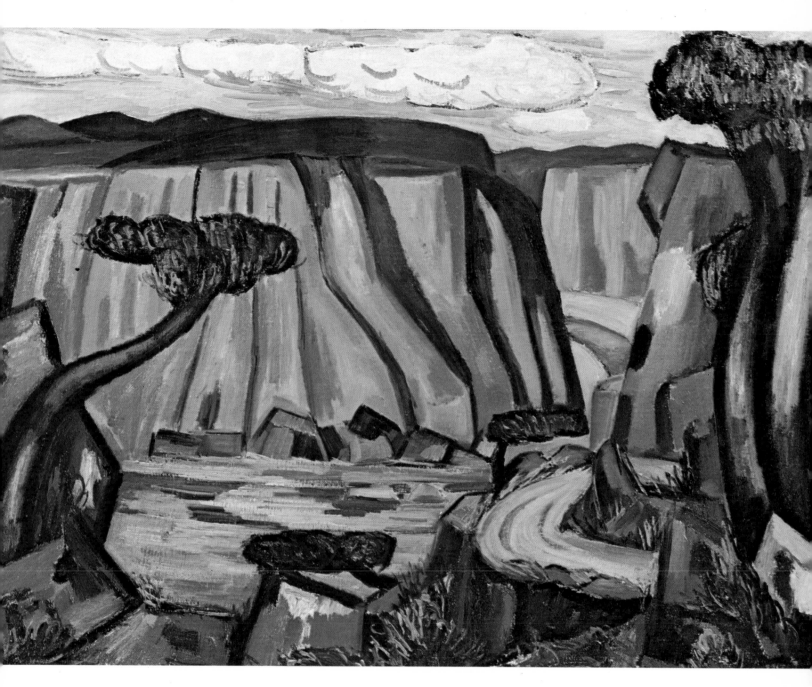

New Mexico Recollection #6. Berlin. Dated 1922–23. 26 x 36½ inches, oil. Marsden Hartley.

Earle Heikka

1910–1941

THE ARTISTIC STRUGGLE of Earle E. Heikka as a sculptor came to an abrupt end with his tragic death at thirty-one years of age. Very few of his original models had been cast in bronze at the time.

His parents were natives of Finland and living in Belt, Montana, when he was born, one of six children. After moving the family to Great Falls, his father died when Heikka was four years old.

During his early school years he developed a stuttering speech impediment, which was a constant embarrassment to him throughout his short life. This handicap, along with dire poverty, contributed to his poor attendance at school. But his interest and ability at sculpturing broadened. He would spend hours modeling animals from laurel gumbo clay.

When he was eighteen, his models, which were made from combinations of wood, leather, cloth, papier-mache, plaster, and metal, were receiving critical acclaim. Most of his work featured pack trains, stagecoaches, and mounted cowboys and Indians in action.

His financial circumstances improved as his models began to sell. He was approached by Marshall Field of Chicago with an offer to market his entire production of western sculptures, which he refused.

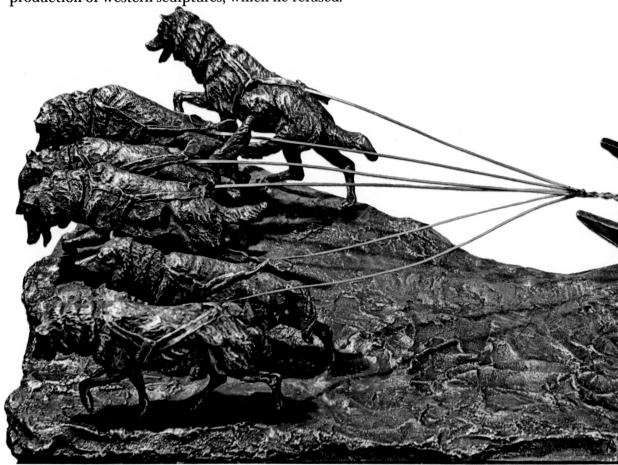

After his marriage in 1934, Heikka built a log cabin studio-home near Great Falls, where he and his wife, Virginia, were raising their four children. Keeping the hectic pace of a hard-working artist found him relaxing more and more in the historically famous Mint Saloon.

Despite his talent, which bordered on genius, tragedy seemed to surround Heikka's life. It started with the death of his father, his speech defect, and then the suicide of his brother, Mike, his hunting and fishing companion.

Just before his own death, his behavior became abusive and threatening, and it is claimed he ended his life with a bullet. But there also is enough evidence to question this conclusion; his death could have been accidental. Either way, the life of a brilliant sculptor was prematurely ended. Thirty-five years passed before his work was again appreciated.

His sculptures and original models are in the collections of the Museum of Native Cultures at Spokane, Washington, the C. M. Russell Museum at Great Falls, Montana, the National Cowboy Hall of Fame in Oklahoma City, and many others.

Bringing in Nanooksoah. H. 10 inches L. 30 inches, German silver. Earle Heikka.

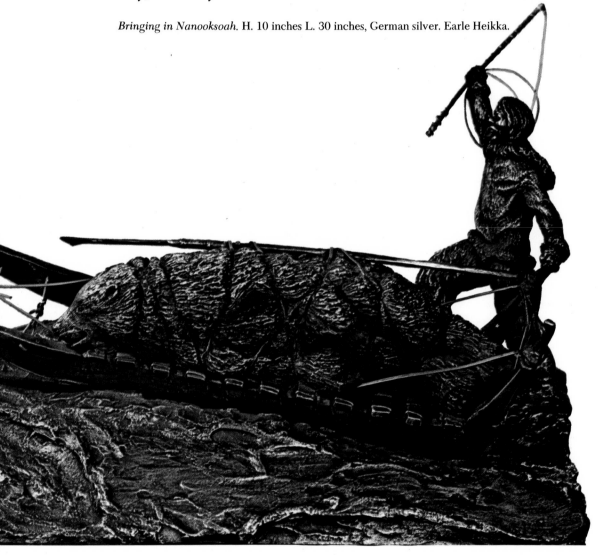

William P. Henderson

1877–1943

BORN IN MEDFORD, MASSACHUSETTS, William Penhallow Henderson experienced a rather unstable childhood. The family followed the father through his diverse careers, which took them from cattle ranching in Uvalde, Texas, back to Medford, to banking in Clifton, Kansas, and eastward once again, in time for young Henderson to enter high school and the Massachusetts Normal Art School in Boston.

Henderson later studied at the Boston Museum of Fine Arts, with Edmund C. Tarbell, where he won the Paige Traveling Scholarship for study in Europe in 1901. After two years abroad, he returned to America to teach at the Chicago Academy of Fine Arts. In 1905 he married Alice Corbin, poet and editor. Henderson collaborated with his wife, illustrating several of the children's books she wrote.

While in Chicago, he designed the scenery and costumes for the production of *Alice in Wonderland* at the Chicago Fine Arts Theatre. He also painted the Midway Gardens murals, commissioned by Frank Lloyd Wright.

Summer vacations were spent in the Southwest with his wife and daughter, Alice. In 1916 the Hendersons moved to Santa Fe, New Mexico, where they built a studio on the Camino del Monte Sol. Henderson helped form the New Mexico Painters Society in 1923.

He also branched out into the design and construction of furniture and homes, starting the Pueblo-Spanish Building Company. His two principal buildings in Santa Fe are the reconstructed Sena Plaza and the Museum of Navajo Ceremonial Art, now known as the Wheelwright Museum. His buildings have stood the test of time, both physically and aesthetically. The exquisite sculptured mural of a corn plant in the entrance to the Museum is not only symbolic as a ceremonial form, but is another indication of the many facets in the talent of this fine artist, muralist, architect, craftsman, and teacher.

Greatly influenced by Cezanne, Van Gogh, Renoir, and Whistler, Henderson's paintings were always original and represented a distinctly personal feeling and spontaniety. He sketched the hills, the town, the wood gatherers and their burros, the goats, the Spanish boys, and the Indians and their ways. Henderson saw beauty and possibilities in everything he viewed. He died at Tesuque, Santa Fe County, New Mexico.

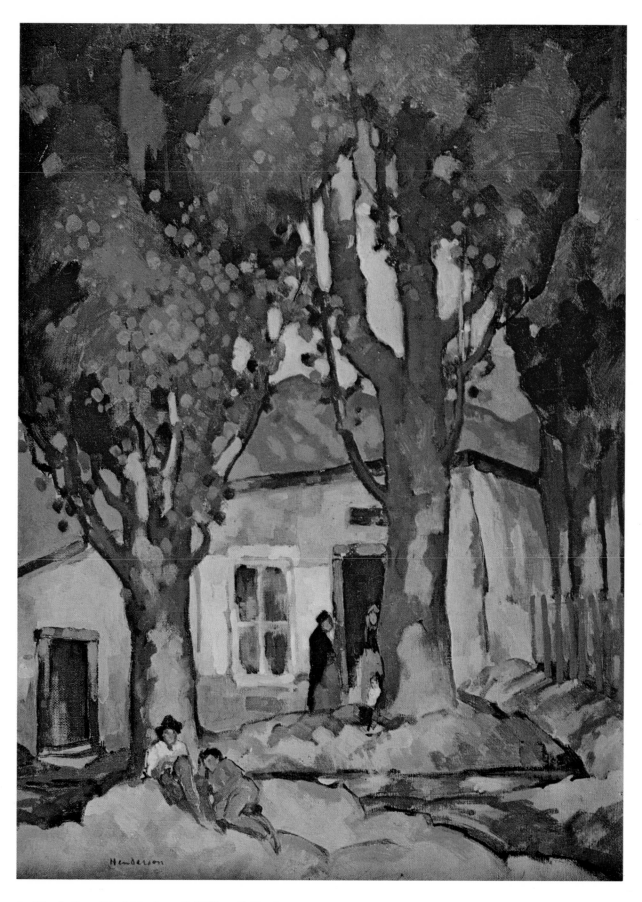

La Tienda Rosa. 24 x 18 inches, oil. William P. Henderson.

Thomas Hinckley

1813–1896

RECOGNITION AND SUCCESS came relatively late in life for Thomas Hewes Hinckley, who was one of this country's superior painters of wild and domestic animals.

As a boy, Hinckley, the son of a sea captain, studied art in Philadelphia, where he worked for a merchant. He also attended evening art classes, conducted by William Mason, which were his only formal instruction.

Most of his early career was spent as a sign painter and portraitist in his hometown of Milton, Massachusetts, where he maintained a studio. In 1851, at the age of thirty-eight, he went to London for further art study. Here he was greatly influenced by Sir Edwin Landseer, England's famous animalier, and by the Flemish masters.

Hinckley studied the survival habits of the deer while on the private island of Naushon as the guest of William Swain, Esq. He produced many beautiful paintings of these graceful, stately animals. Hinckley not only had great knowledge and understanding of the deer but of other creatures of the woods as well.

His paintings of dogs and game were exhibited at the Royal Academy in London, in 1858, followed by showings at the Pennsylvania Academy of Fine Art, The National Academy of Design in New York City, and the American Art Union in New York. Hinckley's work was reproduced in *Antiques* magazine in 1901, in *Connoisseur* magazine in 1907, and in the *Karolik Catalogue*.

He painted his subjects in their native habitat, and was equally noted for his detailed landscapes, which served as backgrounds. For inspiration, Hinckley used the fertile pastures, trees, streams, and flowering marshlands of New England. His painting techniques were that of the Hudson River School. Although he was not a landscape artist, there was a great deal of landscape in his animal paintings. His technique resembled that of his contemporary, Arthur F. Tait.

Later in his life, Hinckley went to California where he painted deer and elk on the rocky promontories along the Mendocino coast. This was virgin land, and the animals were undisturbed by man and were not afraid.

He died in Milton, Massachusetts.

Windgap. 36 x 29 inches, oil. Thomas Hinckley.

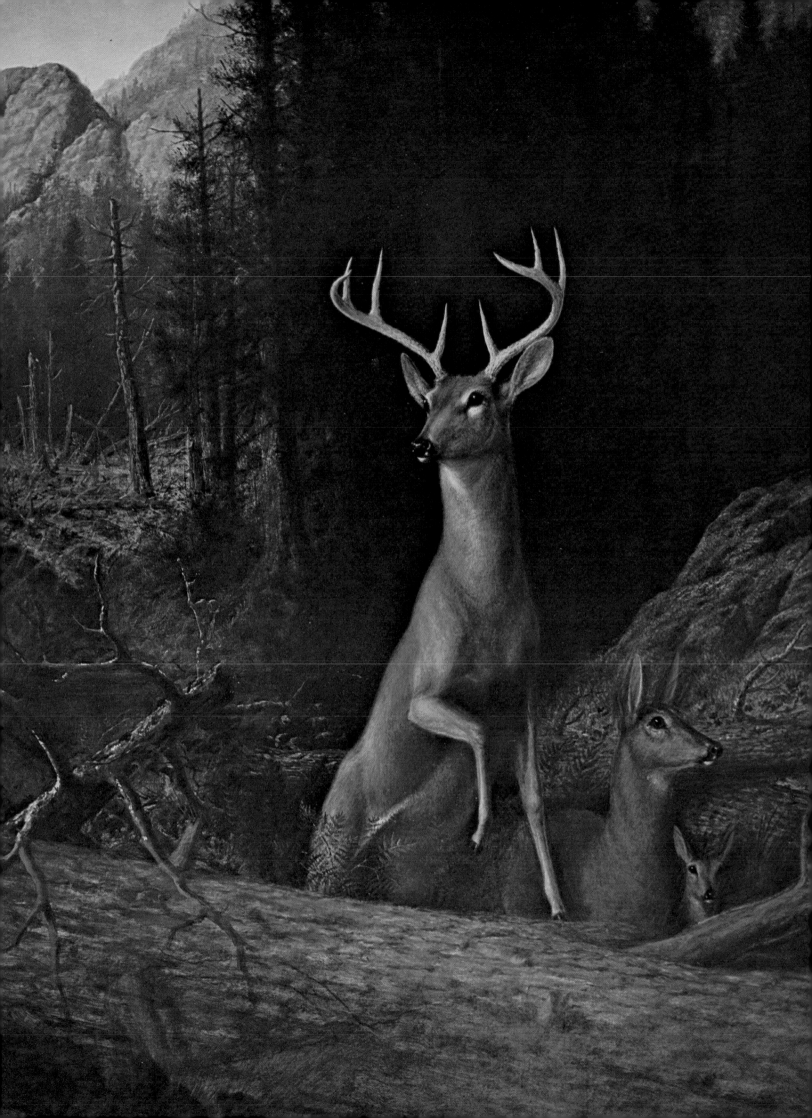

Joseph Hitchins

1838–1893

THE SON OF AN ENGLISH ART COLLECTOR, Joseph Hitchins had the opportunity to study under Europe's great masters. He found fulfillment, however, in the little town of Pueblo, Colorado, living near the ever-changing grandeur of the mountains. He was one of the first artists to establish himself there, "becoming Pueblo's best known artist."

Born in England, Hitchins received an early art education from his father, who owned a vast and priceless collection of fine paintings. As a boy, young Hitchins visited virtually all of the major galleries in Europe and studied at the famed Dusseldorf School in Germany. His awareness of art was instilled through the process of assimilation from his very earliest years.

Following his father's death, Hitchins went to Canada and lived in Montreal briefly before moving to Colorado. In Pueblo, where the Rockies were the subject of many of his paintings, he executed a number of his finest canvases representing the scenery of the San Luis Valley, the Valley of the Arkansas, Spanish Peaks, and the north and south views of Cheyenne Canyon. Southern Colorado was a never-ending source of inspiration.

A tireless and rapid worker, Hitchins spent hours at a time in his studio, often forgetting about meals or exercise. His penchant for work eventually caused a severe breakdown in his health, which led to his death at the early age of fifty-five.

He was noted for the atmosphere of his paintings, the blending of colors, and the selection of tones. One critic noted that "in his strong points, he had no superior in the world."

Many of Hitchins' works are owned by Colorado collectors; and one of his most famous, "The Arkansas Valley," was purchased before the turn of the century by a New Yorker for the sum of $10,000. One of his most celebrated and prophetic paintings, "Admission of Colorado," commemorating Colorado's admission to the Union in 1876, was completed before the actual event. It is now in the collection of the Colorado State Historical Society. A reproduction of this painting was published in the October 1976 issue of the *American Heritage* magazine.

Works by Hitchins are in the Denver Public Library in Denver, Colorado, in the Museum of New Mexico at Santa Fe, and private collections.

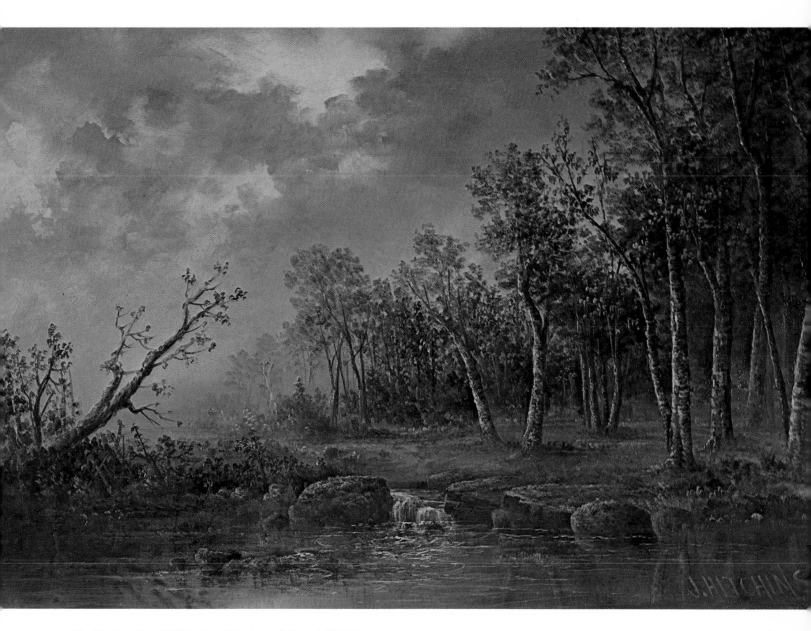

The Birches. Dated 1891. 20 x 30 inches, oil. Joseph Hitchins.

Charles Hittell

1861–1938

AS A NATIVE OF SAN FRANCISCO and the son of early California pioneers, Charles Joseph Hittell helped preserve the heritage of the early West through his artistic endeavors.

He is perhaps best known for the development of his collection of paintings of California adobe structures. Most of the final thirty years of his life, spent in Pacific Grove, California, were devoted to these paintings and to the collection of relics of the Old West. His home was a treasure house of collector's items of early California.

As an artist, Hittell specialized in western scenes and displayed a mastery of detail in reproducing cowboys, Indians, trappers, adobes, missions, landscapes, seascapes, horses, cattle, other native animals, and birds.

Hittell's father, Theodore, was an artist, newspaper editor, and California historian. Along with his brother, John S. Hittell, the elder Hittell authored the *Bancroft History of California,* a four-volume work which was gleaned from Spanish archives.

Young Hittell learned to draw in the San Francisco public schools and later attended the San Francisco School of Design. From 1884 to 1893 he attended the Royal Academie in Munich and the Academie Julien in Paris.

Hittell, who liked to be called Carlos, played the role of a Wild Westerner while in Europe. He often wore a ten-gallon hat that had been given to him by Buffalo Bill, brandished six-shooters, and performed tricks, much to the amazement of the Parisian art students.

After returning to the United States, he painted western subjects and served for a period as field artist for Frank Chapman during his California research for the American Museum of Natural History, New York City.

He is represented in that museum's collection with seven large background landscapes. Hittell's work is also included in the Zoological Museum at Berkeley, California, and the San Francisco Public Library, which has drawings dating back to when he was a boy of twelve years. In 1915 he won recognition at the Panama-Pacific International Exposition. His work is in many private collections and other museums.

Hittell died in Pacific Grove and was survived by his wife, Dr. Amy Bowen Hittell.

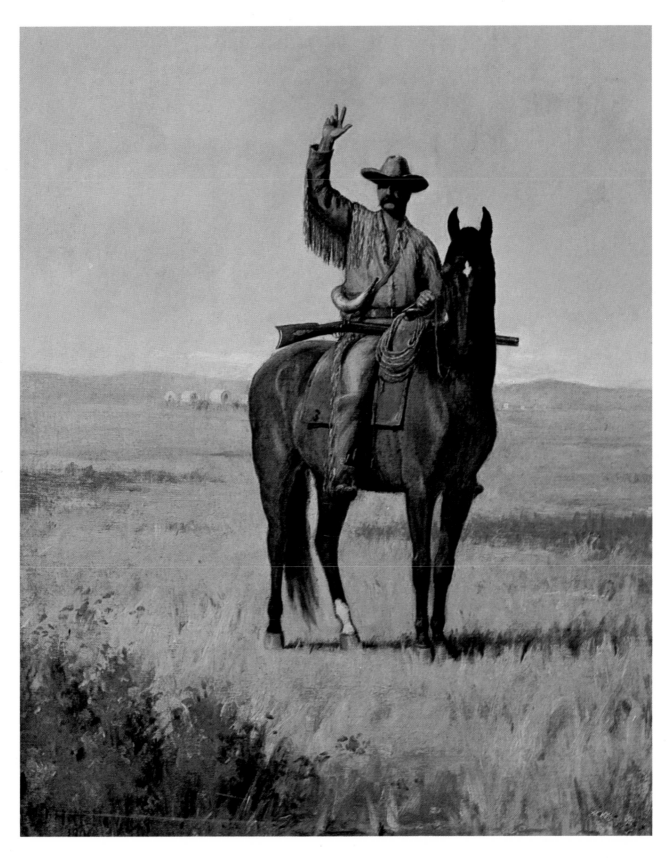

Signal of Peace. 20 x 16 inches, oil. Charles Hittell.

Ransom Holdredge

1836–1899

AFTER HE DIED A PAUPER in the Alameda County Infirmary in California, a newspaper obituary referred to Ransom Gillet Holdredge as a "well-known artist and character about town."

Before his death, which was hastened by despair and heavy drinking, Holdredge established himself as one of California's great landscape artists. Many critics felt his work surpassed that of his contemporary colleague William Keith. The press rated Holdredge as the ranking landscape painter of that particular period.

Born in New York City, most of his early life was spent in the San Francisco area. In his younger years, he served as head draftsman at the Mare Island Navy Yard. Although he was without formal art training, Holdredge spent his spare time painting scenes of the bay and Sierra Mountain landscapes. His vacations were given to sketching and painting in the Southwest, the Northwest, the Rockies, and western Canada. Many of his landscapes included Indians and were authentic scenes witnessed by the artist.

Holdredge's friends recognized his genius and helped provide him with enough money to go to Europe in 1874 for formal training, which included two years of study in Paris.

Upon his return to the United States, he became a staff artist for *Scribner's Magazine* and painted in the field during the Sioux War. He was with United States troops at the time General Custer was massacred at the Battle of the Little Big Horn.

Holdredge spent the final ten years of his life in San Francisco. He helped found the San Francisco Art Association, which later became known as the Mark Hopkins Art Institute. He was a member of the Bohemian Club, where he hobnobbed with such friends as Charles Warren Stoddard and Robert Louis Stevenson.

He had great talent for painting landscapes and seascapes, but had always wanted to be a portrait artist. Holdredge said his disappointment over failing to achieve this goal contributed to his affinity for the bottle, which eventually compromised his art and led to his poverty in his final years.

Holdredge was penniless when he died and was buried at county expense. His only known survivor was a sister, Jennie, who lived in San Francisco.

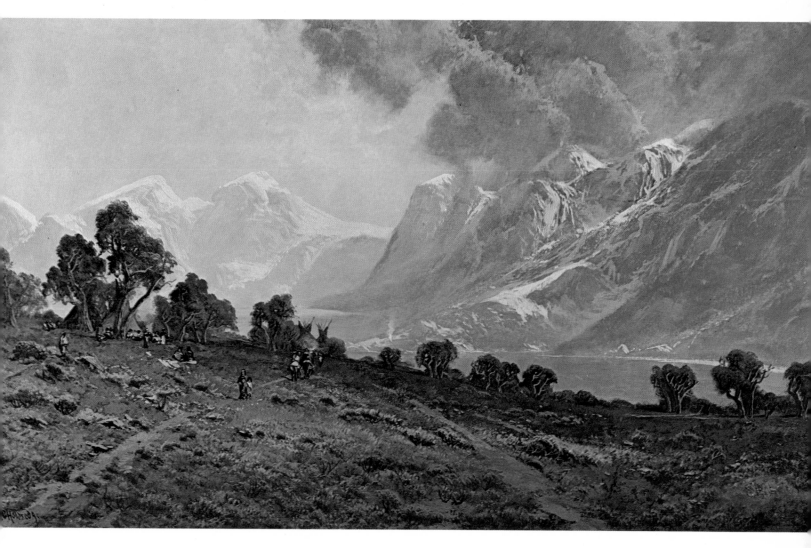

Indian Encampment in the Sierras. 30 x 50 inches, oil. Ransom Holdredge.

William H. Holmes

1846–1933

HARRISON COUNTY, OHIO, was the birthplace of William Henry Holmes. He began his study of geology when he replaced Thomas Moran, in 1872, as an artist with Ferdinand V. Hayden's Yellowstone expedition. He was mainly a self-taught artist, and this knowledge of geology was an invaluable asset to the truthfulness of the mountain paintings he was about to sketch. He was with Hayden in Colorado in 1873–76; then he returned to Wyoming, and by 1878 he was a full-fledged geologist.

Holmes made a tour of Europe in 1879. The next year his services were sought by Clarence E. Dutton to execute territorial landscapes for Dutton's book, *Tertiary History of the Grand Canyon District and Atlas*. He was appointed geologist of the expedition. Only three other artists had preceded Holmes to the Grand Canyon. They were Thomas Moran, John E. Weyss, and Baron von Egloffstein.

Wallace Stegner wrote, "Holmes is thus, both for the extent of his coverage and the authenticity of his pictures, the most important early artist of the Grand Canyon. The nine panoramas that Holmes made for Dutton's *Atlas* represent the highest point to which geological or topographical illustration ever reached. To open the *Tertiary History Atlas* to any of its double-page panoramas is to step to the edge of forty miles of outdoors."

After his return from this last expedition, he turned to archeology and museum administration and was successively head curator of Chicago's Field Museum and the National Museum in Washington. He was in Texas and Mexico in 1884–86 to participate in the study of the Pueblo Indians while acting as curator of aboriginal pottery for the National Museum. In 1902 Holmes succeeded John Wesley Powell as Chief of the Bureau of Ethnology, which he subsequently left to become Director of the National Gallery.

There is nothing like a mountain to give permanence to one's fame, and Holmes has at least two western peaks named for him. He was a member of the Washington Watercolor Club and the Society of Washington Artists.

These impressive contributions to art and science have been amplified by his easel paintings, especially his delicate traditional watercolors, which have received a number of awards. One of his watercolors is in the collection of the National Portrait Gallery in Washington, D.C.

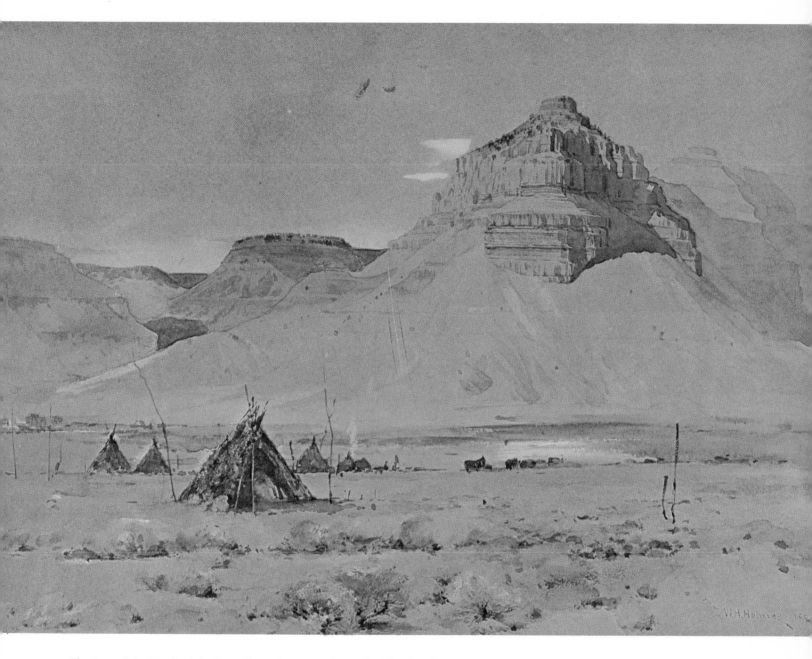

The Area of the Mouth of the Green River Canyon in the Book Cliffs of Utah.
10 x 14½ inches, watercolor. William H. Holmes.

Russell V. Hunter

1900–1955

BORN IN HALLSVILLE, ILLINOIS, Russell Vernon Hunter spent most of his life in New Mexico and the surrounding area, and was well known there as an artist, designer, teacher, and administrator.

Hunter's family moved to Las Vegas, New Mexico, when he was a child. After attending college at James Millikin University in Decatur, Illinois, he began his teaching career at Cerillos School near Santa Fe, New Mexico. During the 1920s he taught at the New Mexico State Teachers College at Silver City and at the Otis Art Institute in Los Angeles, where he studied under S. McDonald Wright.

For a brief time he taught in New York City at the Roerich Museum, where he also became interested in furniture design. But, during the height of the depression in 1932, he returned to his home in Curry County in eastern New Mexico.

In 1934 Hunter opened a vocational school for handicrafts in Puerto de Luna, New Mexico, and the same year was married to Virginia McGee. A son, Skillman Cannon Hunter, was born in 1935. From 1935 through 1942 Hunter was state director of the federal WPA art program in New Mexico. Then, during World War II, he spent five years working as an administrator with the USO.

Although continuing to paint and write numerous magazine articles, Hunter served from 1948 through 1952 as administrative director of the Museum of Fine Arts in Dallas, Texas. His next post was director of the Roswell, New Mexico, Museum, where he stayed until his death.

He was noted for his paintings of windmills, cattle, general stores, and the flat horizons of eastern New Mexico. He had an affectionate, slightly distorted and anecdotal style of painting, where forms were simplified and colors selected for their descriptive purposes. Hunter did several murals, including one for a church in Clovis, New Mexico, and another for the courthouse in Fort Sumner, New Mexico.

Jerry Bywaters, director of the Dallas Museum, wrote: "Hunter was endowed with many unusual qualities of perception and communication. As a painter, he could translate the familiar into something of special import. Most unusual for these times . . . was a sense of the spiritual quality in the artist, which deserved to be developed and convincingly demonstrated."

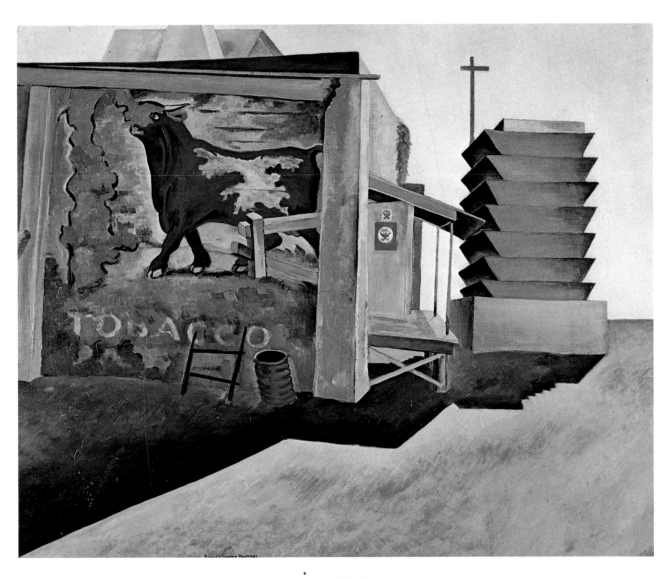

American Mural. Texico, New Mexico. 24 x 30 inches, oil. Russell V. Hunter.

Joseph Imhof

1871–1955

JOSEPH ADAM IMHOF first developed his deep interest in the American Indian when he took a steamship to Europe in 1891; by coincidence, Buffalo Bill Cody's Wild West troupe was also aboard.

Imhof was born in Brooklyn, New York, and was largely self-taught as an artist. He also was an excellent draftsman and lithographer. Finishing high school at the age of fifteen, he rented a studio in New York City, where he did lettering for Currier and Ives.

After three years, he saved enough money for his first trip to Europe aboard the steamship *Noordland.* Imhof was so intrigued with the Indians in Buffalo Bill's troupe that he spent several months with the show after it reached Antwerp.

He studied art in Antwerp, Munich, and Paris, before returning home to begin a study of the Iroquois Indians living in New York and Canada.

Imhof also invented a new process of color printing; the royalties provided money to finance his life as a painter and amateur anthropologist.

In 1897 he married Sarah Stuart. They made several return trips to Europe, before going to the southwestern United States to study the Indians there. Their first visit to New Mexico was in 1905. He built a studio in Albuquerque, in 1906, and traveled throughout the region doing sketches for his paintings.

The Imhofs went back to New York in 1913, intending to go on to Europe. Because of World War I, they remained in New York before returning to Taos, where they built a new home sixteen years later. It was there that he earned the title "the Grand Old Man of the Pueblos."

Imhof is best known for his series of sixty paintings based on the importance of corn in the secular and religious life of the Indian people. The paintings were done between 1950 and 1955, and were completed just two weeks before his death.

His skill as a printmaker reflected his European training; he was the first artist in Taos to have a lithographic press.

Following Imhof's death, his wife presented his corn paintings, along with his rare artifacts and books, to the University of New Mexico as a permanent memorial. Many of his other paintings are owned by the Harwood Foundation in Taos and the Museum of New Mexico in Santa Fe.

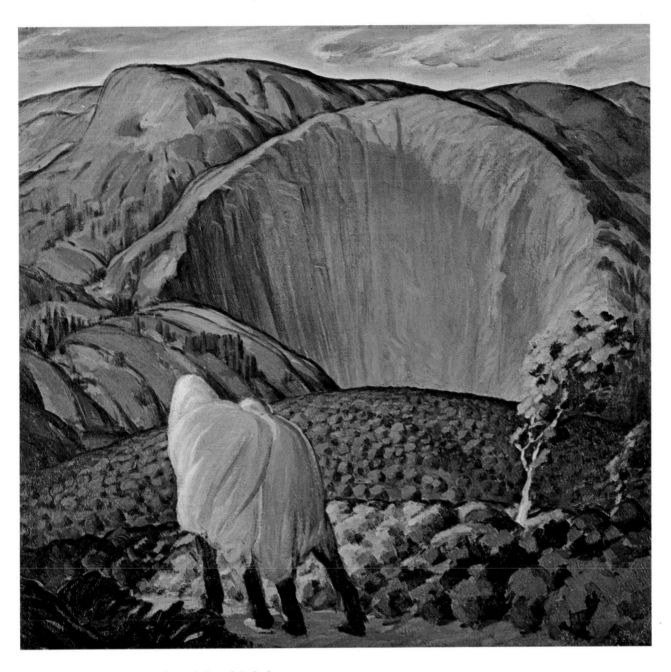

Two Taos Indians. 22 x 24 inches, oil. Joseph Imhof.

Will James

1892–1942

ANTHONY AMARAL, author of *Will James, The Gilt Edged Cowboy,* wrote: "The books that flowed so prolifically from James' pen, and his great gift as painter and illustrator, still keep his name perpetually alive."

Will James was born Joseph Ernest Nephtali Dufault in Quebec, Canada, of French parentage. His father was a merchant and hotel owner.

By the time he was five years old, he was drawing fine examples of cats, dogs, and horses. At ten he collected abandoned pulp magazines from his father's hotel. He could not read English, but he saved the illustrations to copy. These, and stories told by the trappers, created the desire in the boy to become a cowboy and ride horses in the wide open spaces.

In 1910 he had a short stay in jail when he was falsely accused and arrested by the Mounted Police for killing a sheepherder in a barroom fight. After weeks of confinement, he was suddenly released without knowing that he was no longer under suspicion.

He changed his name to Will James because of this incident. He also felt that dropping his French Canadian name would offer him better opportunities across the border in Montana. He thought that unless a man was born in the West, he would never have the chance of becoming a top ranch hand. His book, *Lone Cowboy, The Story of My Life,* was universally accepted as his autobiography, a lie which he perpetuated, and one which eventually led to his downfall.

James married his wife, Alice, in 1925. She did not know of his relatives in Canada with whom he kept secret contact. James was greatly influenced by his wife, who encouraged and helped him with his writing. He had instant success with his illustrated books and cowboy stories, which appeared in many of the current magazines. Artists Charles Dana Gibson and Maynard Dixon were friends and a great help to James' career.

In fifty short years, James' fame and fortune were dissipated; he lost contact with his Canadian family; his wife, friends, and ranch in Montana were gone. Driven by a fear of exposure and scandal, he died in Hollywood of complications from acute alcoholism.

James wrote and illustrated approximately twenty-one books and numerous stories for magazines, many translated into Braille and foreign languages, and were sold throughout the world.

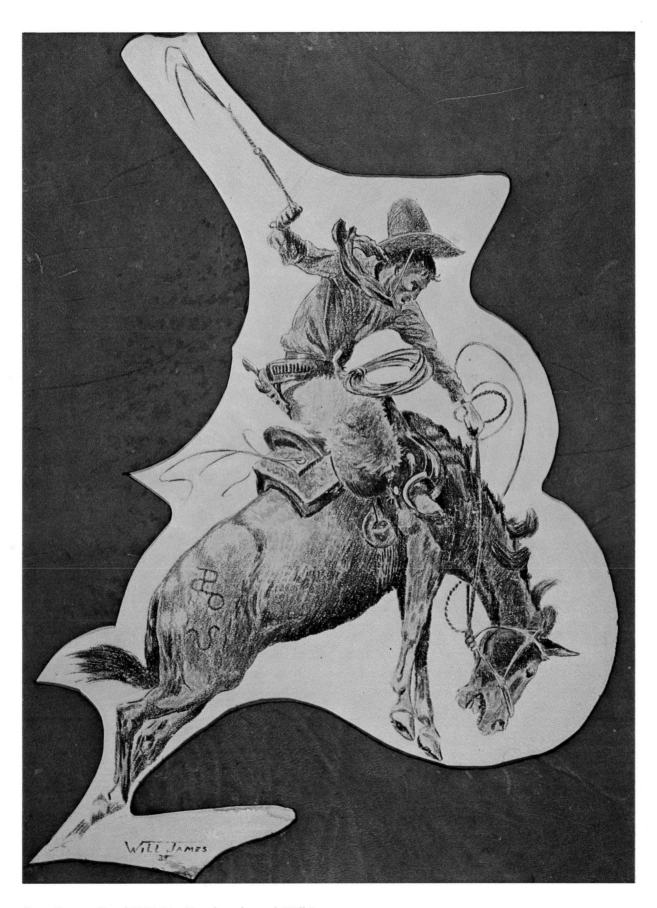

Bronc Busting. Dated 1935. 24 x 18 inches, charcoal. Will James.

Raymond Jonson

b. 1891

A BRILLIANT, INNOVATIVE, and prolific artist, Raymond Jonson has been called a "one-man task force for modern art in New Mexico and a powerful counterforce to provincialism."

The son of a Baptist minister, he was born in Charitown, Iowa. His father, on coming to America from Sweden, had changed the spelling of his name from Jonsson to Johnson, and in 1919 Raymond Johnson changed it again to Jonson. The Reverend Johnson moved frequently from church to church in mid-western communities before the family settled in Portland, Oregon.

While working as a newspaper carrier for the *Portland Oregonian,* the boy was fascinated by the paper's editorial cartoonist and decided that he wanted to be an artist.

In 1909 he was the first pupil to enroll in the art school of the Portland Art Museum. A year later he entered the Chicago Academy of Fine Arts, where he met B.J.O. Nordfeldt, who became a longtime friend and teacher.

Like so many artists of the period, Jonson was greatly influenced by the 1913 New York Armory Show, which was exhibited in Chicago. He was one of the few artists living in the area who realized its true significance.

Jonson spent thirteen years in Chicago working as an artist, teacher, and stage designer. He made several trips westward before moving with his wife, Vera, to Santa Fe in 1922, where they built a home and studio. His wife died in 1965.

Jonson has not enjoyed the national reputation he would have acquired had he lived in New York or Chicago. His works are owned by forty-six museums and are in numerous other public collections. But he has never been given a major show; he has spent many years as an isolated figure among New Mexico's painters.

His most enthusiastic benefactor is the University of New Mexico at Albuquerque, where he served as a professor. In 1947 the university built the Jonson Gallery, which included a studio, living quarters, and storage space for the artist who is now its director. The University, which owns almost 700 of Jonson's works, bestowed upon him an honorary degree, Doctor of Humane Letters, in 1971.

A very comprehensive book entitled *The Art of Raymond Jonson, Painter,* by Ed Garman, was published in 1976.

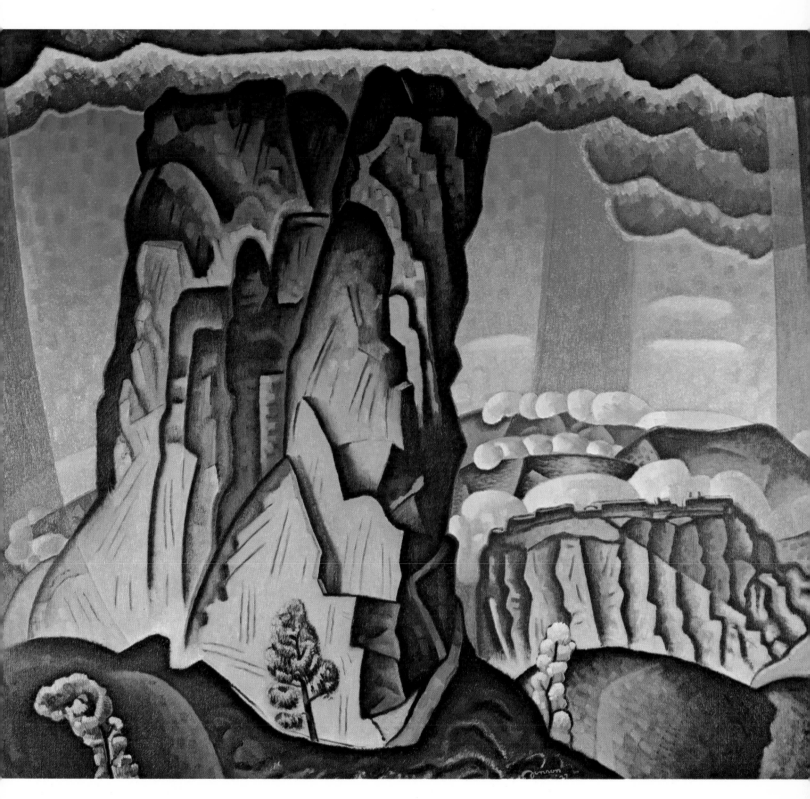

Pueblo Series, Acoma. Dated 1927. 37 x 44 inches, oil. Raymond Jonson.

Amedee Joullin

1862–1917

PERHAPS BEST KNOWN for the landscapes he painted in and around his native San Francisco, Amedee Joullin was among the first artists to portray the life of the southwestern American Indian.

Interested in the brilliant color of that region, Joullin went to New Mexico in the early 1890s and spent several months with the Pueblo Indians. Living in an adobe hut and eating primitive food, he realized that this was the only way to see their life as it really was.

At first, the superstitious Indians were wary of their white visitor, but he gradually won their trust. In 1892 he started a series of paintings of Indian life, which were both moving in content and extremely accurate in detail, such as in the designs of the handmade blankets and baskets. Joullin said of his work, "I have always adhered strictly and truthfully to nature; it has been the only guide I have had."

Joullin's Indian series received considerable attention when exhibited at a New York City show, and this led to a commission to paint the spike-driving ceremonies marking the completion of the Northern Pacific Railroad system. The twenty-foot wide mural was displayed at the Montana State Capitol in Helena.

Born in San Francisco, Joullin's parents were of French descent and were among the earliest of the white settlers in California. Both his father and grandfather were painters of note. He attended the public schools in San Francisco and entered the School of Design there, where he studied for eighteen months under the famed French artist, Jules Tavernier.

Joullin went to Paris for two more years of study under Bouguereau and Robert-Fleury, then returned home to open his own studio and teach at the School of Design in San Francisco with another distinguished California artist, Emil Carlsen.

In 1898 he made a nine-month tour to Mexico and painted several oils of the Indians there. His wife Lucile, also a noted artist who specialized in landscapes and Indian subjects, accompanied him on the trip.

He died in San Francisco following a six-week illness, and his widow moved to Isleta, New Mexico, where she painted until her death in 1924. They were survived by a son, Emile, a violinist.

Indian Woman with Burden Basket. 30½ x 24 inches, oil. Amedee Joullin.

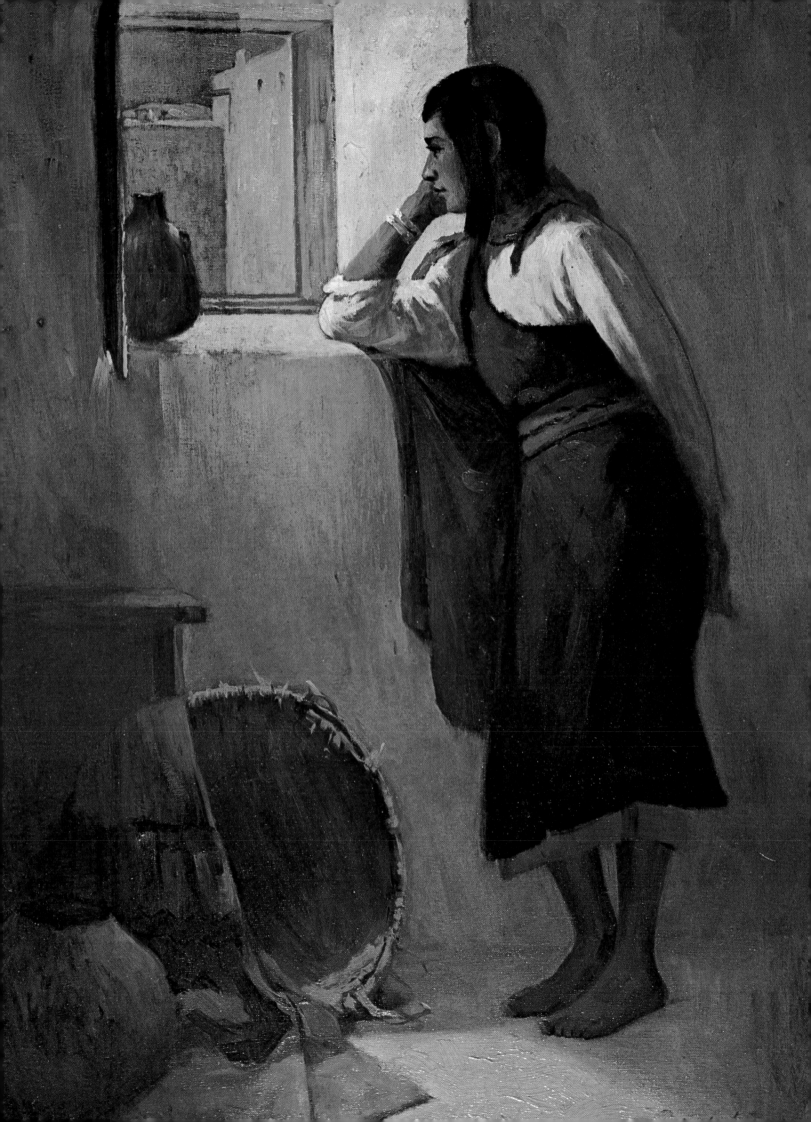

Karl Kauba

1865–1922

FOR A MAN WHO PROBABLY never visited the United States, Karl Kauba is now considered one of the great sculptors of western American subjects.

His life remains somewhat of a mystery. But there are historians who believe he may have briefly visited this country in the late 1880s. The consensus is that Kauba totally created his powerful works from his studio in Vienna, Austria. All of his western bronzes were cast in Vienna and were patterned after photographs, illustrations, and artifacts sent to him by a correspondent in America.

Art collectors today rank Kauba in a class with Remington and Russell. His sculptures—considered excellent examples of Viennese bronzes with their polychrome finish—show soldiers and Indians of the American West in realistic form and intricate detail. Some of his works capture the high drama of frontier life with scenes of violent, massive movement. Others are portrait busts or standing figures. He portrayed the Indian with great skill, and his horses are authentic Indian ponies.

Kauba was born in Austria and studied as a watchmaker before delving into art in the Vienna academies under Carl Waschmann and Stefan Schwartz. During that period in Europe, there was an enormously popular interest in western America. German writer Carl May wrote extensively about it, and this stimulated Kauba's interest, as did the American Wild West shows.

Many of Kauba's sculptures were exported to the United States between 1895 and 1912, but their value was not fully realized until the 1950s. Most are small or medium size.

The president of the Roman Bronze Works in Vienna that cast the works of Remington and Russell said; "I like Kauba's work. The fellow was an artist. But if we tried to cast those statues today, the price would be prohibitive, just doing properly all that wealth of artistic detail."

The lure of the American West is indeed worldwide. The West's inspirational power was felt by the early artists many decades ago. The western endeavors of these European and American sculptors and painters, some of whom had never seen the western frontier or experienced the actual excitement of the scenes they portrayed, in many cases, are considered historical and irreplaceable treasures.

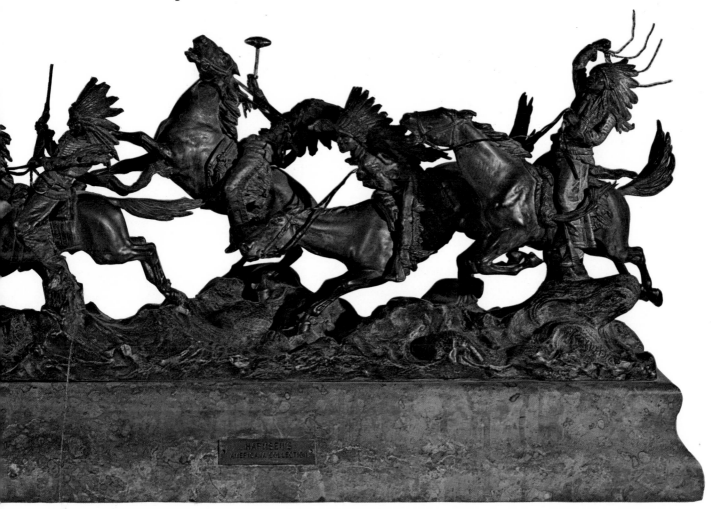

The Raid. H. 9 inches L. 28 inches, bronze. Karl Kauba.

Henry Keller ANA

1869-1949

HENRY KELLER'S DEEP INTEREST in art and nature was manifested in his early youth when he painted landscapes on his mother's treasured window shades at their Cleveland, Ohio, home. Surviving this unappreciated beginning, he became one of the finest unheralded American artists of his period.

Keller was born at sea on a ship off Nova Scotia while his German parents were on their way to settle in Cleveland.

At the age of eighteen he began art study at what eventually became the Cleveland Institute of Art. A year later he rode freight trains and Erie Canal barges to New York City to visit the Metropolitan Museum of Art.

When Keller was twenty-one, he went to Germany to study. Returning to Cleveland a year later, he was employed as an apprentice with a lithography company, while continuing his studies at the Art Students League in New York and the Cincinnati School of Art. His contemporaries at that time were Walter Kuhn, Arthur B. Davies, Jerome Myers, and George Luks, leaders in the new movement in American art.

Keller was married in 1893. In 1899 he returned to Europe to study animal drawing and anatomy at Dusseldorf under Julius Hugo Bergmann, and at the Royal Academie of Bavaria in Munich under Johann Zugel, who was considered one of the great animal painters of the day. A Keller painting won a silver medal at the Academie.

In 1902 he became an instructor at the Cleveland Institute of Art and remained there until his retirement in 1945. As a teacher, Keller was a hard taskmaster. And when it came to his own paintings, he also was very exacting. A witty and colloquial man, he was a rabid fact finder, which is reflected in his paintings.

Keller was elected an associate member of the National Academy of Design in 1939.

Living most of his life in Cleveland, Keller first visited Taos, New Mexico, in 1920 and returned there in 1931.

During the last fifteen years of his life, he spent his summers painting the areas around La Jolla and Palm Springs in Southern California.

Keller died in San Diego, California, where in his final years he had lived with his son, Albert; he also left another son, Leslie.

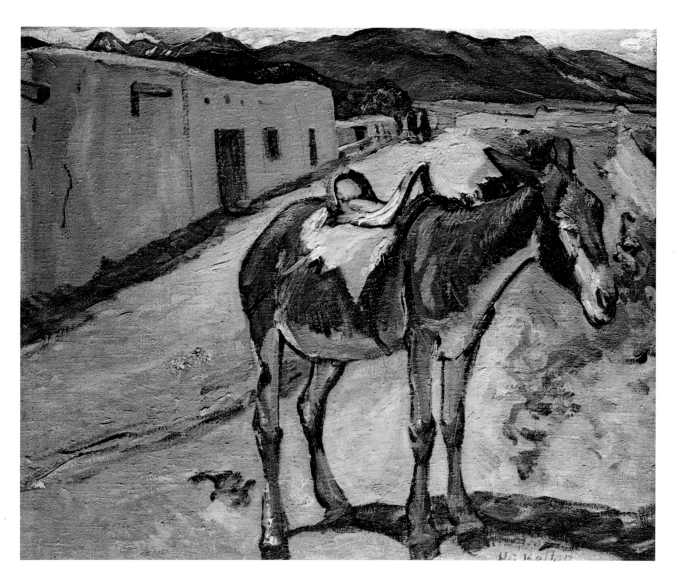

Pueblo Stop. 22 x 27 inches, oil. Henry Keller.

Edward Kemeys

1843–1907

HE WAS A SCULPTOR with the foresight to see that a magnificent part of our nation's heritage was disappearing before civilization's relentless advance. Edward Kemeys became one of America's first animal and Indian bronze delineators with his early efforts in the 1870s.

His work is little known outside of museums because many of his fine pieces have never been cast and have been held at the Smithsonian Institution since 1907, a gift from Kemeys. A documentation of Kemeys' masterpieces throughout the United States and establishment of their historical relevance has recently been completed in Washington, D.C. The talent of this man, however, is well-known to art historians. The historical rediscovery of Kemeys is an extraordinary event in American sculpture.

Edward Kemeys was born in Savannah, Georgia. The impetus for Kemeys' early interest in animals was provided on a train returning to New York from Illinois and a chance meeting with "Grizzly Adams," who was traveling with his show of American animals.

During the Civil War, Kemeys enlisted as a private in the 65th regiment and later took part in the battle of Richmond. He was promoted to the rank of captain.

Returning to New York, he opened a studio. There he met an unknown sculptor modeling a head of a wolf. After this meeting Kemeys produced his first bronze sculptures, "Wounded Wolf" and "Wolf at Bay." This was a period of great productivity, where he used his small examples as models to sell the larger versions to his clientele. Some of those commissions grace civic centers, buildings, and parks throughout the United States. His finest works are possibly the bronze lions at the main entrance to the Art Institute in Chicago.

In 1873 Kemeys spent a year traveling in the American West with Richard Audubon, grandson of John Audubon. Recognizing the American wilderness as his true source of subject matter, he lived with the Indians, hunters, and trappers, and became a favorite of Theodore Roosevelt.

Edward Kemeys married Laura Swing in 1885 and settled in Bridgeton, New Jersey. They had one son, William. In 1902 they moved to Washington, D.C., where Kemeys died and was buried in Arlington National Cemetery with full military honors.

118

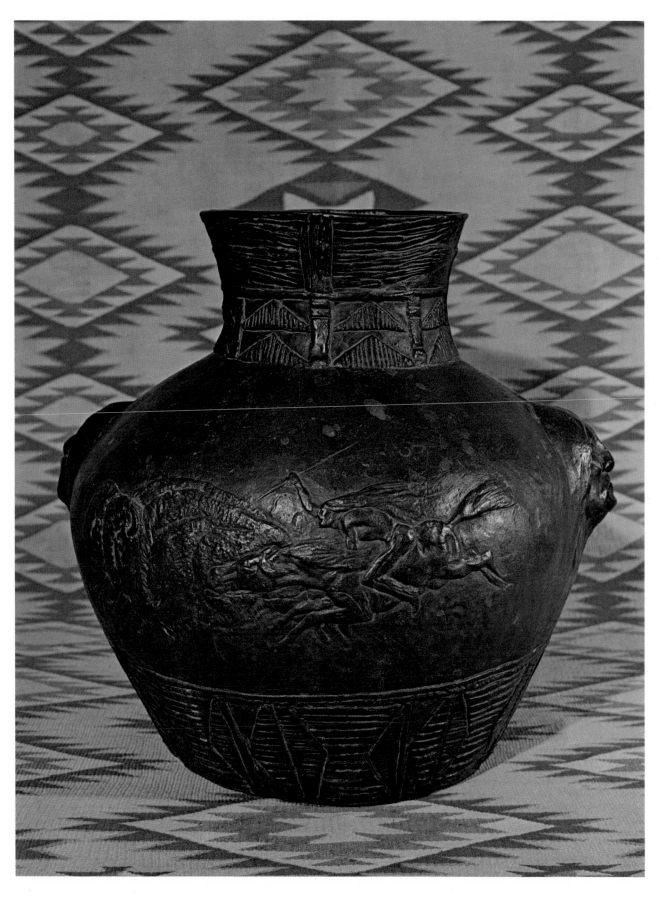

Bas-Relief Pot. H. 13 inches, bronze. Edward Kemeys.

W. H. D. Koerner

1878–1938

BORN IN GERMANY, William Henry Dethlef Koerner was two years old when he sailed with his family to America; they located in Clinton, Iowa. His father was a shoemaker, and the family was extremely poor.

From his earliest childhood, there was only one thing he wanted to do—to be an artist. W. H. D. Koerner drew everything in sight, using old house paint, crayons, pencils; he made his own canvas. One canvas was started in spring, painted over in the summer, and repainted in the fall with that season's vivid colors. It was to be his masterpiece—despite the fact his mother used it at one time to stop a leak in her hen house roof.

When he was eighteen, his father gave him a gold watch, a little money, and his blessing to go to Chicago to work as a quick-sketch artist for the *Chicago Tribune.* Koerner possessed a photographic memory; with a glance he was able to fix details in his mind for transfer into a truthful picture. He later gained recognition as a master of the vignette.

In 1905 the Koerners went to New York so the youth could study at the Art Students League. There he won the George Bridgman Award, which provided a much-needed scholarship. He also served on the Board of Control of the League for two years. In 1907 he went to Wilmington, Delaware, to attend the seminars conducted by the master illustrator, Howard Pyle.

Koerner's tremendous feeling for the West began in 1919 while he was illustrating a series of stories, *Traveling the Old Trails,* by Emerson Hough, for the *Saturday Evening Post.* This exposure led to his specialization in western scenes. In his quest for authenticity, Koerner spent long hours in New York's Public Library and the Museum of Natural History. From 1924 on, his research was augmented by summer sketching trips to Montana and other western states to see firsthand the activity of the real West. Always accompanied by his wife and daughter, they roughed it in old cabins.

After Koerner's death in Interlaken, New Jersey, Mrs. Koerner kept intact the many artifacts in the studio and his magnificent oil paintings, which remain today as part of the "Koerner Studio Collection." Their daughter, Ruth Koerner Oliver of Santa Barbara, California, has made the collection available for exhibits in prominent places. Many of Koerner's paintings are now in private collections and museums, and his fame as an artist will be magnified by the future generation of Western Art collectors.

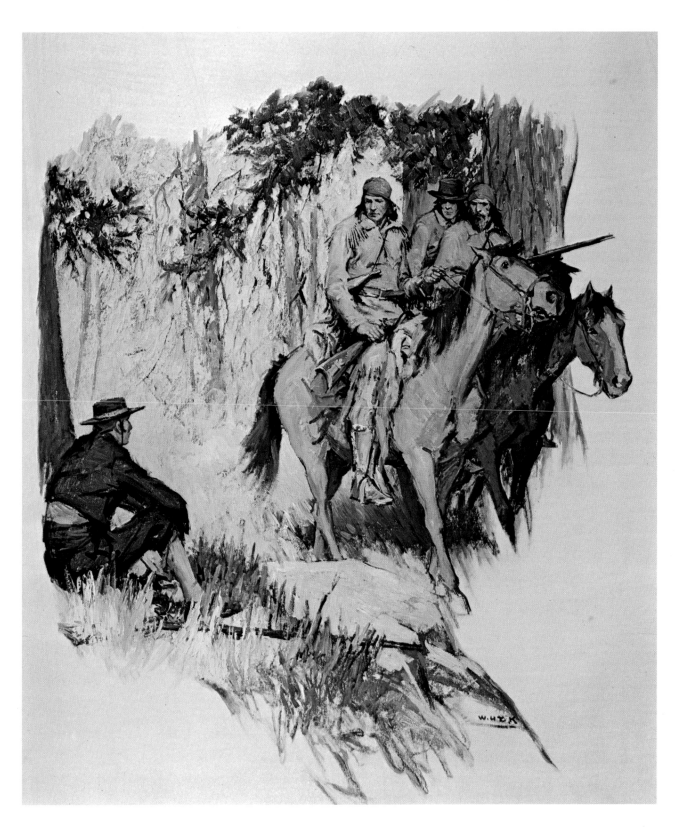

Trappers Wintering Near Monterey. Dated 1932. 36 x 30 inches, oil. W. H. D. Koerner.

Pawel Kontny

b. 1923

A LISTING OF THE COUNTRIES in which Pawel August Kontny has painted would read like the United Nations roster. In oils, watercolors, and pastels, he has captured the spirit of cities and rural scenes around the world.

Born in Laurahuette, Poland, the son of a wealthy pastry shop owner, he spent much of his youth with a pencil or chalk, decorating anything in sight. To his family's regret, he went to Breslau to study architecture. They wanted him to work in the family business.

His studies were interrupted by the war. While traveling through many countries as a soldier artist, he sketched the varied landscapes. In 1945 he was captured and made a prisoner of war in Italy.

After the war, Kontny entered the Union of Nuremburg Architects to help create building designs to replace rubble left by the war. He also met his wife, Irmgard, a dancer with the Nuremburg Opera Company.

Exhibitions in many countries brought him a number of friends who encouraged his talent. When internationally known museums and galleries in Europe and the United States exhibited his work with success, he slowly gained the recognition he deserved.

His wartime sketches are a long way from his present artistic expressions. His work is full of contrasts, in which objective and abstract art seem to touch. He favors architectural subjects in his paintings, which are built up with the aid of marble dust into one-fourth-inch thick structures, giving a three-dimensional effect pleasing to the eye and touch. Kontny says his paint formulation consists of only two ingredients—marble dust and a good grade of oil paint. He has prepared his own marble dust for years. "As for my palette, I prefer a flat table and use a large piece of glass on which to mix my colors."

He uses heavy weight masonite panel instead of canvas because of the thickness of his paintings. His clever color technique even seems to catch the feeling of a breeze in the air. He paints with luminous simplicity, depth, and originality.

The Kontnys moved to Denver, Colorado, in 1969 where they make their home and maintain a studio. Painting the American West has become a new challenge and adventure to the artist. They are the parents of a son, Mario, and a daughter, Yvonne.

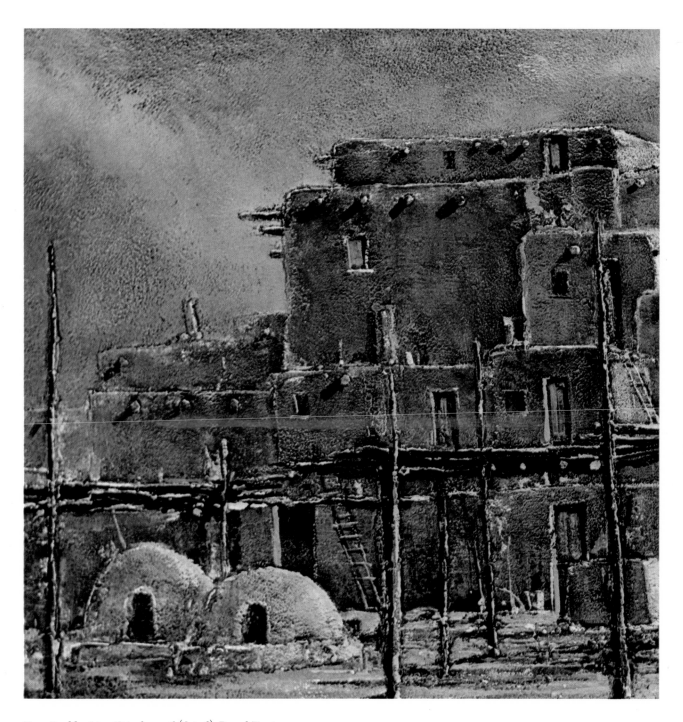

Taos Pueblo. 24 x 48 inches, oil (detail). Pawel Kontny.

Charles Lanman ANA

1819–1895

A DESCENDANT OF A WEALTHY eastern family, Charles Lanman spent most of his life in Washington, D.C. He had an insatiable desire to explore the American frontier, and his avocation was painting it and writing about it.

Lanman made numerous trips to the Mississippi Valley, the Greak Lakes region, and the Appalachian Mountains on horseback, on foot, and by canoe. His sketches and paintings were published in periodicals in the United States and England, and many of his articles were bound into volumes, which are in museums and Americana collections.

Lanman was the great-great grandson of James Lanman, who came from England to settle in Boston about 1724. His grandfather, James Lanman, was United States Senator from Connecticut from 1819 to 1825. The artist was born in Monroe, Michigan, where his father was a lawyer.

When he was ten years of age, Lanman went to live with his grandfather in Connecticut and attended Plymouth Academy near Norwich. In 1835 he went to work for an East India mercantile house in New York City, and in his spare time began the first of many exploratory trips into the eastern and western wilderness.

Little is known about Lanman's artistic training, but he did study under the noted Asher B. Durand. In 1846 he was elected an associate member of the National Academy of Design. His art has the flavor of the Hudson River School, much of it showing the influence of Albert Bierstadt.

Lanman worked briefly as a newspaperman, taking over the editorship of the *Monroe Gazette* in 1845 and moving to the *Cincinnati Chronicle,* as associate editor, in 1846. He later joined the staff of the *New York Express.*

In 1849, he became librarian for the War Department in Washington and married Adeline Dodge. The following year he took a position as private secretary for Daniel Webster. Following Webster's death in 1852, he wrote a book about the famed statesman and diplomat.

Lanman remained in Washington in many posts: librarian for the Department of the Interior and the House of Representatives; American secretary to the Japanese legation; and librarian of the Washington city library. He also wrote thirty-two distinct works.

Lanman died at his Georgetown home.

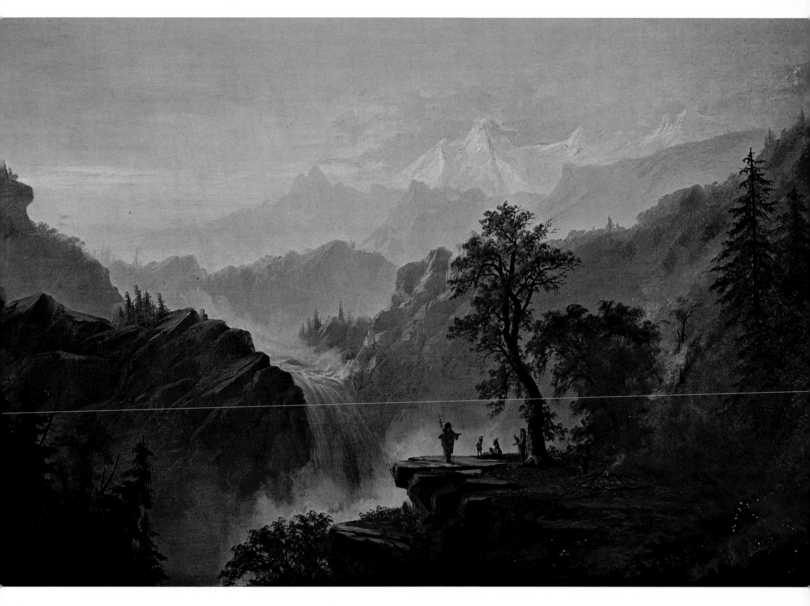

Campfire on the Ledge. 29 x 47 inches, oil. Charles Lanman.

Harry Learned

1842–unknown

MANY ARTISTS living on the eastern seaboard during the 1800s suffered poor health. This was a prime factor in their migrating to the West. Tuberculosis brought Harry Learned to Colorado.

Learned was born in Glasgow, Scotland; as a young man he immigrated to New York City. Here he painted theatrical posters, curtains, and drops. In his spare time he traveled and painted in the New England states, particularly Vermont. He taught art in Vermont and also in New York City.

Learned left New York City because of his poor health and declining career. He arrived in Leadville, Colorado, and lived near his cousin, George F. Robinson, an early pioneer who operated a mill in nearby Climax. The town of Robinson, Colorado, was named for the Robinson family. Robinson was the subject of many Learned paintings.

Colorado art historians refer to the illusive Harry Learned as an "itinerant scenic artist painting in the San Juan area of Colorado in 1874. Being very accomplished in his portrayal of mountain scenery, it is hard to believe that he was self-taught."

Finding a wealth of beauty in the surrounding Rocky Mountains, Learned remained in Leadville for about five years; he painted landscapes, mining scenes, and mining towns.

For his friends and admirers, he did hundreds of little paintings on diagonal slices of wood cut from pine and spruce trees. He continued to do theatrical painting in opera houses in Fort Collins, Greeley, and Denver, Colorado. He also taught painting in Leadville and at the Academy of Music in Denver.

Learned was known to have been active in Colorado until 1896. There were several published notations of his artistic activities in the *Rocky Mountain News* in Denver until that time. After 1896, his whereabouts or events leading to his death have never been determined.

Coloradans are indebted to Harry Learned for the historical preservation his work has contributed to the pictorial records of this state. His paintings are in the collections of the Denver Art Museum, the Colorado Historical Society, the Denver Public Library, other museums, and many private collections, as silent reminders of Colorado's scenic beauty.

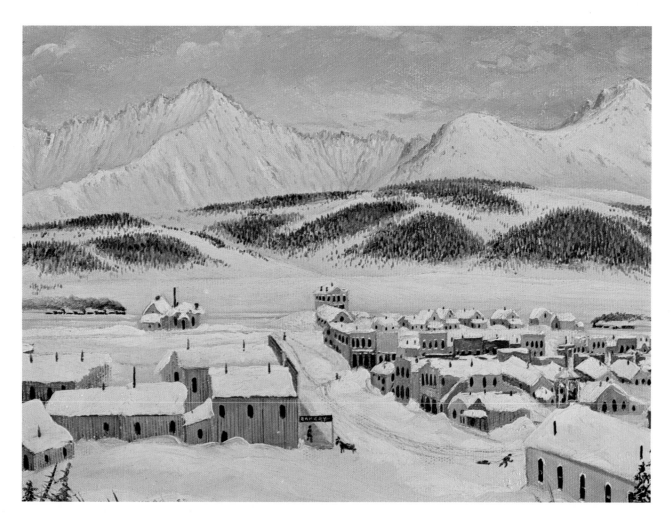

Robinson, Colorado. Dated 1887. 10 x 14 inches, oil. Harry Learned.

Ward Lockwood

1894–1963

WARD LOCKWOOD IS GENERALLY thought of as a New Mexico artist and was one of the West's most respected art educators. He first visited Taos in 1926, and thereafter spent much of his life in that area.

He was born in Atchison, Kansas, and as a boy was overwhelmed by the desire to paint. In 1914 he went eastward to study at the Pennsylvania Academy, where he felt the influences of modern art. In 1917 he enlisted in the Army and served in France. He said, "That period now seems alternately a ghastly dream and an exciting adventure." The period of readjustment for Lockwood was confusing and frustrating.

Two years after his discharge in 1919, he returned to Paris to study. His style of painting at that time was a mixture of Cezanne, Van Gogh, and impressionism, which were his environmental influences.

Lockwood and his wife, the former Clyde Bonebrake, moved to Taos in 1927, where they bought and remodeled an old adobe house on Ledoux Street and built a studio there. He became immersed in many of Taos' local projects and civic causes, and spent considerable time attending Indian ceremonials at the local pueblos. He was a popular and respected figure and became a collector of artifacts.

He studied with the famous "Taos Ten," but the abstract art of John Marin and Andrew Dasburg's cubism also greatly impressed him. Lockwood became involved with the government-sponsored art programs, and he did many murals for the WPA.

In the summer of 1932 Lockwood served on the faculty of the Broadmoor Art Academy in Colorado Springs, Colorado. In 1938 he became chairman of the Department of Art at the University of Texas and, subsequently, an instructor at the University of California at Berkeley and at the University of Kansas at Manhattan.

Lockwood again served in the Army during World War II, advancing to the rank of colonel before his discharge in 1945. In 1948 he returned to California to teach. The new environment greatly influenced his painting. His scenes of the San Francisco East Bay and his summertime works in Taos were both abstract.

In 1961 he returned to Taos to live out his final years. At the time of his death, there were 400 paintings in his studio collection.

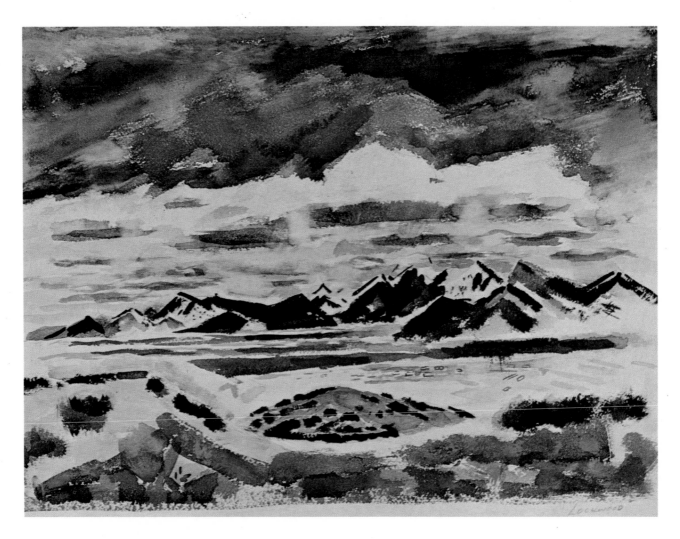

Winter Valley. 14 x 18 inches, watercolor. Ward Lockwood.

Waldo Love

1881–1967

THE CONTRIBUTION CHARLES WALDO LOVE made to America's western heritage lives on at the Museum of Natural History in Denver, Colorado. His talented brush created many of the amazingly real panoramas that form the backgrounds for the museum's wildlife exhibits.

Love was born in Washington, D.C., where his mother, Dr. Minnie C.T. Love, was studying for her medical degree and his father was working toward a law degree. The family moved to Denver, Colorado, in 1893; his mother became a well-known physician and one of the founders of the Children's Hospital.

Love attended the Reed Art School in Denver and the Art Students League in New York City. He also studied in Paris at the Academie de la Grande Chaumiere and Academie Julien.

After his return from Europe, he worked as a commercial artist in New York City, then joined the staff of the Colorado State Historical Society Museum. In 1937 he began his twenty-year association with the Denver Museum of Natural History.

The circular views of Colorado scenery in the dioramas at the Museum are wonderful examples of Waldo Love's ability. He was a master craftsman in this intricate type of painting, skillfully creating atmosphere, perspective, and color with just the right amount of realism. The background paintings recede from the animal exhibits in the foreground yet tie in with the primary tones of the wildflowers and birds.

After his retirement, Love continued to work on special assignments for the Museum. He painted thirty-three of the panoramic scenes in the Museum's habitat groups, which, at the time of his death, were viewed by approximately 700,000 visitors annually.

In describing his work, Love said, "It is a question of trying to find out what nature does, and do likewise. But I also must achieve a feeling of daylight under the fluorescent lights, which isn't so easy, since the brightest light in the backgrounds is comparable to a cloudy day. Because of this I use a very high keyed palette."

He also executed many easel paintings of mountain and woodland scenes.

The Waldo Loves were the parents of a daughter, Mary, and two sons, Dudley and Charles.

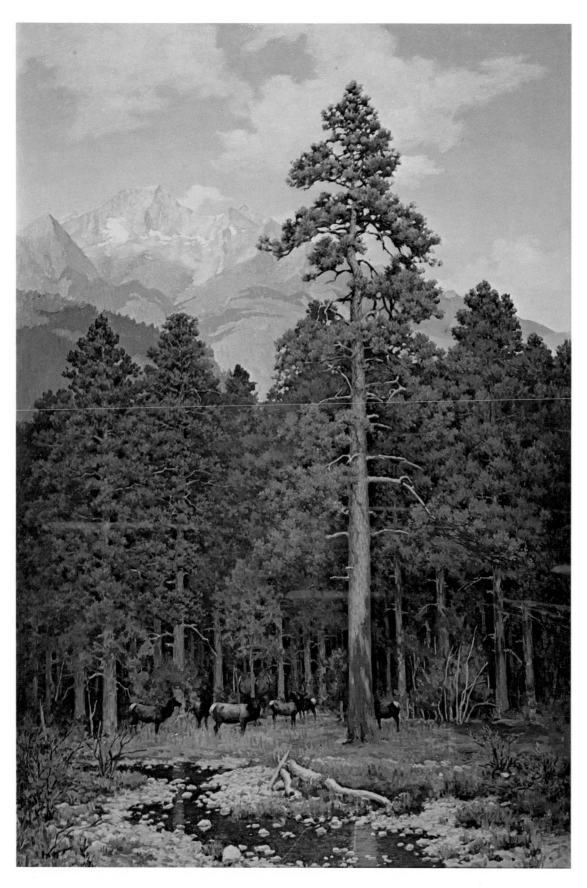

Chair Mountain, Colorado. 43 x 29 inches, oil. Waldo Love.

Fernand Lungren

1857–1932

IT TOOK SEVERAL YEARS and several stops before Fernand Harvey Lungren made it to the southwestern United States to paint. And it took several more years before he received due acclaim as one of the great western artists and illustrators of the Southwest.

Born in Hagerstown, Maryland, the son of a doctor, Lungren grew up in Toledo, Ohio. He showed little inclination for formal schooling, but at the age of seven he was considered a child prodigy in art. At sixteen he was a bank clerk, making sketches on the backs of checks in idle hours.

At his father's insistence, he enrolled at the University of Michigan as an engineering student, but dropped out two years later to study art in Cincinnati, at the Pennsylvania Academy in Philadelphia, and at the Academie Julien in Paris.

In the early 1890s in Cincinnati, Lungren met Joseph H. Sharp, who interested him in going west. The Santa Fe Railway gave him the chance. It offered traveling expenses plus a nominal sum for all accepted drawings. Lungren spent eight months in and around Santa Fe, New Mexico, visiting the Indian pueblos and painting life there. In 1893, he went back to Arizona to witness the nine-day Hopi Snake Dance ceremony. He was initiated into several Indian tribes and into the Hopi priesthood. When Lungren returned to Cincinnati, his paintings of the "open spaces" were largely misunderstood by the critics, as they knew little about the country he was trying to introduce to them.

In 1904, Lungren made a trip to the Sierras. Until then he had painted landscapes primarily as a background for Indian life. Now, in a country offering infinite variety, the landscape itself became the artist's obsession.

In the following years, Lungren and his wife, Henrietta Whipple, set up a permanent home and studio in Santa Barbara. There he painted the desert and the Sierras; and it was then that his earlier work became fully appreciated.

Several years after the death of his wife, Lungren helped found the Santa Barbara School of Art. He remained active in the school until his death. His biography, by John A. Berger, was published in 1936. Lungren's studio collection of paintings and Indian artifacts became the property of the Santa Barbara State College.

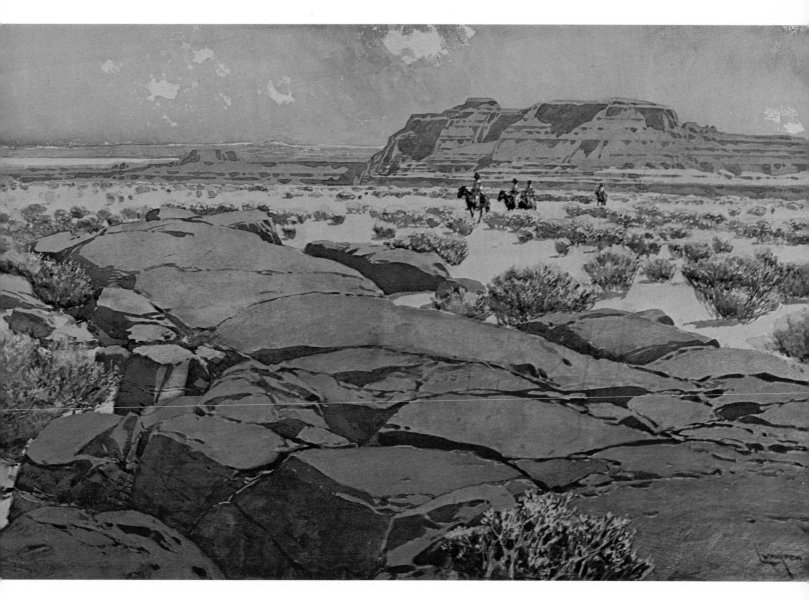

Indian Riders. 16¼ x 17½, watercolor. Fernand Lungren.

Leal Mack

1892–1962

AFTER FIFTY-FOUR YEARS Leal Mack finally found the quiet, simple life he loved in Taos, New Mexico. He was born in Titusville, Pennsylvania, and as a boy worked in a buckwheat mill owned by his father and uncle. Although he never lived on a farm, he spent much time on his uncle's land. Many of his rural subjects are memories of this period. The man who appears in several paintings is his Uncle Will.

Mack always liked to draw, but his parents refused to give him art lessons because, "there were no other artists in the family." Instead they favored piano lessons; but the young boy, who also loved music, wanted a violin.

After saving enough money from his work, he bought a violin and subsequently went to California, where he studied music. He played in an orchestra in a silent movie house and in dance bands making five dollars a night.

He was able to put enough money aside to pursue his first ambition—art. This brought him back to the Pennsylvania Academy of Fine Art in Philadelphia, where his talent was quickly apparent. He soon set up a studio in Wilmington, Delaware, with Pitt Fitzgerald.

His illustrating career was helped by his friendship with students of Howard Pyle, including Harvey Dunn, N. C. Wyeth, and Frank Schoonover. Wyeth particularly was impressed with Mack's potential and invited him to study at his Chadds Ford, Pennsylvania, school. He met his wife here.

His paintings reflect the tutelage of N. C. Wyeth, who also heavily influenced Henriette, Carolyn, and Andrew Wyeth; Peter Hurd, and John McCoy. The Chadds Ford group is characterized by individuality in depicting a deep respect for the world's simple elements. N. C. Wyeth's pupils communicated an intimate concern with the loveliness of nature's seasonal, changing drama.

After fifteen years of illustrating for the leading magazines of the day, the Depression came, and Mack returned to Pennsylvania to manage a mill for ten years, painting only at night in a loft studio.

In 1946 the Macks moved to Taos, New Mexico, having previously known a few of the artists living there. "This is the place I have been looking for," Mack exclaimed, after seeing it for the first time. And there he stayed until his death.

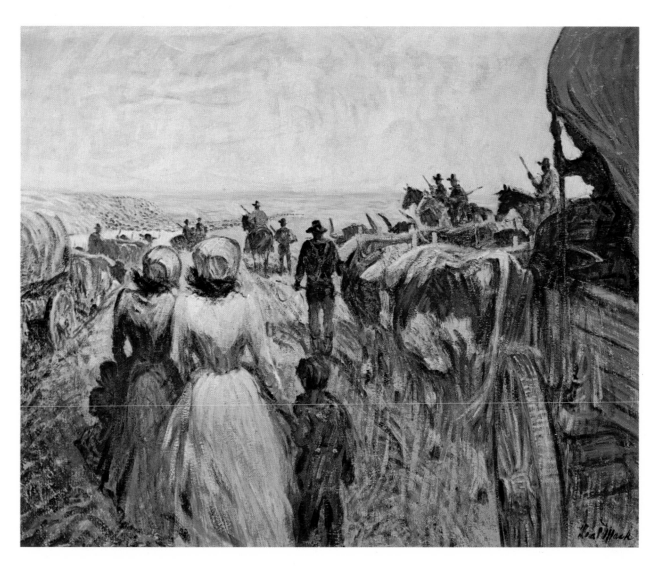

Great Expectations. 32 x 40 inches, oil. Leal Mack.

Roy Mason NA AWS

1886–1972

DURING HIS CAREER, Roy Martell Mason portrayed a wide range of outdoor subjects with superb realism and control of color. His work won many awards, including the Gold Medal from the American Watercolor Society, and was shown in many prestigious exhibitions throughout the country.

"Mason's thirst for the great outdoors was satiated partly by rod and gun and partly by his wonderful brush," said artist Vernon Nye. "A skilled sportsman, his paintings revealed a firsthand knowledge gained through many hours spent in the field. . . . Like a breath of October air, his paintings appealed to a wide range of tastes."

Mason would make rapid sketches of outdoor scenes, convert them to larger drawings in charcoal, remove the excess charcoal so that only a faint pattern would remain and then apply paints. He felt better pictures could be created this way, rather than to paint a scene directly.

He was born in Gilbert Mills, New York, the son of Frank and Elizabeth Mason. His father farmed and also worked as a gunstock engraver for the Batavia Gun Company. The elder Mason encouraged his son in art and in his spare time taught him to hunt and fish. They enjoyed a rare and rewarding father-son relationship.

In 1902, young Mason took a correspondence course in art, which he later referred to as his "formal art training." He also served as artist for his high school newspaper in Batavia, New York.

In 1907, Mason's father started his own engraving business. Young Mason composed the drawings and the elder Mason did the engraving. The firm prospered. As a young man, he won a watercolor painting contest and a trip to Puerto Rico. His paintings of the island inspired his professional career.

Mason then joined a Philadelphia lithographic company and eventually became head of its art department, a position he held until 1946. He also maintained his own studio in Philadelphia.

In New Hampshire in 1926, Mason met Chauncey Ryder, an artist he had long admired, and the two became friends and often painted together.

In 1959, Mason and his wife, Lena, moved to LaJolla, California, where the artist spent his final years. "Two things make for a happy life," he once said, "to be able to paint and to be married to the right wife."

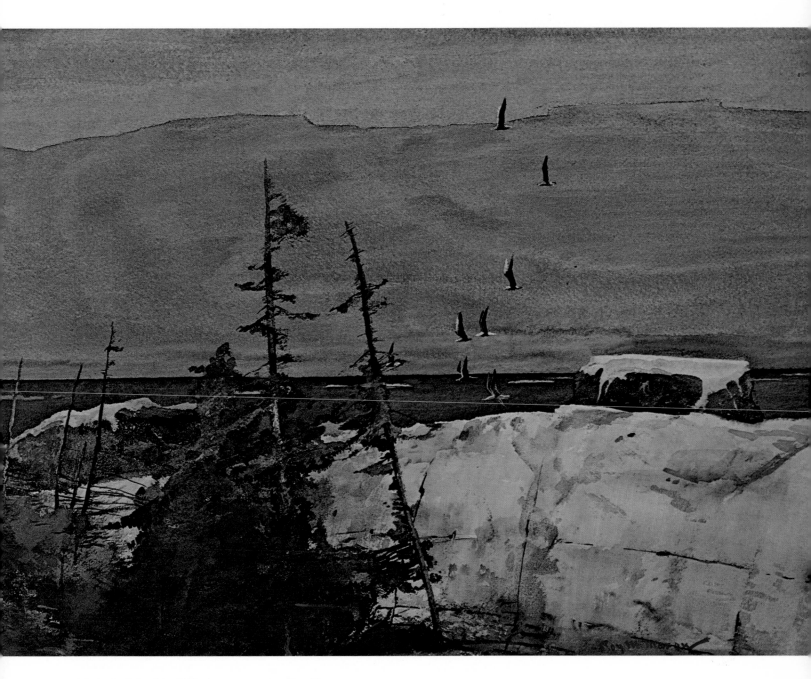

Admiralty Inlet. 22 x 30 inches, watercolor. Roy Mason.

Clarence McGrath

b. 1938

CLARENCE McGRATH IS DESCRIBED in an article published by the *American Artist* magazine, April 1975, as "a John Wayne western type, unaffected and friendly, but paradoxically a technical virtuoso—a nearly classic painter of scenes, character portaits, and still life."

One of five children, Clarence McGrath was raised on a forty-acre farm that his father sharecropped in Duncan, Arizona. The children all worked on farms, ranches, or herding sheep to help support the family.

McGrath was interested in art at an early age, and his parents encouraged him to paint in his spare time. As a teenager he was capable of finished art work. His friend and neighbor in Duncan, the western realist painter Hal Empie, influenced his work, as did his high school art teacher and later his college art teacher at Eastern Arizona Junior College. McGrath also studied briefly at the Arizona School of Art in Phoenix.

In the late fifties he went to the Arizona State Fair and found out a man could paint for a living. Before that, he thought he had to earn a living in order to paint.

He met an itinerant portrait artist from the Philippines, who sketched effective portrait studies on ochre paper and shared his techniques with McGrath. The next year, McGrath was sketching at the fair, then at a concession at the local shopping center.

By this time he had a wife and two children to support. When the Phoenix season ended, he moved to Southern California to make a living doing portraits at Knott's Berry Farm. But the season was off there also, so he went to work in a warehouse instead. In his spare time he studied with Phil Gilkerson, Sergei Bongart, and Leon Franks.

In 1962 he was awarded the J. F. and Anna Lee Stacey Fellowship Award, providing funds for a painting trip to Central America. He was enjoying enough financial success from his art to give up his warehouse job. But it was just at this time that his wife died. To recover from the tragedy, he sold everything and moved to Mexico. Since McGrath had grown up and worked alongside Spanish-speaking neighbors, he was very much at home in Mexico. He speaks Spanish fluently.

He is living in Baja California, Mexico, with his second wife, Florida, his two children from his first marriage, and three adopted children.

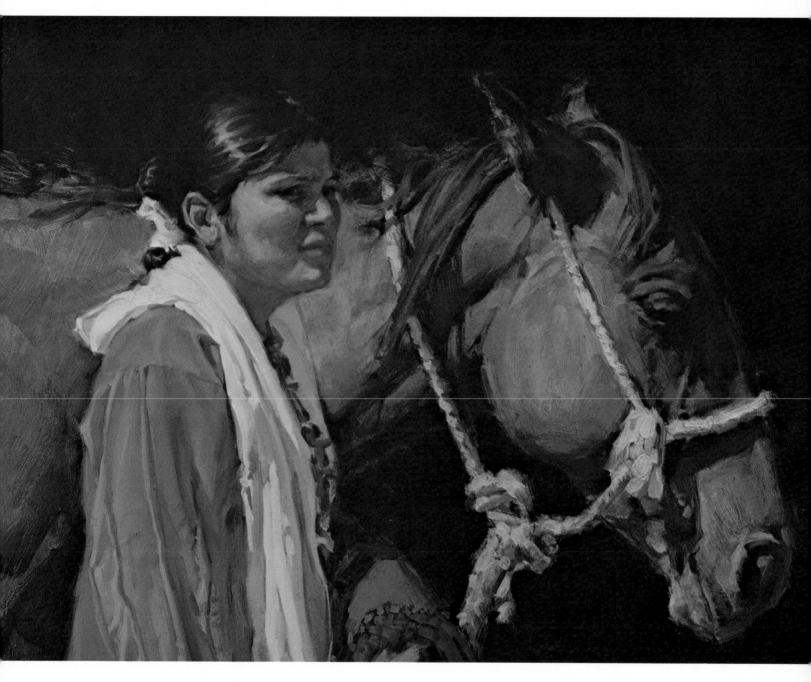

Silk and Velvet. 18 x 24 inches, oil. Clarence McGrath.

F. Luis Mora NA

1874–1940

THE SON OF A FAMED SPANISH PAINTER and sculptor, Francis Luis Mora developed a unique style of art that was both Spanish and modern American in flavor and technique.

During his long diverse career, he was best known as an illustrator, a muralist, and portrait artist in both watercolor and oil. Yet he also did etchings and sculptures. By the time he was eighteen years of age, Mora was doing illustrations for many of the leading magazines and periodicals of the day. His career was maturing early.

As a muralist, he was commissioned in 1900 to do a panel for the Lynn, Massachusetts, Public Library, and a mural for the Missouri State Building at the Louisiana Purchase Exposition of 1904. As a portrait artist, Mora did paintings of Andrew Carnegie and President Warren Harding.

He was born in Montevideo, Uruguay, the son of artist Domingo Mora and a French mother, Laura Gaillard Mora. His early life was spent in South America. His parents brought him to the United States; his father taught art at Perth Amboy, New Jersey; Boston, and New York City.

Young Mora's promising art career was encouraged and fostered by his father. After attending Manning's Seminary at Perth Amboy, and the New York and Boston public schools, he was sent to the school of drawing and painting at the Boston Museum of Fine Arts, where he studied under Frank Benson and Edmund Tarbell. Subsequently he was a pupil of H. Siddons Mowbray at the Art Students League in New York and later made various trips abroad to study the works of the old masters.

Mora eventually taught painting at the Art Students League, the Grand Central and New York Schools of Art in New York City. In 1904 he became an associate member of the National Academy of Design and two years later was elected a full member.

He spent most of his life in New York City and in Gaylordsville, Connecticut, with ocassional trips west to gather material for his Indian and western scene paintings. Enjoying the outdoors, which he loved to paint, he also fished, ice skated, and rode horseback. He was married twice and had a daughter, Rosemary, by his first wife. His brother, Joseph Jacinto Mora, also was a noted southwestern painter and sculptor.

Luis Mora died in New York City.

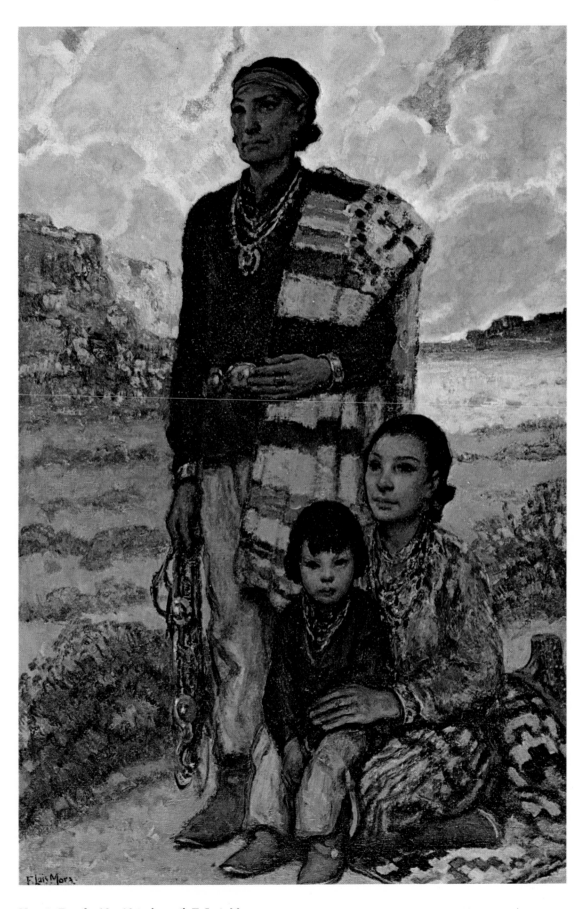

Navajo Family. 18 x 12 inches, oil. F. Luis Mora.

Alfred Morang

1901–1958

"I DON'T BELIEVE IN ART FOR ART'S SAKE; I believe in art for people's sake." This remark epitomized Alfred Gwynne Morang—artist, musician, writer, and self-styled philosopher. His vitality and joy of living are reflected in all of his work.

Born in Ellsworth, Maine, Alfred Morang was an intelligent, sensitive child. His natural creativity was nurtured by his mother. At the age of twenty-one he was well launched into the aesthetic world. A gifted violinist, he played professionally in symphony orchestras and dance bands.

Following the death of his mother in 1922, Morang went to Boston to further his study of art and music. Here he met Dorothy Clark, a fellow art and music student he married in 1930.

Morang and his bride settled in Portland, Maine, where he found a position as a violin instructor. By 1936 Morang had published eighty-seven short stories and a few poems and articles.

A year later he was forced to seek a drier climate because of tuberculosis. The Morangs moved to Santa Fe, New Mexico. Not the type to surrender to illness, he spent his first three years teaching art and writing at the Arsuna School of Fine Arts in Santa Fe. In addition, he was publicity director for the American Foundation of Transcendental Paintings, Inc. This avant-garde organization conformed with Morang's personal philosophy— "shatter the rules if you need to." It was only natural that he should support a school of art that encouraged the painter to give free rein to his spontaneity.

Communicating his zest for art over the air on his own half-hour radio program, he volunteered this service for seventeen years for no payment. He wrote a regular column for a Santa Fe newspaper entitled "Art In The News." He also conducted the Morang School of Fine Arts. He was a great admirer of the French Impressionists, and his friend John Sloan became a great influence on his work.

His first marriage ended in divorce after twenty years. After a second marriage and divorce, Morang spent his remaining years in a "Thoreau-like" existence. He was found burned to death from a fire that had swept through his little adobe house, his kitten alive in his arms. His body was cremated and his ashes kept by the Museum of New Mexico for two years and then scattered over Santa Fe from a plane.

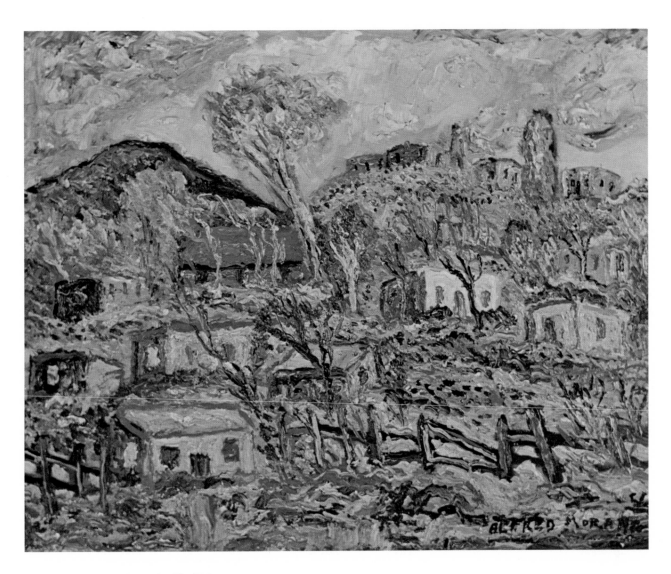

Santa Fe. 16 x 20 inches, oil. Alfred Morang.

Walter Mruk

1883–1942

OF THE FIVE EARLY SANTA FE PAINTERS, Wladyslaw R. Mruk and Jozef Bakos had known each other before they joined forces in New Mexico. They were both from Buffalo, New York, where Walter Mruk was born, and both were of Polish parentage. They studied together at the Albright Institute and with John Thompson in Denver.

In 1920 Mruk worked in the Santa Fe area as a forest ranger and drew political cartoons for the *Santa Fe New Mexican*. He was a very introspective man, who had a great love for nature and outdoor living.

When "Los Cinco Pintores" (the five painters) organized into a group—consisting of Mruk, Bakos, Fremont Ellis, Will Shuster, and Willard Nash—they held their first of several annual exhibitions at the Museum of Art. At that time Santa Fe was a town of 7,000, with a large and flourishing art colony. There was a cross-pollination of ideas between the Santa Fe colony and the artists living and painting in Taos. Los Cinco Pintores were a great contrast to the earlier artists as they were regarded by the more established citizens as "a wild bunch."

Will Shuster and Mruk shared an interesting adventure when they went into the Carlsbad Caverns to paint, long before the caverns were developed into a public attraction. They were lowered into the caves in buckets and they painted by lantern light.

El Palacio quoted in 1925, "This collection of canvases has created a stir in the art world, not only because the visit of Mruk and Shuster was the first that resulted in paintings of the cavern, but Mruk's canvases are said to be imaginative to a high degree. He filled the cavern with mythical grotesques in an effort to interpret his reaction upon entering the dim lit interior. The work is accepted as a distinct achievement, although decidedly unusual and difficult of treatment. Art critics have differed over the paintings, but all have conceded an impressive result."

Walter Mruk's art is the least known of the five painters, as examples of his work are rather rare. It has been over a half-century since the five young men formed "Los Cinco Pintores," but their paintings are still widely known and collected.

After exhibiting in the Modern Wing of the Museum of Art in Santa Fe, he returned East to live out his life in Buffalo, New York.

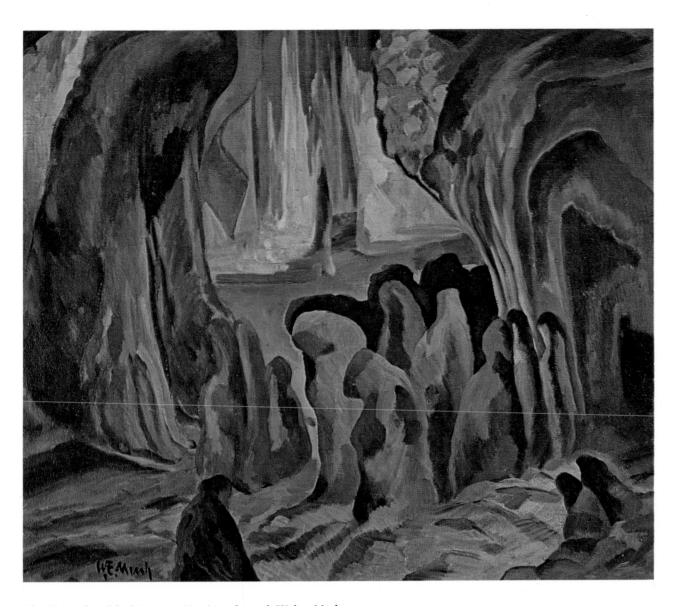

The Ghost of Carlsbad Caverns. 20 x 24 inches, oil. Walter Mruk.

Dan Muller

1888–1977

IF EXPERIENCE IS THE BEST TEACHER, Dan Cody Muller certainly would have no peer as a western artist.

Muller was born in Montana, and his father, a freelance scout and long-time friend of Buffalo Bill Cody, was one-fourth Piegan Blackfoot Indian. When Muller was nine years old, a bronc riding accident claimed the life of his father. He was then adopted by the legendary Cody. He spent many years as a working cowboy, traveling from Canada to Mexico by horseback and appearing frequently for eighteen years in Cody's Wild West Show, an education in itself.

Many of Muller's firsthand experiences in the Old West are depicted in his oils, watercolors, and pastels. His work is done in a documentary style, which is punctuated with great authenticity. He was careful to portray exact detail in the clothing and gear of his subjects, as well as in the background scenes. He also had a keen knowledge of horseflesh.

"I'm not upholstered with any elegancies of diction," Muller once wrote, "my education being sadly corrupted with years of such surroundings as cattle, hosses, cards, and . . . a mite of horse larceny. I'm of the old school of cowpunching, when cowboying was done with a tough bronc, a good saddle, and a stout rope, and one followed the chuckwagons and slept under the stars. The sum total of my education adds up to only six months—three months each term for two winter seasons in a one-room country schoolhouse. I found school dull—and that is just the way it found me."

Muller painted the three largest murals at A Century of Progress Exhibition in Chicago in 1933, and he illustrated many books. He also did illustrations for the first issue of *Esquire Magazine*. He authored several books, including *My Life with Buffalo Bill* and his famous illustrated *Book of Horses*.

His paintings are owned by museums and private collectors throughout the United States, Canada, Europe, and South America.

In his latter years, Muller moved to Wisconsin and established a studio and home there.

"Now I often drift back to the days and the men I have met on life's trail," he once said. "I relive the scenes of those days now long gone by, on canvas, and try to make them historically correct in every last detail."

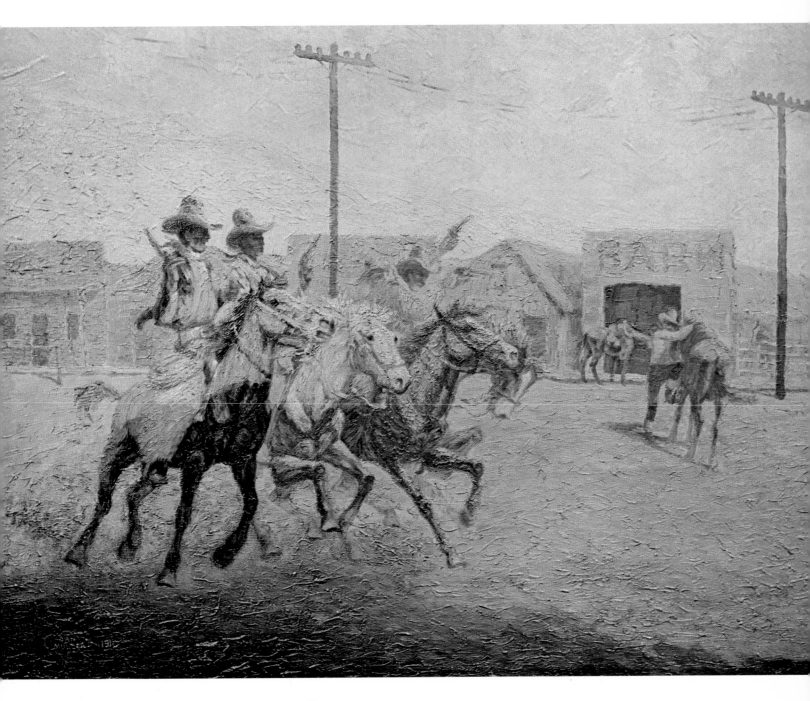

Town. Dated 1910. 28 x 36 inches, oil. Dan Muller.

Ernest Narjot

1826–1898

IN HIS QUEST FOR GOLD in 1849, Ernest Narjot did not strike it rich, but instead he became one of the pioneer painters of the West.

Narjot went to California in 1849. The trip was made from his native France by sailing ship around Cape Horn, rather than by traveling across the western plains in covered wagons with the prospectors. His motivation was gold; and it was not until 1865, when he returned permanently to San Francisco, did he devote his full energies to painting California and its people and preserving its robust history.

His full name was Ernest Etienne Narjot deFranceville. Both his parents were artists. Narjot received his formal art training in Paris, becoming a painter of note before being enticed by the gold discoveries in America.

He had little luck in the gold fields; after three years, he joined a mining expedition that went to Mexico. He spent thirteen years there, mining and painting scenes along the border between Mexico and Arizona in his spare time. In 1860 in Sonora, he married Santos Ortiz.

After returning to the United States, Narjot set up a studio in San Francisco and traveled throughout the state. He painted landscapes, as well as portraits and sketches of the gold miners and of Indian life. He also illustrated a book on early life in California.

As his reputation grew, Narjot was commissioned to paint several murals and frescoes for churches and public buildings. The climax of his career came when he was asked to decorate the ceiling for Leland Stanford's tomb, which was located on the campus of Stanford University.

While finishing the project, he accidentally splashed paint in his eyes, which eventually led to his blindness. Narjot lived the final months of his life with failing eyesight and deteriorating health. His wife, who could speak little English, was forced to sell many of his paintings to support the family, which included their daughter and grandchildren.

A Narjot benefit was held by prominent Bay Area artists—William Keith, Thomas Hill, Arthur Mathews, and Amedee Joullin—who sold their paintings to provide money for the stricken artist.

Many of Narjot's unsold works were destroyed in the San Francisco earthquake and fire of 1906.

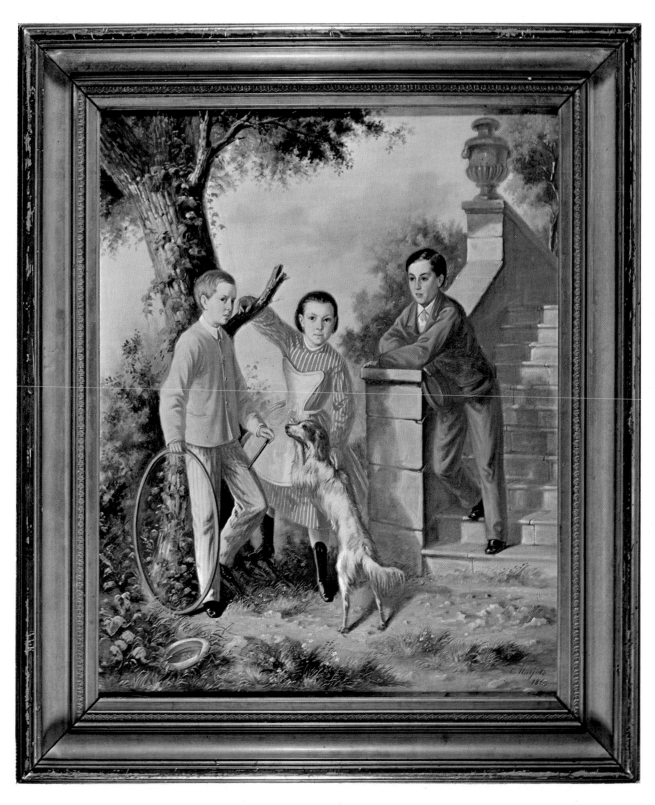

The Grandchildren. 27 x 22 inches, oil. Ernest Narjot.

Willard Nash

1898–1943

WILLARD AYER NASH WAS the most abstract painter among the five members of the Santa Fe, New Mexico, group known as "Los Cinco Pintores." Nash, along with Will Shuster, Jozef Bakos, Fremont Ellis, and Walter Mruk, brought a new art style to New Mexico, and a new lifestyle.

"The five nuts in the adobe huts," as they called themselves, were noted for their rather eccentric way of life. But they helped create a new sense of community involvement in Santa Fe, promoting numerous benefit events to aid the Indians in the area, especially during the drought years.

Sponsored by a Detroit art patron, Nash had an advantage over his fellow Pintores, who struggled for years before their paintings brought them financial rewards and a comfortable living.

He was born in Philadelphia, but spent most of his early life in Detroit, where he studied art under John P. Wicker. Nash made his first trip to Santa Fe in 1920 to gather data for a mural he was painting, and returned there the following year to make his home. Along with the other Pintores, he built a studio on Camino del Monte Sol.

Influenced by Cezanne, Nash also became immensely excited by the Fauve colors and John Marin's abstractions. The academic style of painting he brought from the East soon took on new boldness, and he developed a great command of color. One of his mentors in New Mexico was Andrew Dasburg, known as the American champion of cubism. Working in both oil and watercolor, all of his paintings have a cool, intellectual quality. He was known also for his simplified nudes.

"I am an individualist and a self-analytical one," he said. "I am an experimenter in art and I have worked through many phases, going step by step deeper into the mysteries of aesthetics."

In the 1920s Nash's work was shown in the Modern Wing of the Museum of New Mexico. The work of the same group was shown at the Whitney Museum in New York City in 1932 and 1935.

He taught at the Broadmoor Art Academy in Colorado Springs, Colorado, and at the San Francisco Art School.

Nash left New Mexico in 1936 for what he called "self-imposed exile" in Los Angeles, where he died.

150

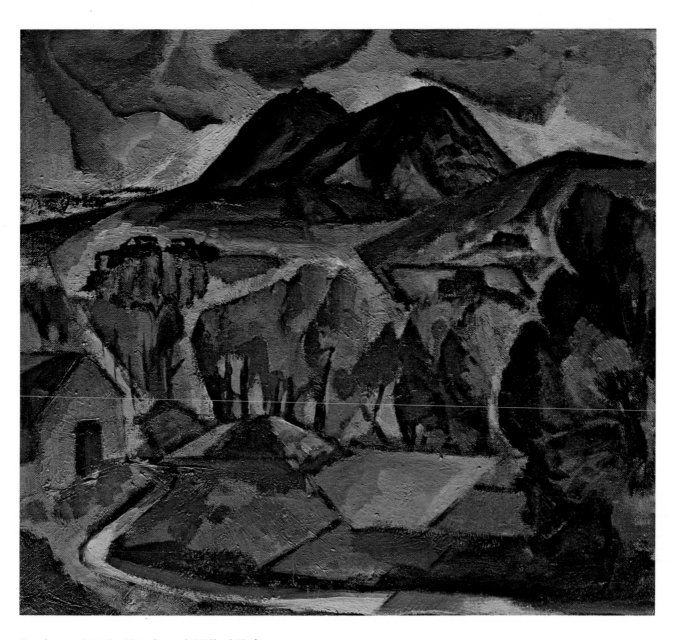

Landscape # 2. 18 x 20 inches, oil. Willard Nash.

Victor Nehlig NA
1830–1909

A NATIVE OF FRANCE, Victor Nehlig was born in Paris, where he studied under Leon Cogniet and Abel de Pujol. At the age of twenty he immigrated to the United States and settled in New York City. His paintings met with tremendous success, and he was elected an associate member of the National Academy of Design in 1863.

On his way to America, he stopped for a short time in Cuba to paint the countryside. It was this visit to Cuba that resulted in the canvas entitled "Mahogany Cutting," which was exhibited at the National Academy in 1871 and brought the artist more recognition.

In Henry Tuckerman's 1867 *Book of the Artists,* Tuckerman stated prophetically, "It is to be hoped that the ambition of this artist will lead him into the field of historic painting . . . a work for which his artistic genius is admirably fitted."

Nehlig was a painter noted for his figures, portraits, and genre paintings of historical events. Depicting American history during our nation's centennial period, his canvases have remained art treasures and will continue to be an astute art collector's valued possession. Illustrations for books were also in his particular field.

After he returned to Europe for additional art study in 1872, Nehlig's later historical painting specialized in Indian subjects. His work is a perpetual reminder that as early as the mid-nineteenth century, European artists were preserving the American heritage and the fast disappearing events of the early American development.

Among his principal historical works are "The Cavalry Charge of Lieutenant Hidden," "The Artist's Dream," "The Captive Huguenot," "Gertrude of Wyoming," "Waiting for My Enemy," "Serenade," "The Bravo," "Hiawatha and Minnehaha," "The Princess Pocahontas," and "Pocahontas and John Smith." This story-telling type of art was a popular medium of the period and serves as an irreplaceable record of places and events past.

Nehlig is listed in many art reference books, and his paintings are in various museums and private collections; they have been shown in numerous outstanding exhibitions.

He was living in New York City at the time of his death.

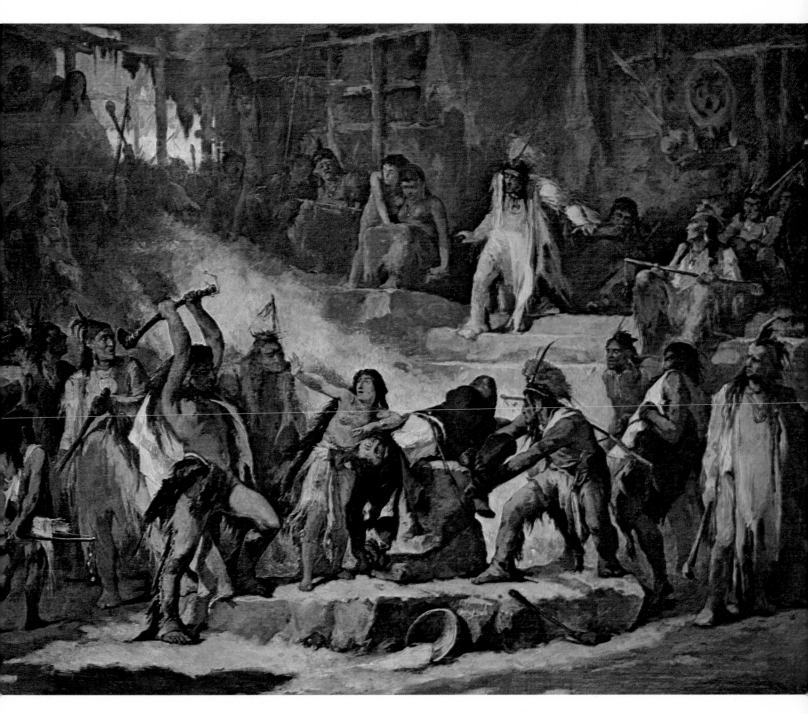

Pocahontas and John Smith. New York. Dated 1870. 20 x 25½ inches, oil. Victor Nehlig.

B. J. O. Nordfeldt

1878–1955

THE VAST AND VARIED ART CAREER of Bror Julius Olsson Nordfeldt included nearly twenty years in New Mexico. He was considered one of the most romantic expressionistic artists of Santa Fe's art colony.

He was born in Tullstrop, Sweden, one of ten children born to Nels and Ingrid Sofia Nordfeldt Olsson. The family came to the United States in 1891, when young Nordfeldt was thirteen, and settled in Chicago.

The artist began using his mother's maiden name when he was about twenty-five years of age to avoid confusion with another artist named Julius Olsson, who had become famous in both the United States and Europe. He legally adopted the name in about 1918.

As a boy, his first job was as a printer's devil with a Swedish-language newspaper in Chicago. His employer urged him to enter the Art Institute of Chicago in 1899. He became an assistant to Albert Herter in painting a mural commissioned by the McCormick Harvester Company for the Paris Exhibition, and in 1900 he was sent to France to view its unveiling.

Nordfeldt remained in France to study and teach, and he was greatly influenced by the work of Manet, Gauguin, and Cezanne. He next went to London to study etching and woodblock cutting. And his etchings financed a year's visit to his native Sweden.

Returning to the United States in 1903, he worked as a portrait artist in Chicago. Nordfeldt moved east in 1907, then returned to Europe, where he remained until World War I. In 1909, he married Dr. Margaret Doolittle.

After the armistice he was persuaded to visit Santa Fe. He was enamored with the country and its people and soon built a home and studio which were decorated with much of his artistic taste and labor.

He remained there until 1940. Nordfeldt's importance as a pioneering modernist was apparent in his non-academic handling of Indians, who he painted with distortion and abstraction using bold color. He also chose simple subject matter, to which he gave an air of mystery. His still life painting reflects the French influence of his earlier training.

Nordfeldt died of a heart attack in Henderson, Texas, where he became ill following a trip to Mexico.

He was survived by his second wife, Emily Abbott, who he married in 1944.

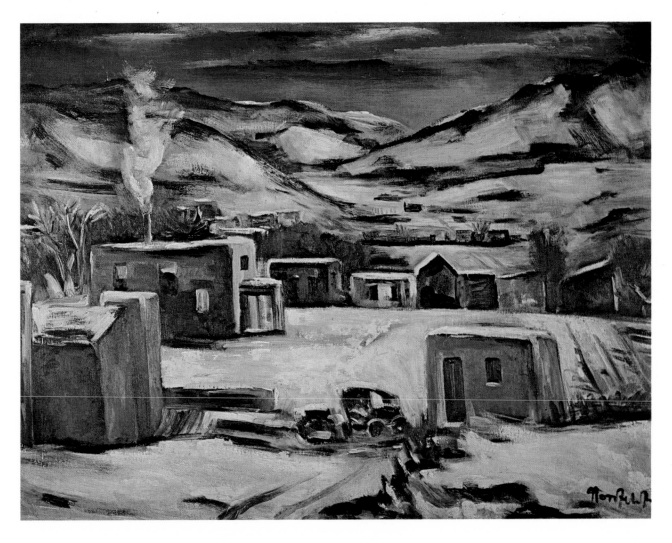

Winter Scene, Santa Fe, New Mexico. 30 x 40 inches, oil. B. J. O. Nordfeldt.

Sheldon Parsons

1866–1943

ORRIN SHELDON PARSONS was born in Rochester, New York. As a teenager, he painted in oils and watercolor, without any previous instruction. After high school, he went to New York City to study at several schools, including the National Academy of Design, where he was tutored by William Merritt Chase and Will H. Low.

Parson's talent for portraits was quickly recognized; he eventually was commissioned to paint President McKinley, Vice President Hobart, Senator Mark Hanna, Susan B. Anthony, and many members of socially prominent families. He also won acclaim for his autumn scenes of the hilly, wooded countryside of Westchester County, New York, and for a series of winter snow scenes painted in the Adirondacks.

After his wife died in 1913, Parsons gave up a successful career as a portrait artist in New York City to start a new life in Santa Fe, New Mexico. He was very ill with tuberculosis when he left New York with his twelve-year-old daughter Sara. It was several months after their arrival in Santa Fe that Parsons recovered sufficiently to paint again.

He was one of the first major painters there, following Carlos Vierra, Kenneth Chapman, and Gerald Cassidy. As Parsons became more familiar with the territory, his work showed greater freedom and a stronger sense of color. His paintings were quickly accepted, and they were exhibited at the Palace of the Governors and the newly built Museum of New Mexico. He was the first director of the Museum, which owns a number of his paintings.

Parsons painted few people into his pictures, doing mostly landscapes in an impressionistic manner and delicate, poetic fashion. In 1916, the publication of the Museum of New Mexico rated him "among the foremost delineators of the artistic aspects of the western desert, mountains, canyons, mission churches, Indian pueblos, Spanish plazas, and historic landmarks."

His wife, Caroline Reed Parsons, had been a noted photographer. Their daughter Sara was once married to artist Victor Higgins; after their divorce, Sara became a top-ranking New York photographer for *Vogue* magazine.

Parsons' paintings are owned by collectors throughout the United States, as well as in South America, India, Australia, Sweden, London, and Paris.

He died in Santa Fe following a heart attack.

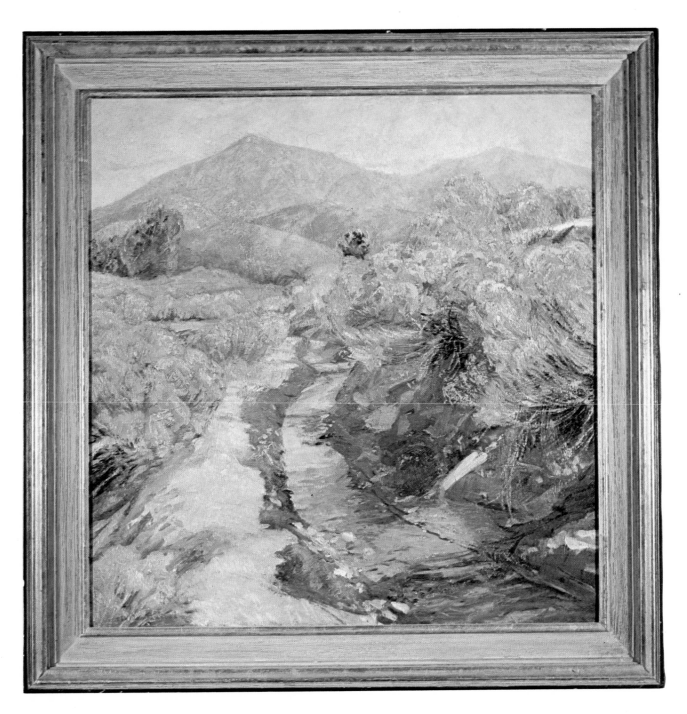

Chamisa. 36 x 36 inches, oil. Sheldon Parsons.

Wolfgang Pogzeba

THE WESTERN AMERICANIZATION of Wolfgang Pogzeba began in 1950 in Denver, Colorado. Since that time he has become a fine contemporary painter, sculptor, and photographer.

His work is a blend of the orthodox western and the unconventional modern, and his sculptures have been acclaimed by proponents of realistic and abstract art.

A bold and imaginative artist, the German-born Pogzeba often distorts figures to achieve full dramatic power. He casts his own bronzes and, in addition to his paintings, drawings, and ink washes, also works in steel sculpture. His accomplishments are not limited to western subjects. In the early 1970s he all but abandoned western bronzes to experiment with other subjects and media; he completed a number of works on the female anatomy in both bronze and fiberglass. He travels extensively and is in the field or on location gathering material firsthand for his diversified art. Pogzeba's interests fall in many different directions: he is also an architect, builder, classical pianist, and knowledgeable art collector.

Pogzeba was born in Munich, Germany, to a Polish father and German mother. He grew up in Germany during World War II and came to the

158

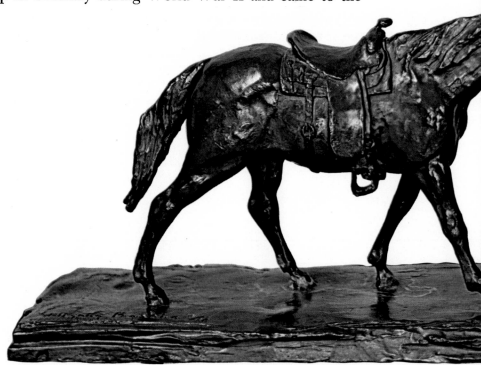

United States with his parents in 1948. After living in the East for two years, the family settled in Denver. Young Pogzeba quickly became enamored with the history of the West and the heritage of his new land.

He attended the Denver public schools and first entered college at the Colorado School of Mines in Golden, Colorado, to study engineering. But that course of study left him little time to pursue his creative inclinations. He transferred to the school of architecture at the University of Colorado.

Later, he attended the University of Mexico in Mexico City, the Kunst-akademie in Munich, and the Ecole des Beaux Arts in Paris. In 1960 he was graduated from the University of Colorado with a degree in art history.

His career began with an exhibition at the Montana Historical Society and flourished with many other major one-man shows in museums and galleries throughout the United States.

A book entitled *Wolfgang Pogzeba, New Vision,* representing his photography of the West, was published in 1977.

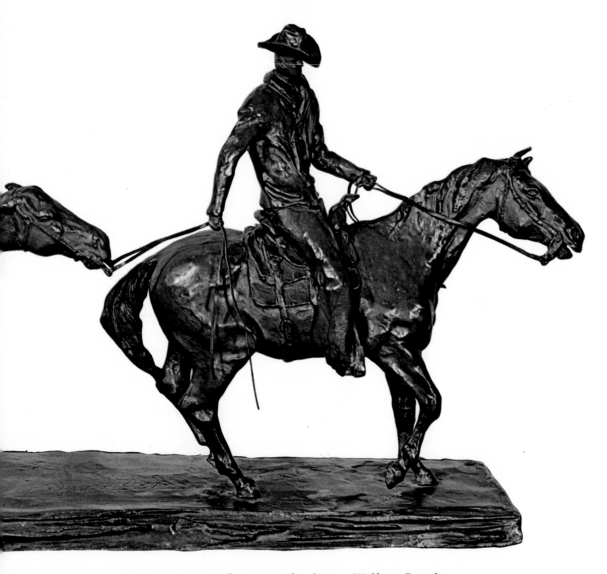

Lost Rider. H. 13 inches L. 29 inches, bronze. Wolfgang Pogzeba.

Marjorie Reed

b. 1915

MARJORIE REED HAS BEEN PAINTING HORSES since she was three years of age. Growing up in Los Angeles, she has always had a love of the desert country and is noted for her faithful and colorful paintings of the stagecoaches and the stage stations of the Old West, a choice of subject matter unusual for a woman artist.

Jack Wilkinson Smith, the noted landscape artist, was her teacher. He quickly became aware of her love of the outdoors, horses, and western history. He encouraged her to roam the countryside, where she became acquainted with Captain William Banning, who had been a stage driver for his father, Phinneas Banning. From him she acquired a knowledge of stagecoaches, the handling of teams of horses and, most important, the romantic history of the Butterfield Overland Stage and Mail Route.

After twenty years of research and traveling the old Butterfield trail in her Model-T with her Alaskan Husky dog for a companion, she began work on a series of paintings to record its story in form and color. The Butterfield Stage ran from San Francisco to the Yuma crossing on the Colorado River.

While she was concentrating on the horses and stagecoaches of the early days, she also was mastering the detail and color of the desert landscape, which was to be the background for so many of her paintings. Her canvases show true-to-life action with the use of a prismatic palette.

After her Butterfield Stage series of paintings was completed in 1957, a book entitled, *The Colorful Overland Stage,* a very historical and interesting documentary, was published, containing twenty color reproductions by Marjorie Reed with text by Richard F. Pourade.

Marjorie Reed, born in Springfield, Illinois, developed an early interest in art as her father was a commercial artist there. In 1927, while Miss Reed was still in school, the family moved to California, where she completed her preparatory schooling at Glendale. She had decided to follow in the footsteps of her father and become a serious painter.

Today Marjorie Reed, now Mrs. Cecil Creese, is one of the desertland's most popular painters, not only from the standpoint of her talent as an artist, but also from the historical contribution she has made to America and particularly the West.

160

She is living and painting in Tombstone, Arizona.

Butterfield Stage Leaving Vallecito. 24 x 36 inches, oil (detail). Marjorie Reed.

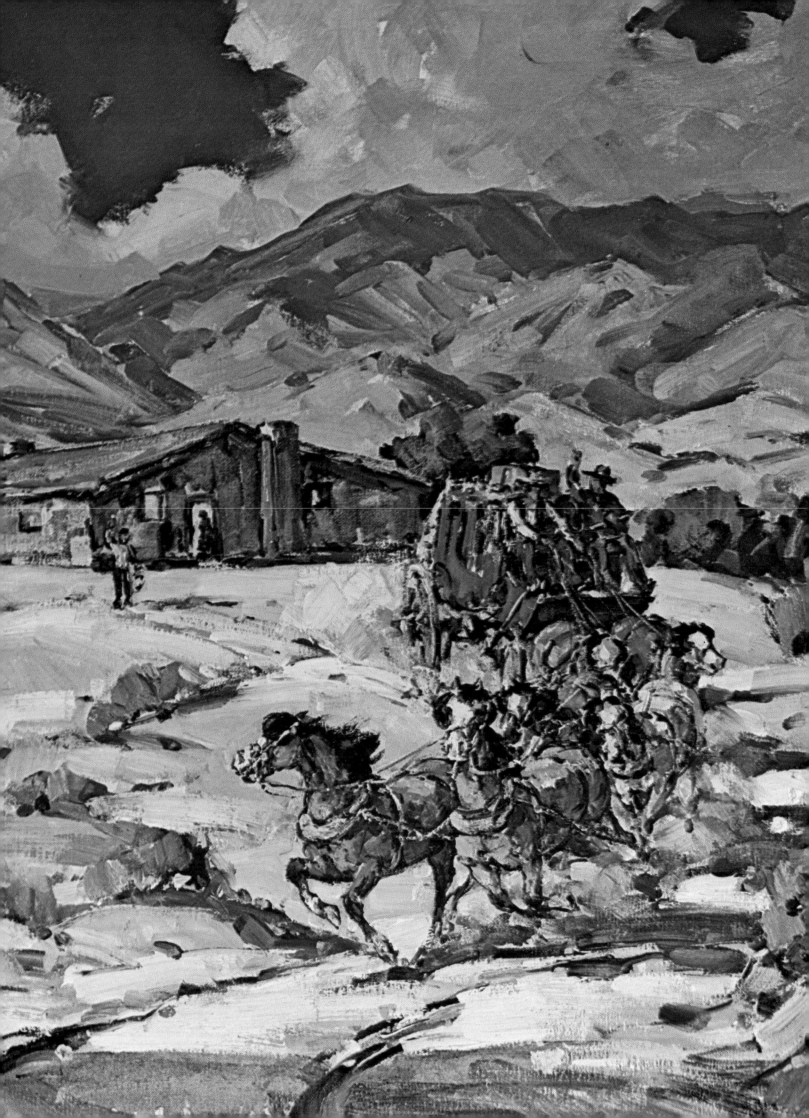

Leonard Reedy

1899–1956

WITH THE DEATH OF Leonard Howard Reedy, known as "Chicago's Cowboy Painter," the West lost one of its most zealous and devoted interpreters. He was a brilliant storyteller with his brush.

Born in Chicago, Reedy directed his talents exclusively to subjects of the Old West and the "New"—a part of the country that he loved. He painted the many rugged and colorful activities that were so typical of the frontier days, as well as recording the life on modern ranches.

He worked in both watercolor and oil, putting on canvas the nostalgic vignettes which reflected both his love and personal knowledge of the country and people involved in this way of life.

During his younger days, Reedy spent a great deal of time on the Great Plains and in the mountains of the West, living in mining and logging camps. He had been a ranch hand and had roamed and lived with the Indians. From firsthand experience he knew the Bad Lands, Grand Canyon, and life in the cattle country.

As a boy, Reedy showed great aptitude for art. The margins of his school books were generously illustrated with his heroes of the West—Indians, cowpunchers, and bandits. He studied at the Chicago Art Institute and the Chicago Academy of Fine Arts.

Many artists have given their lives to western subjects, but few have painstakingly studied the early history, its characters, Indian lore, and way of life from which inspiration for authentic subject matter is acquired.

Typical of Reedy's favorite themes are: "The Unbroken Mustang," "Caught in Stampede," "Sioux on the March," "Besieged by Bandits," "Trouble With the Sheriff," "Attack on the Union Pacific," "Catching Up with the Rustlers," "The Santa Fe Stage Route," "Carrying the Gold Shipment," "Wild Horses," and "Round-up in an Electrical Storm." The titles alone stir up a feeling of excitement and expectancy.

Leonard Reedy vividly stands out as one of the dedicated group of artists who, with their brushes, preserved life in the West, by providing a colorful, lively record of both its past and present. The historical delineators of future generations will be grateful to these uncompromising artists of the twentieth century, who relied on facts rather than fiction.

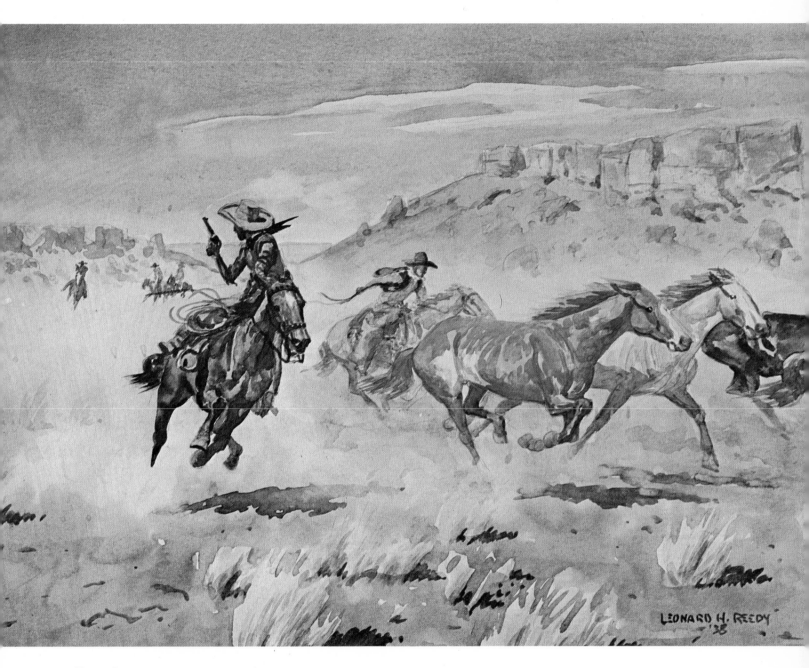

Horse Thieves. Dated 1938. 9 x 12 inches, watercolor. Leonard Reedy.

Frederic Remington ANA

1861–1909

ALTHOUGH RAISED IN THE EAST, the restless Frederic Sackrider Remington spent much of his life in the West, working as a cowboy and sheep rancher, prospecting for gold, and fighting as a soldier against the renegade Sioux. He studied and sketched the land around him with almost photographic eyes. His subjects were of prime importance, and his heroes were the everyday people of the frontier. He insisted on realism in every detail.

Remington was born in Canton, New York, where his father was a newspaper publisher. As a boy, he sketched the horses, Indians, cowboys, and soldiers he dreamed about. When he was seventeen, he was one of the first two students to enter the Yale University Art School.

In 1880 Remington's father died, and the ensuing inheritance prompted him to leave school. He worked briefly at several office jobs, but he could not settle down and grew restless and headed west with his easel, paint, and brushes to find his "Pot of Gold."

Four years later, he married Eva Caten. They moved to Kansas City, where Remington bought an interest in a saloon, after owning a sheep ranch. The other partners in the cantina cheated him out of his investment, and he returned to New York a year later with three dollars in his pocket and hundreds of western drawings.

He took a serious interest in art, entering the Art Students League to improve his technique. Success did not come quickly; by the early 1890s his paintings began to win prizes, and he became in great demand as a magazine and book illustrator. In 1895 his first sculpture, "Bronco Buster," won instant acclaim. His election as an associate of the National Academy of Design was in 1891. Author Owen Wister declared: "Remington is not merely an artist, he is a national treasure."

After achieving both wealth and notoriety, Remington moved to a Connecticut farm, where he established a library and art gallery and surrounded himself with his western artifacts and memorabilia. After 1900 the realism of his work changed somewhat to colorful semi-impressionism, as he sought to change his illustrative style.

Remington died suddenly from an attack of appendicitis in Ridgefield, Connecticut, at the age of forty-eight.

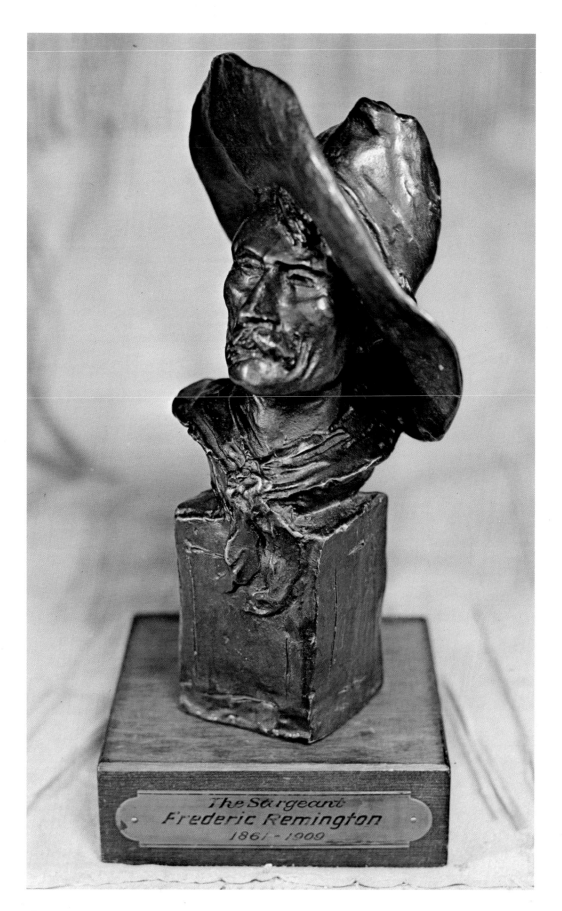

The Sergeant. H. 10 inches, bronze. Frederic Remington.

Louis Ribak

b. 1902

RUSSIAN BORN AND NEW YORK EDUCATED, Louis Ribak went to Taos, New Mexico, in 1944 to develop his own unique and powerful style of painting, one of the most abstract in western art.

A serious artist who was firmly established in the East, Ribak stepped out of the mainstream. He went to New Mexico, partially because of his health, but largely because of his dislike of the New York "art scene" and the looming battle between realists and abstractionists.

"I was afraid of being influenced," he said. "I didn't want to belong to a school and become hemmed in by conventionalism."

Ribak came to the United States when he was ten years of age. As a boy, he trained as a hatmaker, but his talent for art was apparent. He studied at the Pennsylvania Academy of Fine Art in Philadelphia and the Art Students League in New York City, where he came under the influence of John Sloan, who later became a longtime friend.

His paintings, intense in both color and line, were exhibited in the leading museums in both the United States and Europe in the 1930s. Ribak became an American citizen in 1934. In 1942 he was drafted into the military.

Upon his discharge two years later, he immediately headed west. Ribak and his wife, Beatrice Mandelman, also an artist, went to Taos, New Mexico, where they established their home and studio in an adobe house which had belonged to the artist Blanche Grant.

In his new surroundings, Ribak was hardly a financial success; but he never compromised his style. His first showing of New Mexico paintings in New York came in 1946. The artist's growth in his chosen environment is clearly apparent. In 1947 Ribak opened his own Taos Valley Art School which became a successful venture.

He won the First Purchase Award at the El Paso Sun Carnival in 1969. Norman Geske, director of the University Art Galleries in Lincoln, Nebraska, and juror of the show, said of Ribak, "He stands out as a master because of his unique style and his absolute ease in working with painting problems." Many feel this same response to Ribak's work.

Louis Ribak and his wife presently live seven months of the year in Taos. The remaining months are spent in San Miguel de Allende, Mexico.

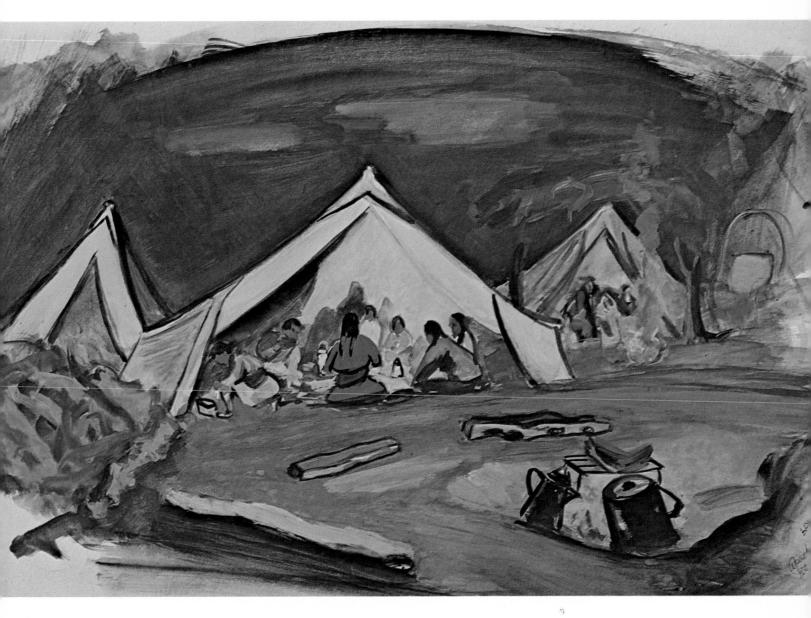

Apache Dinner at Dulce. Dated 1945. 18 x 28 inches, casein. Louis Ribak.

A. L. Ripley

1896–1969

AS AN AVID SPORTSMAN and conservationist, Aiden Lassell Ripley's paintings were dedicated to the orderly preservation of history, ecology, and hydrology. A half century ago he recognized the need for conservation. He painted a wide range of subjects in oils and watercolors, including landscapes, animals, birds, historical themes, and portraits.

Ripley's work, spanning four decades of voluminous production, consistently won prizes throughout the nation. His paintings captured the spring sunlight and the beauty of snow in winter, as well as the open spaces and crowded cities.

He was born in Wakefield, Massachusetts. As a boy he was an accomplished musician and almost followed a music career before enrolling in the Fenway School of Illustration and the Boston Museum School of Fine Arts. A Paige Traveling Fellowship enabled him to paint in Europe for two years.

One of Ripley's major works was a "portrait biography" of Paul Revere, done in fourteen murals, for the Paul Revere Insurance Company of Worcester, Massachusetts.

He was a member of the American Society of Watercolor Painters and the Guild of Boston Artists and is listed in *Who's Who in American Art* and *Who's Who in America*. His work is in the Chicago Art Institute and Boston Museum of Fine Arts and in public buildings in Lexington, Massachusetts, and Atlanta, Georgia.

A man with a great zest for life, he was as happy conversing with neighbors as he was pursuing his loves in nature. Carrying out his interest in conservation, he served on the planning board of the city of Lexington, from 1964 through 1968, and was a member of its Conservation Commission. If he were alive today, he would be saddened by the deplorable condition of our once great wilderness areas and the wanton extermination of our wildlife. He undoubtedly would enter wholeheartedly into the present campaigns for the preservation of our endangered species. America is indebted to men such as Ripley for their foresightedness.

Acknowledging a toast on his seventieth birthday, he quoted the great western artist Charles Russell: "Any man that can make a living doing what he likes is lucky, and I am that."

He died at seventy-three and was survived by his wife, Doris.

168

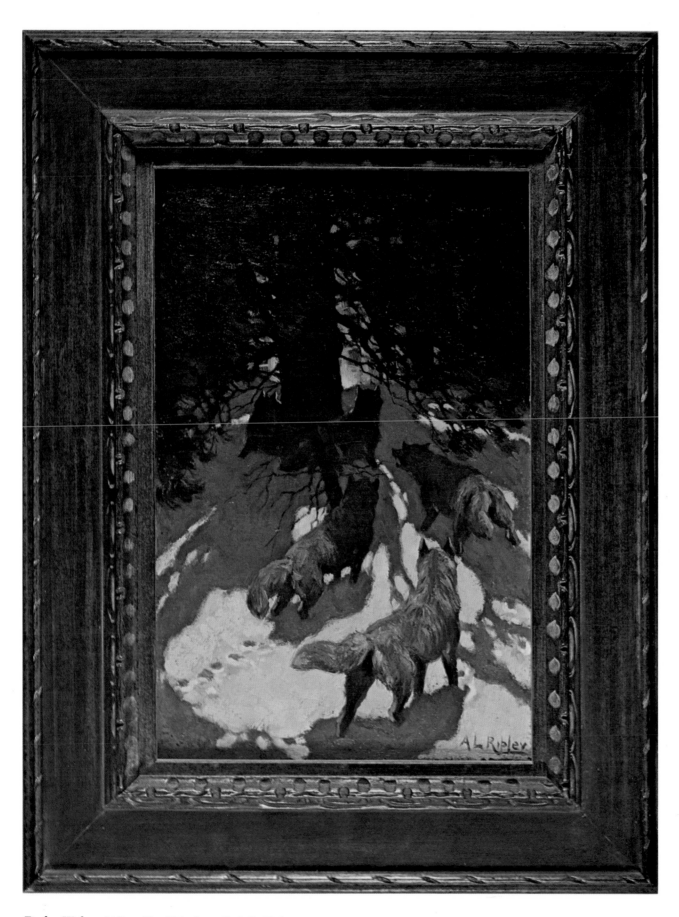

Timber Wolves At Bay. 18 x 12 inches, oil. A. L. Ripley.

Julian Rix

1850–1903

THE LANDSCAPE ARTIST, JULIAN WALBRIDGE RIX, though self-taught, was acclaimed by the art connoisseurs of California as an outstanding painter. He painted extensively on both the Pacific and Atlantic Coasts, and his works—mainly landscapes and sunsets—were noted for their vivid colors. He also painted many Colorado scenes.

Rix began drawing in black and white and followed with pastels and then oils. He also experimented with watercolors, gaining considerable attention from his technique of applying the pigment as if it were oil. Rix made etchings, too, some of which were used to illustrate a story in *Harper's* magazine, in 1889, on the California coastal mountains and forests.

He was born in Peacham, Vermont, the son of Judge Alfred Rix. When he was still a child, the family moved to San Francisco, California. Within a few years, a bereavement separated the family, and the boy was sent to an uncle in Vermont. When he was fifteen, he returned to California to complete his academic education.

Showing an early talent for art, which his father discouraged, Rix became an apprentice in a trading firm. He painted in his spare time; at the age of twenty-two he took a job as a sign and decorative painter. He associated with artists Amedee Joullin and the "Bohemian of Bohemians," Jules Tavernier, with whom he shared a studio.

Seeking a wider horizon, Rix left San Francisco in 1881 and moved to Patterson, New Jersey. Subsequently, he set up a studio in New York City, spending the next twenty years in the East, Midwest, and traveling abroad. Described as "a good-natured Bohemian," he was an independent thinker and worker, ranking among the best landscape painters of the day.

Returning to San Francisco in 1901, Rix spent several months sketching and painting in the mountains and valleys near Monterey and Santa Barbara. He presented one of his famous works, "Summer Landscape," to the Mark Hopkins Institute of Art. Most of his paintings were purchased by collectors in the East and in Europe.

A bachelor all his life, Rix was a life member of the Bohemian Club of San Francisco and a director of the Lotus Club of New York City.

170

He died in New York in 1903, following an operation.

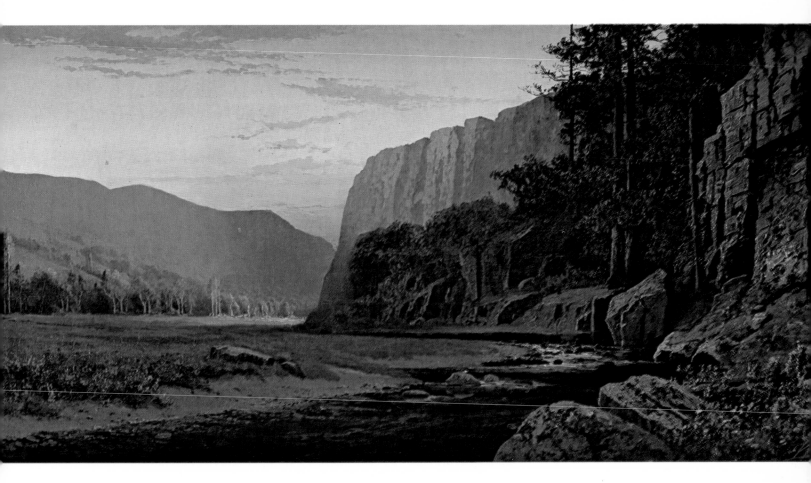

La Barranca Hondo. Carmel Valley, Monterey. Dated 1887. 24 x 50 inches, oil. Julian Rix.

Julius Rolshoven ANA

1858–1930

JULIUS ROLSHOVEN WAS WELL ESTABLISHED as one of the classic eastern painters when he arrived in Santa Fe, New Mexico, in 1916. His aristocratic air set him apart from most of the other artists at work there.

Dressed in a fashionable white traveling suit, followed by a wagon piled high with luggage, his arrival on the Plaza was long remembered by the city's inhabitants.

Rolshoven set up a studio at the Palace of Governors, making Santa Fe his permanent home for three years. During the final eleven years of his life, he divided his time between New Mexico and Italy.

He made friends with the local Indians and painted many portraits and scenes of their life. To soften the harsh southwestern light, he often set up a tent as an outdoor studio. His works were romantic and had the "old master" look that he had developed in Europe.

Rolshoven was born in Detroit, the son of a German jeweler. As a boy, he worked in his father's workshop where he did some designing. His interest in painting was stimulated in 1876 when he attended the art displays at the Centennial Exhibition in Philadelphia.

He tried to enroll at the school of the National Academy of Design in New York City, but his work was not considered good enough to gain admittance. He attended night school at Cooper Union Academy instead and studied anatomy under Ernst Plassman as well. In 1926 he won the coveted election to the Academy as an associate academician. Going to Europe, Rolshoven studied art at the Academie of Dusseldorf and the Royal Academie in Munich; he also studied with Frank Duveneck in Italy. Following his marriage to Anna Chickering, a member of the famous piano manufacturing family, he moved to Paris and attended the Academie Julien.

Rolshoven received the silver medal at the Paris Exhibition, in 1889, and began teaching in Paris and later in London. In 1897, his wife died, and he returned to Italy to live. With the outbreak of World War I, Rolshoven came to the United States. He married Harriette Blazo of California; they honeymooned in Santa Fe and decided to make that city their home.

Returning to the United States from Italy, Rolshoven became ill at sea; he died in New York City.

172

Sun Arrow. 36 x 28 inches, oil. Julius Rolshoven.

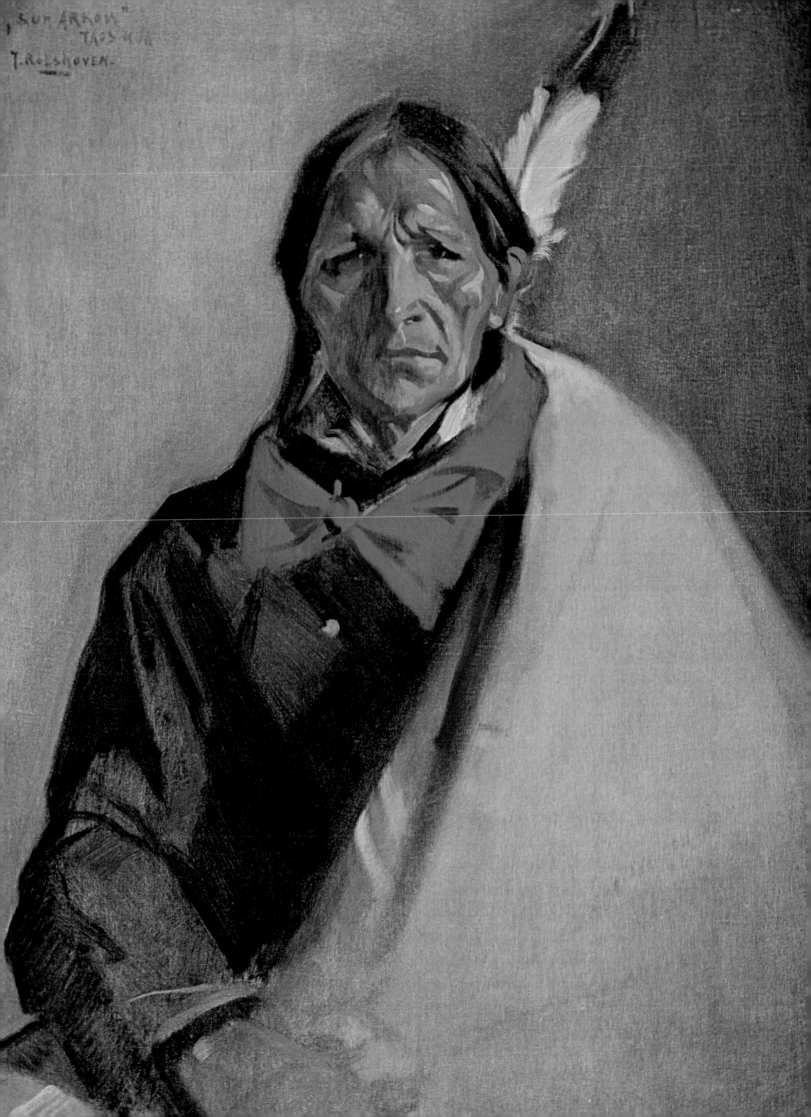

"SUN ARROW"
TAOS N.M.
J. ROLSHOVEN.

Chauncey Ryder NA

1868–1947

A PAINTER, ETCHER, AND LITHOGRAPHER, Chauncey Foster Ryder was born in Danbury, Connecticut. He spent most of his life in the East except for occasional western journeys. Many of his contemporary western artist friends named him a great influence in their creative endeavors.

Before reaching his teens, he had decided to pursue a career in the arts. To achieve this goal, he worked as an accountant, attending the Chicago Art Institute at night. He married Mary Keith Dole in 1892 in Chicago.

In the early 1900s, Ryder went to Paris to study at the Academie Julien and with Raphael Collin and Jean Paul Laurens. His first objective was to become a portrait painter. This disciplined training contributed much to his later landscape compositions, the area in which he ultimately specialized. By 1907 he had gained recognition, winning a Paris Salon award.

After their return to America, the Ryders, having no children of their own, took a ten-year-old girl into their home. She lived with them for many years but was never available for adoption. They later adopted two young sisters, who they raised.

A quiet man of simple tastes, Ryder and his family maintained a summer home in Wilton, New Hampshire, and a camp on an island in Maine where he could paint directly from nature. He found poetry in stripped trees, bare hillsides, sullen waters, and wind-swept fields. Each mountain had its own element of aloofness that spoke volumes about restricted property and privacy, which he apparently foresaw as becoming so precious.

His etchings show an economy of line, yet he was able to transfer the feeling of spaciousness in the great outdoors to the limited space of his copper plates. His paintings have a sense of solidity, well-suited to his subject matter, which is principally concerned with the enduring qualities of nature. To achieve this effect, he used broad color strokes and applied the paint rather thickly, then often molded his forms with a palette knife.

In 1914 Chauncey Ryder was elected an Associate Member of the National Academy of Design in New York City, and a full Academician in 1920. He belonged to numerous professional organizations, and his work is widely represented in Europe and in many museums and collections in the United States.

He died in Wilton, New Hampshire, at the age of eighty-one.

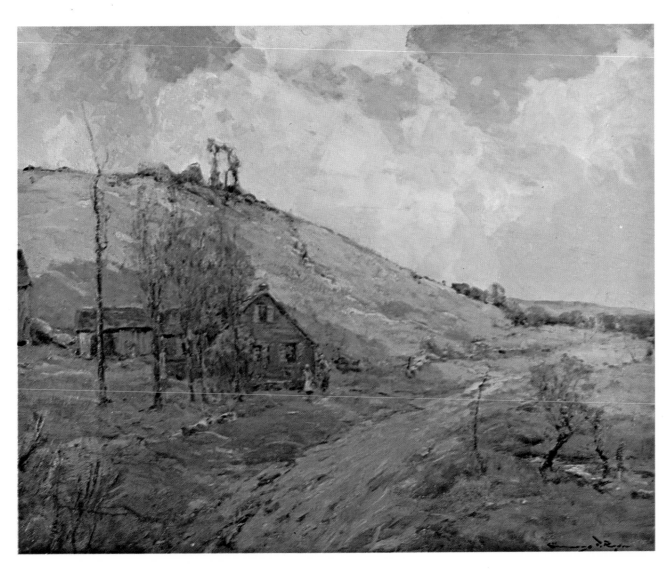

Snug Hill. 32 x 40 inches, oil. Chauncey Ryder.

Mathias Sandor

1857–1920

IN THE SIXTY-THREE YEARS that Mathias Sandor lived, he made an enviable name for himself in the art world. He is known as a portrait, miniature, and landscape painter. "His westerns are very scarce and considered a very desirable addition to a collection."

Sandor's meticulous, realistic style of painting may be attributed to the fact that he was a miniature painter, especially on ivory. He used a subdued blending of color and peaceful, quiet subject matter.

Sandor was born in Szeged, Hungary. After leaving high school, he was employed in the office of an exporting house in Budapest. Because of his intense interest in art, America seemed to be the logical place to look for the opportunity to continue his artistic career.

Upon coming to the United States, in 1881, he continued his study of art in his spare time. He attended art classes at the Art Students League, in New York City, under George de Forest Brush.

Sandor returned to Europe to study at the Academie Julien in Paris, from 1885–86, and under Francios Flameng and Gabriel Ferrier, from 1889–90.

Returning to America, he supported himself by painting miniature portraits and landscapes. Sandor also created designs for commercial purposes.

His diversification in art was due to the intermingling influences of his European and American training. Traveling throughout the world, he painted in Arizona, New Mexico, Canada, Mexico, and many European countries. His paintings of the Hopi Indians and their pueblos in New Mexico brought him recognition.

Sandor exhibited at the American Art Association in Paris, the National Academy of Design in New York, the Watercolor Club, and many other important art salons of his time.

One of his miniature portraits hung in the place of honor at the Paris Salon in 1905. He also was a member of the Artist's Fund Society, the American Federation of Arts, the Salmagundi Club, the Municipal Art Association, and the Republican Club in New York.

Maintaining a studio and residence on Madison Avenue in New York City, he spent his summers in the White Mountains of New Hampshire.

Sandor never married. He died in New York City.

San Estevan Church. Acoma, New Mexico. 43 x 33 inches, oil. Mathias Sandor.

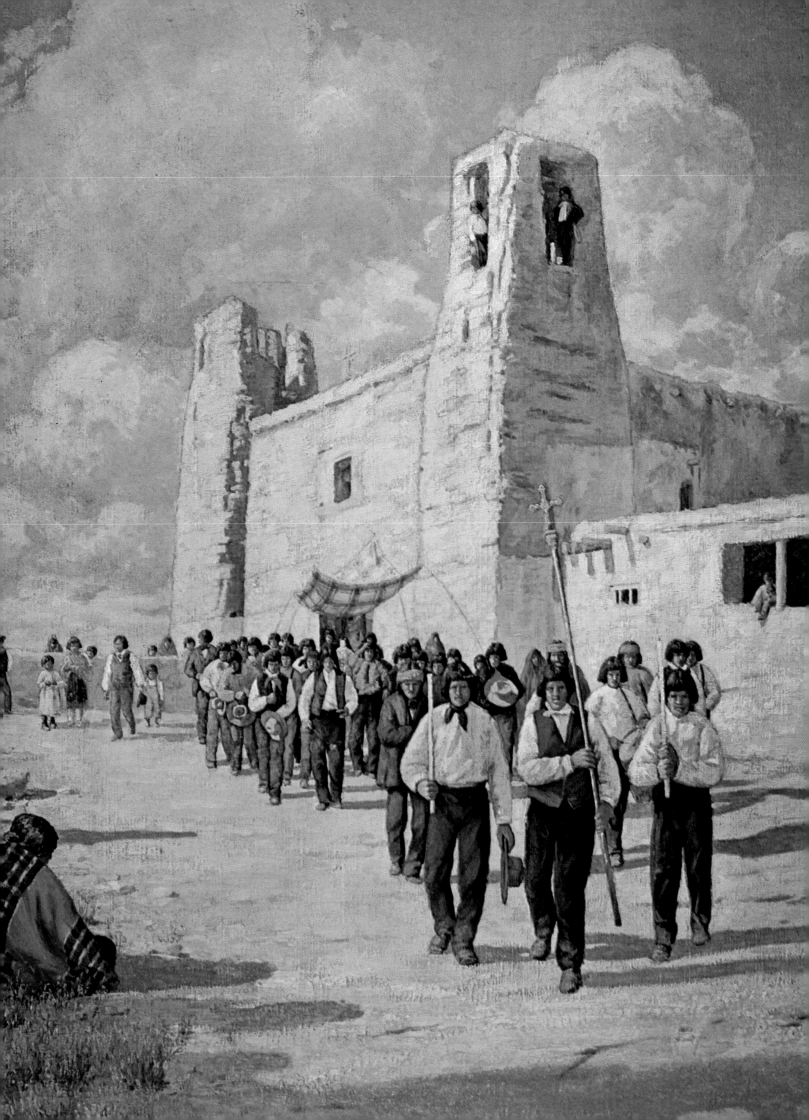

Frank Sauerwein

1871–1910

THE ARTISTIC CAREER of Frank Paul Sauerwein was hampered and shortened by a severe case of tuberculosis. But because of it, he went to the American Southwest where he became a most distinguished painter.

His weakened condition prevented Sauerwein from painting for long periods of time. Yet before his death at the age of thirty-nine, he had painted numerous Indian scenes, the missions of California, the mountains of the West and many genre paintings of the Southwest.

According to his obituary in *The New York Times* of June 15, 1910, Frank Sauerwein was born in Yonkers, New York. His father, Charles D. Sauerwein, was an artist.

In 1890–91 he registered in the beginner's class at the Pennsylvania Academy of Art in Philadelphia as Frank P. Sauerwen. This marks the first known time Sauerwein left the "i" out of his last name. Most of his paintings in later life are signed F. P. Sauerwen. He was graduated from the Philadelphia Museum School of Art in 1888.

Between 1891 and 1900 he spent much of his time in Denver, Colorado, where his older sister, Amelia, had gone because of tuberculosis. In 1898 he was listed as a member of the Denver Artists Club and chaired its committee to hang paintings for its fifth Annual Exhibition.

From his studio in Denver, Sauerwein traveled throughout the West, and a journey to a Ute Indian reservation with artist Charles Craig sparked his interest in western art.

In 1901 he and his sister moved to California, where she died. Freed from the responsibilities of caring for her, he made a long trip to Italy, Spain, Sicily, and other European countries.

Sauerwein's watercolors and oils were realistic renderings of landscapes and Indian life, with delicate finesse in stroke and color. The Santa Fe Railway purchased one of his works, and others were sold through the Fred Harvey System at the El Tovar Hotel at the Grand Canyon.

In 1906 he became seriously ill in Denver and went to California, then to Arizona, and finally settling in Taos, New Mexico. After selling his home there, it was enlarged to become a charming hotel, The Taos Inn.

A bachelor all of his life, Sauerwein moved back east. He died in Stamford, Connecticut.

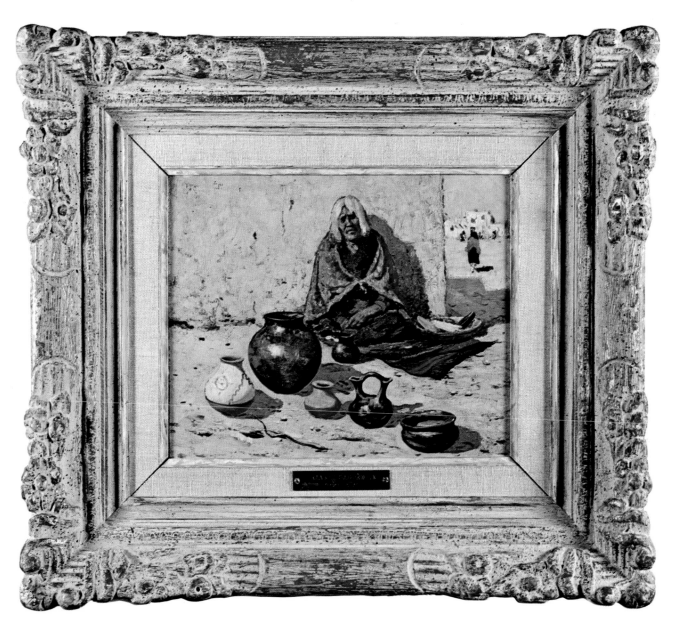

Esperando Los Turistas. 8 x 10 inches, oil. Frank Sauerwein.

F. Grayson Sayre

1879–1939

A WELL-KNOWN CALIFORNIA ARTIST, Fred Grayson Sayre was born in Medoc, Missouri, the only boy among five children. In his early years he worked in the zinc and lead mines there and also manufactured leather goods. His first creative job as an artist was for an engraving company in Houston, Texas.

Almost entirely self-taught, Sayre had two months of formal training under J. Laurie Wallace in Omaha, Nebraska.

Moving from Houston to Chicago, a near fatal bout with diptheria dramatically changed his art career. He was thirty-seven years of age and a highly successful illustrator when he became seriously ill.

The doctors urged him to move to California to preserve his health. Traveling through the Southwest by train, he was enchanted by the beauty of the desert sunset. He vowed to return to the desert—which he did three years later—and went on to become one of many fine landscape artists of the southwestern United States.

From 1919 through 1922 he lived in Arizona, painting during the day and working as a bookkeeper for a mining company at night. His first exhibition of sixty-four watercolors in San Francisco in 1922 was a success. A critic wrote, "The mystery of his pictures is that the purple, blue, roseate, and pink haze which, under varying conditions, hangs over mountains, canyons, and desert, actually seems to vibrate. To mix such a color from pigments, that it seems to live and move like heat waves rising from sand, would seem to be impossible."

These paintings paved the way for a gradual transition into oils, and five years later he won first prize in that medium at the Artclub of Los Angeles. He was a charter member of the Painters and Sculptors Club of Los Angeles in 1923 and president in 1929.

In the heart of the Coachella Valley at Indio, California, Sayre built a home and studio where, with his wife Ruth and daughter Barbara, he spent his winters sketching the beauties of the region. In this climate he was allowed complete freedom for travel twelve months of the year.

Coincidentally Sayre died in Glendale, California, the same day Frank Tenney Johnson, another noted western artist, passed away in Pasadena.

His daughter, Barbara Harmon of Taos, New Mexico, has also reached success with her imaginative paintings.

180

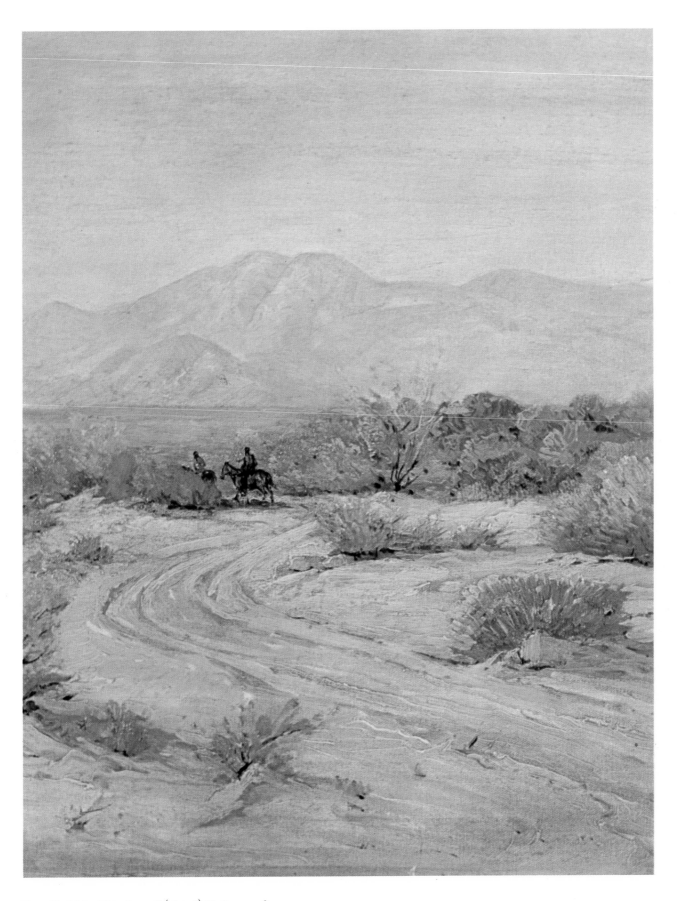

Days End. 24 x 30 inches, oil (detail). F. Grayson Sayre.

Frank Schoonover

1877–1972

FRANK EARLE SCHOONOVER was born in Oxford, New Jersey. As a boy spending his summers in the Pocono Mountains, he foresaw his future as an illustrator of adventures on the frontier and in the wilderness. His drawing skill developed early.

A full-page advertisement in the *Philadelphia Inquirer* was the turning point in Schoonover's life. It was placed by Howard Pyle, the famous American illustrator, who was inviting art students to enroll in his Philadelphia classes to study the fundamentals of illustration.

At the time, young Schoonover was studying to enter the Presbyterian ministry. But his interest in art, coupled with Pyle's invitation, proved too tempting, and Schoonover went to art school instead. Later he became a protege of Pyle and one of his famous contemporaries.

Recognition and success did not come instantly at Pyle's school. Far from it. Schoonover was behind most of the other students and was assigned to preparatory classes under James Wood, drawing cones, cubes, and spheres with a charcoal stick. Next came work in oils and watercolors. The eager Schoonover lived for the hours he could spend in the back row of Pyle's composition class, where the master critiqued the works of other students.

Schoonover went on to study under Pyle at the Drexel Institute in Philadelphia and at Chadds Ford, Pennsylvania. Pyle had a fatherly concern for Schoonover and felt he had the talent and capacity for work necessary for greatness. He fulfilled his teacher's prediction.

Schoonover illustrated numerous books and magazine articles and taught at the John Herron Art Institute in Indianapolis and at his own studio in Wilmington, Delaware.

Although he spent most of his life in the East, Schoonover was assigned to illustrate many western and frontier subjects. In 1903 he made the first of two trips by dog team and snowshoe to the Hudson Bay area of Canada to observe, sketch, and paint the Indians of that region. He also went to the Mississippi Bayou to illustrate a story about "Jean Lafitte, the Pirate of the Gulf," which was published in *Harper's Magazine.*

He lived his final years in Trenton, New Jersey.

A biography of Frank Schoonover's life, by his son Cortlandt Schoonover, was published in 1976.

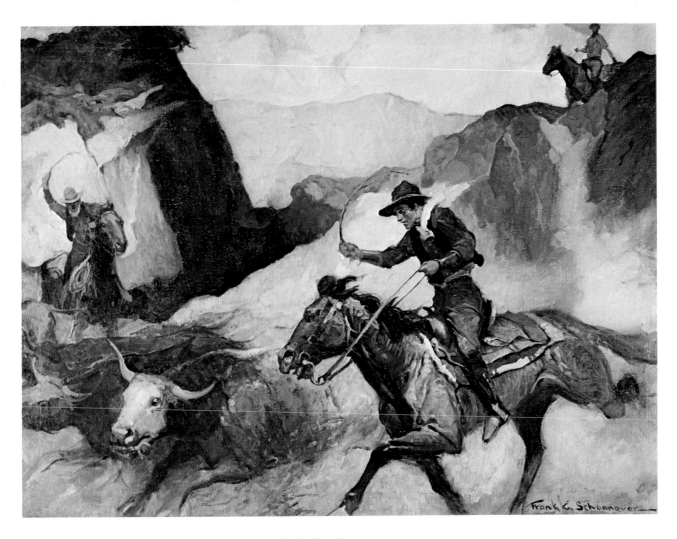

The Cattle Drive. Dated April 1907. 28 x 38 inches, oil. Frank Schoonover.

Charles Schreyvogel ANA

1861–1912

CHARLES SCHREYVOGEL SPENT MOST OF HIS LIFE as an impoverished portrait painter before recognition of his western paintings brought him seemingly overnight fame.

Born in New York City, his parents were German immigrant shopkeepers. He worked as an apprentice lithographer before going to Munich, Germany, in 1886, for formal art training as a pupil of Carl Marr and Frank Kirchbach.

Returning to the United States, he spent much time sketching the horses, cowboys, and Indians in Buffalo Bill's Wild West Show. He also visited the veteran cavalrymen stationed on Governor's Island to sketch them and listen to their stories of the West.

His career was influenced by Dr. William Redwood Fisher, a noted art patron. Dr. Fisher encouraged Schreyvogel and supported his interest in western art, acquiring many Schreyvogel paintings for his own collection.

In 1893 Schreyvogel made his first trip west, visiting the Ute reservation in Colorado. But the resulting paintings didn't sell, and he returned to doing commissioned portraits and continued as a lithographic artist. By 1894, he saved enough money to marry Louise Walther, who had been his fiancee for quite some time. His portraits provided a very meager living.

In 1901 his work entitled "My Bunkie," a portrayal of a cavalryman rescuing a fellow soldier from hostile Indians, won the first prize at the National Academy of Design. The selection stunned the eastern art establishment as "Western Art" was not considered to be on the same esthetic level as "American Art." He was elected an associate member of the Academy the same year.

Because of his insistence on accurate details in his work and the time-consuming research it involved, Schreyvogel completed only seventy-five western paintings before his death. He finished several sculptures.

The mild-mannered artist worked at his studio in Hoboken, New Jersey, and at his farm in West Kill, New York, but made annual trips to the western United States. He specialized in military scenes.

He died in Hoboken, New Jersey, from blood poisoning caused by a chicken bone lodged in his gum.

His studio and collection are now on permanent display at the National Cowboy Hall of Fame and Western Heritage Center in Oklahoma City.

184

Sevaro, Chief of Capota Ute. 30 x 24 inches, oil. Charles Schreyvogel.

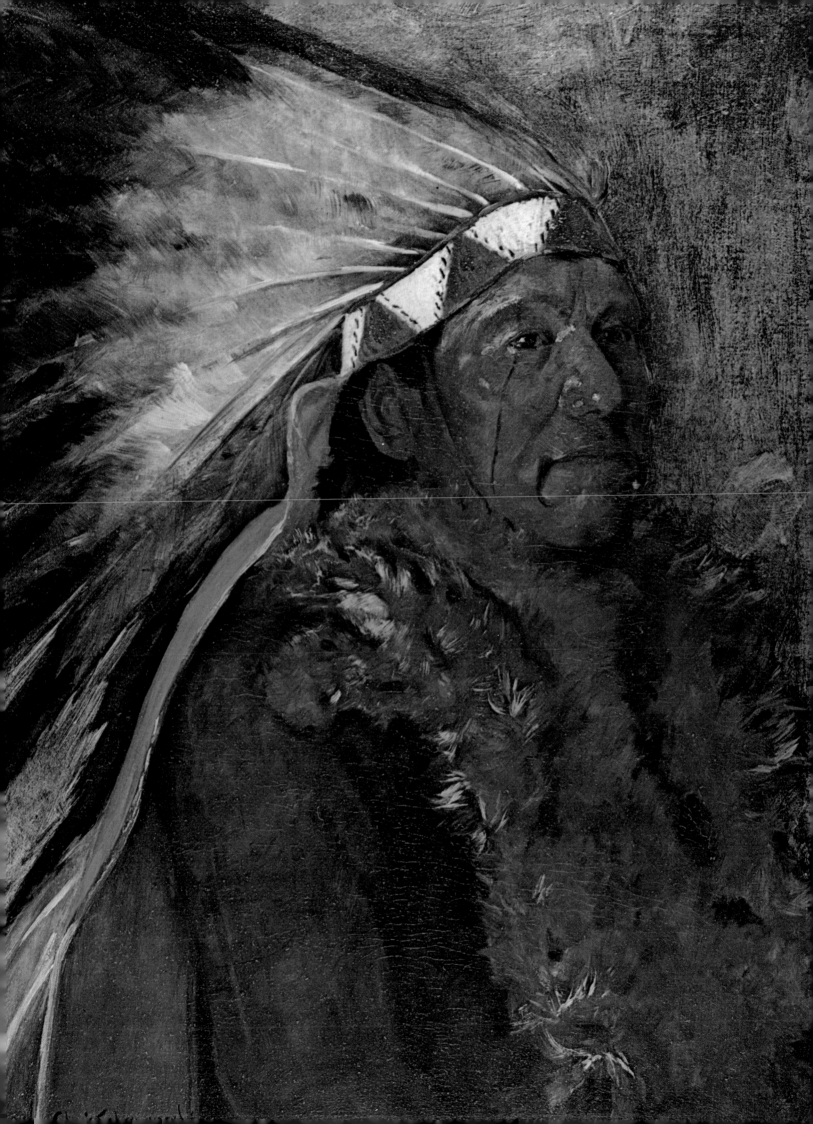

Conrad Schwiering

b. 1916

KNOWN AS "PAINTER OF THE TETONS," Schwiering was born in Boulder, Colorado. His father was attending summer school classes at Colorado University at the time. The elder Schwiering was a frustrated artist who compensated for his own lack of opportunity in the arts by encouraging his son to follow his artistic inclination, but as a hobby only.

In Laramie, Wyoming, which was home to the Schwierings, the young artist was persuaded to enroll at the University of Wyoming. He also proceeded with his art studies in his spare time under Robert Graham, who taught classes in Denver. Later he studied under Raphael Lillywhite in Laramie, then Bert Phillips in Taos. Returning to Laramie he graduated from college with a bachelor's degree in Commerce and Law.

In 1939 he married his wife Mary Ethel, who taught school to provide an income. They lived in New York where Schwiering studied under George Bridgman and Charles S. Chapman at the Art Students League. He also studied with, and was befriended by, Carl Rungius.

After he won a medal of merit at the Grand Central School of Art, Chapman told him to "go back West where you can paint the things you know and love." The Schwierings settled in Jackson Hole, Wyoming, where lean years followed. He did everything from digging ditches to picking turkeys. "An artist should work at various jobs. It gives him experience with people in different life situations," Schwiering once noted.

Being one of the original members of the National Academy of Western Art at the Cowboy Hall of Fame in Oklahoma City, he feels this group has the promise of being one of the most significant forces of art in America.

Schwiering expresses dismay at the overt exclusion of western art by eastern so-called critics and art museums. He says, "These critics might just as well be ignored. If we get enough of the best-qualified, knowledgeable artists together, we'll wind up with a strong group that will make a tremendous impact on the art of America in spite of the dilettantes."

The Schwiering home and studio sits on a knoll just off Antelope Flats, eight miles from the Grand Tetons, with one of the most magnificent views in the world. He is grateful for the opportunity to live near the beautiful Tetons and to record the fast disappearing scenes of today's West.

186

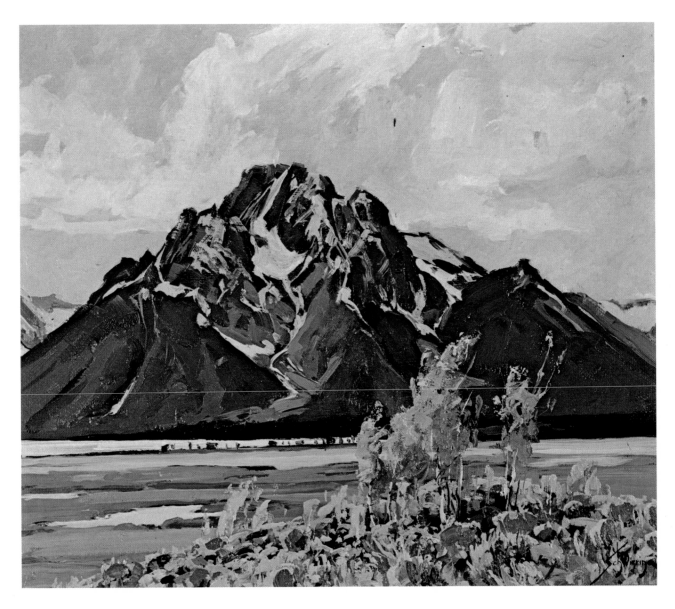

The Tetons. 24 x 20 inches, oil. Conrad Schwiering.

Julian Scott ANA

1846–1901

HIS TALENT WAS DISCOVERED in a most unlikely situation—on the inside walls of a military hospital during the Civil War. Julian Scott, a young Vermont soldier, who had joined the Army as a musician, captured a rebel prisoner near the Union lines and conducted him into camp. During the encounter, Scott was injured. Winning a medal for his bravery, he was placed on the staff of General William Farrar "Baldy" Smith. During his convalescence, he amused himself with rough drawings of camp scenes sketched on the walls near the hospital patients.

A New York merchant, a connoisseur of art, visited the hospital and was taken by the spirit and expression of a soldier's face drawn on the crude interior wall. The gallantry and artistic tendencies of young Colonel Scott gained him the friendship of this man who eventually provided for Scott's education. Scott became an accomplished draftsman and painted many authentic scenes of the hospital, the camp, and the battlefield.

At the close of the war, Scott entered the schools of the National Academy of Design in New York and finished his studies in Paris. He was elected an Associate of the National Academy in 1870.

To conduct the eleventh census of 1890 among the Indians, the United States Census Bureau sent a group of special agents throughout the country. Among these were artists Julian Scott, Peter Moran, Gilbert Gaul, Walter Shirlaw, and Henry Poore. From the efforts of this group, and many others, there resulted the 683-page document entitled *Report on Indians Taxed and Not Taxed,* one of the most exhaustive sources of information on Indians ever to be printed and bound into book form.

Scott has credit for most of the illustrations with over thirty drawings or paintings, both in color and in black and white, appearing in the book. His report was on the Moqui Pueblos of Arizona.

In 1892 a book, *The Song of the Ancient People,* by Edna Dean Proctor, was illustrated with eleven aquatints by Julian Scott, who had lived for a year with the Moqui and used those Indians as subjects.

Most of the Indian portraits from his western trips belong to the University of Pennsylvania's Museum of Art.

Scott was born in Johnson, Vermont, and died in Plainfield, New Jersey.

188

Tonto Apache, Arizona. Dated 1891. 12 x 10 inches, oil. Julian Scott.

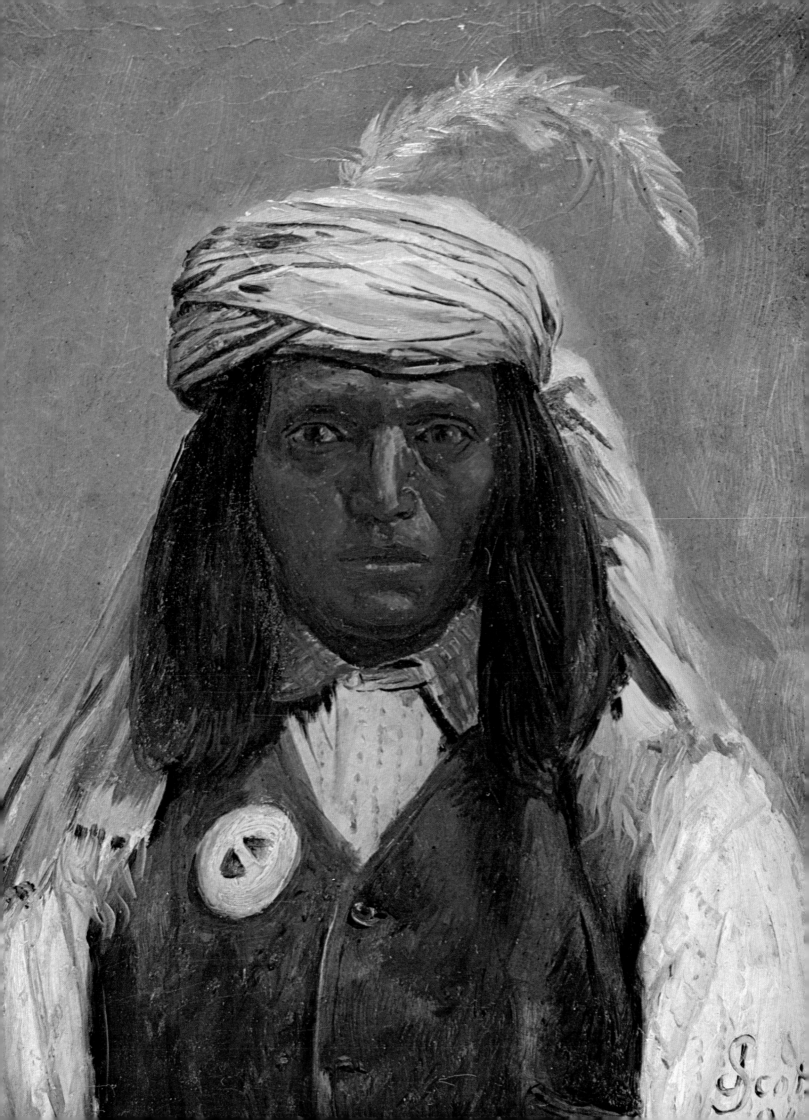

James Sessions

1882–1964

FOR OVER FIFTY YEARS James M. Sessions was considered one of the forefront group of American watercolorists. Today, Sessions' paintings and prints continue to have an appreciative market throughout the country.

Sessions received his art training at the Chicago Art Institute. His most frequently painted subjects grew out of his interest in the sea and his deep love of it. Thus, the great majority of his paintings are of the sea—the coastal scenes of New England, the shores and boats of the Bahamas, and, most notably, the World War II naval battle scenes of the Pacific war.

The demands of his work as an illustrator took him into fields far from the oceans as did the Great Plains of the West, which he painted with great understanding and feeling for pioneer life.

He was born in Rome, New York, and, as a young boy, served as a wheelsman on grain and ore vessels in the Great Lakes and later as bosun's mate in the United States Navy.

In the earlier part of the Second World War, he was used as a camouflage expert and later was commissioned to make a pictorial record of the naval battles of the Pacific Theatre. In preparation for the officially sponsored paintings, he was permitted to view the official United States Navy moving pictures and photographs not publicly released. Throughout his life, Sessions studied the records of great naval battles and talked, whenever possible, with those who had fought them. The result was accuracy displayed with Sessions' own brand of dash and skill.

A tribute to his work came from the Metropolitan Museum of Art, which gave this series one of the few one-man shows in its history. Following this, the art museums in Cleveland and Milwaukee, as well as the Art Institute of Chicago, gave shows.

In 1959, the *Chicago Tribune* commissioned Sessions to paint the Chicago arrival of the heavy cruiser *Macon* leading a flotilla of twenty warships as part of the St. Lawrence Seaway dedication and the International Trade Fair. This picture was published in the *Chicago Tribune;* it was later presented to the Great Lakes Naval Training Center.

James Sessions died in Chicago and was survived by his widow Chrysanthy and a son by a former marriage, Harold E. Sessions.

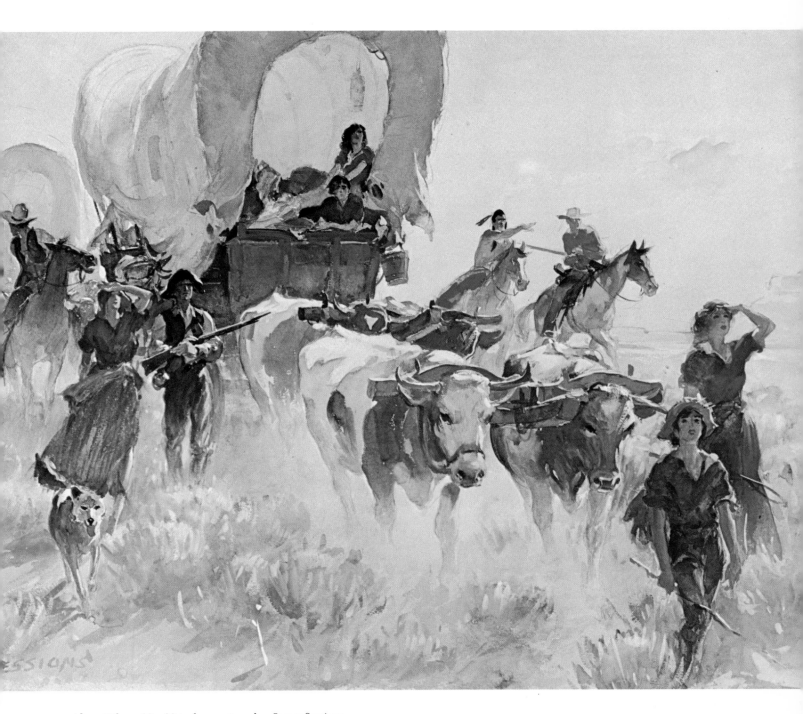

Almost There. 20 x 28 inches, watercolor. James Sessions.

Bill Sharer

b. 1934

WITH VERY LITTLE ART TRAINING as a child, William E. Sharer was in his mid-twenties before he decided to pursue art as a career. But his natural ability and determination eventually paid off.

Working in oils, watercolors, and pastels, Sharer could be called a varied subject painter, using still life composition, painting frequently in his highly imaginative style.

Born and raised in Roswell, New Mexico, and being on his own after the age of fifteen, Sharer joined the Marine Corps following his graduation from high school. Sharer almost decided to make a career of the service, but he returned to civilian life and spent two years making blueprints for oil companies. The veteran's benefits available through the G.I. Bill forced him to make a decision on his education, so he enrolled at the American Academy of Art in Chicago. He studied there for three years under William H. Mosby and Joseph Vandenbrouck.

Returning west, he moved into an isolated mountain cabin in Colorado that had belonged to his mother. For the next six months he lived alone, painting the surrounding wilderness.

In 1962 Sharer took his paintings to an art gallery in Taos, New Mexico, and finally moved there in an attempt to establish himself. But recognition came slowly. He lived on $600 the first year, trading his paintings to a local restaurant for meals. Yet, he stayed with his goal, refusing to take part-time work. He knows what it means to be a "starving artist."

The second winter he was able to rent a studio for very little money from the Harwood Foundation in Taos.

In 1969, Sharer's paintings were accepted for the Allied Artist Show in New York City, and he not only won a cash award, but the portrait was purchased for the permanent collection of the American Academy in Chicago. He captured a National Arts Club prize the same year. In 1971 he won the Stacey Scholarship and in 1972 the Jane Peterson Prize for figure painting.

Sharer moved to Santa Fe, New Mexico, in 1969, then to Denver, Colorado, in 1975. The February 1973 *American Artist* Magazine featured a story about Bill Sharer, using one of his paintings on the cover. His former wife, Sandra Wilson, was the model for the delicate, appealing work.

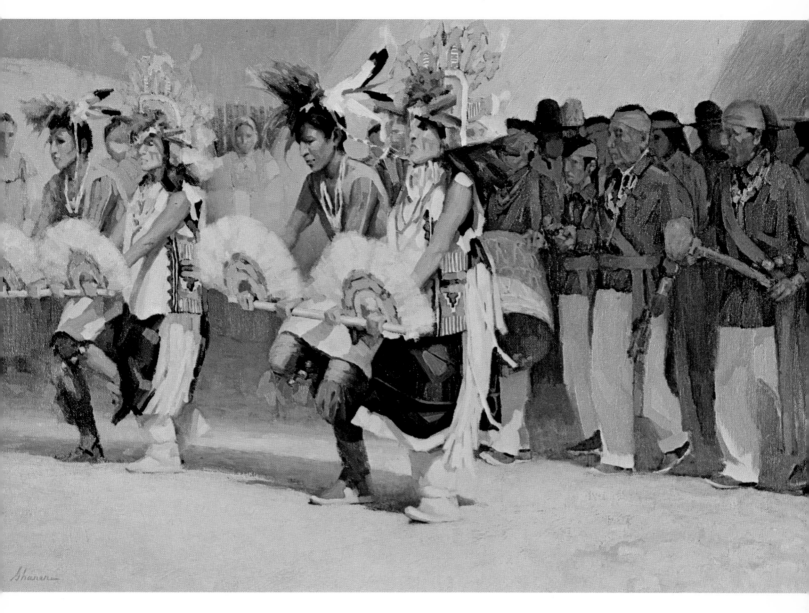

Butterfly Kachina Dancers, Gallup Ceremony. Dated 1968. 20 x 30 inches, oil. Bill Sharer.

John Sloan

1871–1951

LOCK HAVEN, PENNSYLVANIA, WAS THE BIRTHPLACE of John Sloan, who left high school in 1888 to take a job with a book and print dealer. His skills as an artist were basically self-taught, but he studied briefly at the Pennsylvania Academy of Fine Art in Philadelphia and at the Spring Garden Institute. He was also a pupil of Thomas Eakins.

While still in Philadelphia, Sloan became a member of the group that eventually became known as "The Eight" or "The Ashcan School." It included Robert Henri, William Glackens, George Luks, and Everett Shinn, and New Yorkers Maurice Pendergast, Ernest Lawson, and Arthur B. Davies. All became newspaper illustrators in New York City, and mixed socially with the celebrities of the sports, theater, and academic worlds. They were called "The Eight" from their number and "The Ashcan School" from the subjects they chose to paint.

Sloan became art editor of *The Masses*, a Socialist paper for which he drew scathing cartoons about the injustices inflicted on the poor by the rich. He taught art for years and exhibited regularly.

As was the custom, artists left New York City in the summer. It was on one such journey in 1919 that Sloan took a trip to Santa Fe, New Mexico. He was so struck by the Southwest he returned almost every year for the rest of his life. It was there he developed the use of boldly cross-hatched strokes, which characterized some of his works.

John Sloan was famous by the time he was forty years old. But oddly enough, he never did achieve financial security, always teaching and writing to help support his wife and himself.

During the Depression he sent out a very moving letter noting that he was sixty-two years old and would probably die in the next few years. He asked, "In the event of my passing, is it likely that the trustees of your museum would consider it desirable to acquire one of my paintings?" He pointed out that "after a painter of repute dies, the prices of his works are at once more than doubled. John Sloan is alive and hereby offers these works at one-half the prices brought during the last five years." The letter went to sixty institutions and brought one sale.

194

He died in Hanover, New Hampshire.

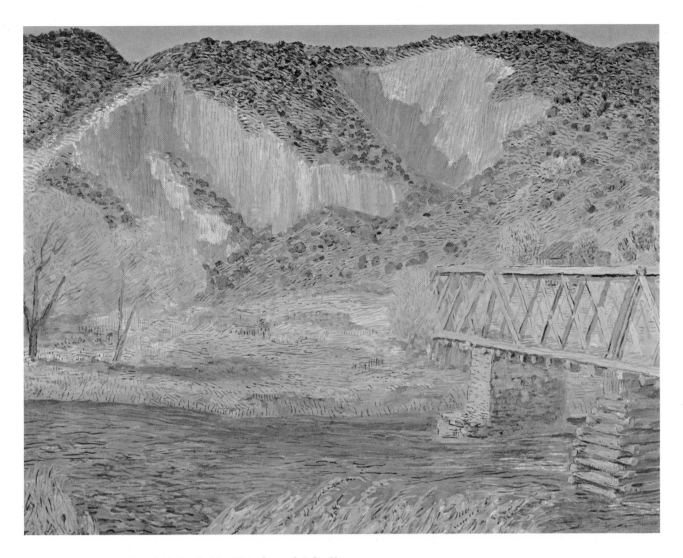

Rio Grande Canyon. Dated 1948–49. 21 x 18 inches, oil. John Sloan.

George Smillie NA
1840–1921

AS A MEMBER of one of the few great family dynasties in the arts, George Henry Smillie was the son of James Smillie and the brother of James Jr. and William Smillie—all four reaching fame as artists and engravers.

New York was the lifelong home of George Smillie, but he traveled throughout the United States—including the West—in search of subjects for his masterful landscapes.

He was born in New York City. Educated there in private schools, he received his first art lesson from his father and later became a pupil of James McDougal Hart. By the time Smillie was twenty-four years of age, he was elected an associate member of the National Academy of Design and was painting much in the manner of The Hudson River School, a style which remained an influence on his work.

In 1871 he made a sketching trip to the Rocky Mountains and the Yosemite Valley. For many years thereafter he painted western scenes in watercolors and oils. Many were mountain landscapes; a few depicted Indian life.

He married Nellie Sheldon Jacobs in 1881; she was a painter of genre pictures and a member of the American Watercolor Society. She had been an art student of George Smillie's older brother James.

The following year, Smillie was elected a full academician of the National Academy of Design, and he served as its recording secretary for ten years. He also was a member of the American Watercolor Society and was treasurer for four years.

He and his wife made an extended tour of Europe in 1884. Upon their return they made their home in Bronxville, New York, where they shared a studio with brother James.

Smillie's paintings became favorites with collectors; his work was purchased by the Corcoran Gallery in Washington, D.C., the Metropolitan Museum of Art in New York, the Rhode Island School of Design, the Lotus Club of New York, and Union League Club in Philadelphia.

He won the first prize of the American Art Association of New York in 1885, and he received medals at the Louisiana Purchase Exposition of 1904 in St. Louis and from the Society of American Artists in 1907.

Smillie died at his Bronxville home. His wife and three sons survived him.

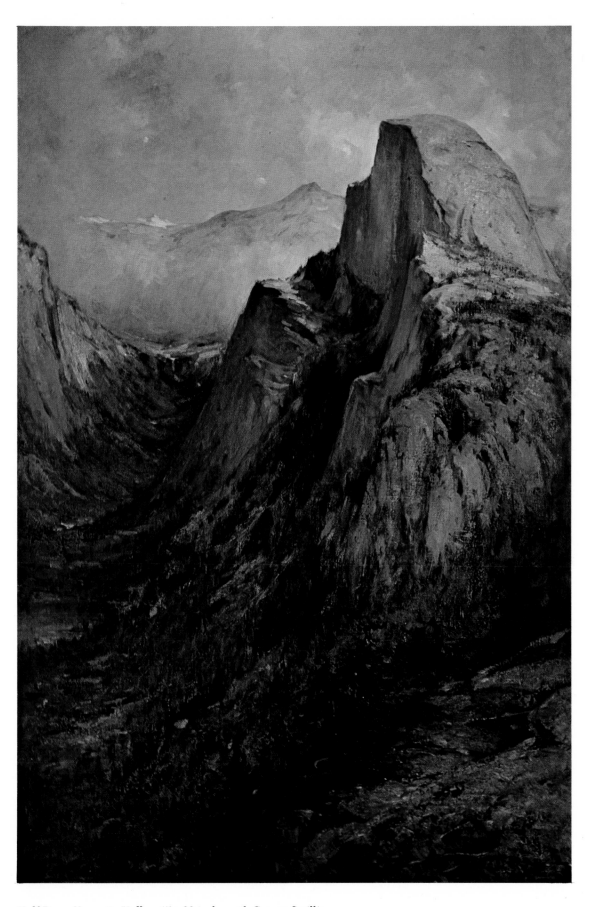

Half Dome Yosemite Valley. 45 x 30 inches, oil. George Smillie.

Will Sparks

1862–1937

WILL SPARKS WAS NOT ONLY a fine western artist, he was also considered one of the outstanding citizens of his adopted state of California.

Painting for fifty years, he completed about 3,000 works, most of them colorful scenes of California, New Mexico, Arizona, and Mexico. A man of keen intellect, he spent forty of those years as a journalist and writer. He spoke French, German, and Spanish fluently.

Sparks was born in St. Louis, Missouri, where he attended public schools, Washington University, and the St. Louis School of Fine Arts. Finishing his first sketch at age twelve, it was sold for five dollars. He almost pursued a career in medicine after majoring in anatomy at the St. Louis Medical College. But his inclination and ability brought him back to the artistic world; he very quickly became known in the local art circles.

Spending his meager savings, Sparks went to New York in 1884, then to Paris to study at the Academies Julien and Colarossi under Bouvert and Cazin. He became associated with Louis Pasteur. Sparks' medical education made his services to the scientist invaluable in making anatomical drawings.

Returning to the United States, he headed west, first to Denver, then to Fresno and Stockton, California, where he continued to work for various newspapers. His former experience was important in this publishing field.

When he left the *Fresno Expositor,* the paper printed an article about him that said in part, "Sparks can write, put up presses, speak Choctaw, shovel coal, drink beer and lie with great ingenuity, and he can paint—which is his real forte." This he did with great imagination.

Sparks moved to San Francisco in 1891, and it became his permanent home. Perhaps his most famous series of paintings were thirty-six works depicting all thirty-two of California's original Spanish missions, which he executed between 1887 and 1919. A second series was completed in 1933. He painted many blazing sunset and moonlit nocturnal scenes.

A friend of many notable Californians, he was a member of the Bohemian Club, the San Francisco Art Association, the Sequoia Club, and the Society of California Artists. In 1904 Sparks became a member of the faculty of the University of California. His work there was mostly confined to anatomical drawing for the medical classes.

Sparks died in San Francisco, survived by his second wife.

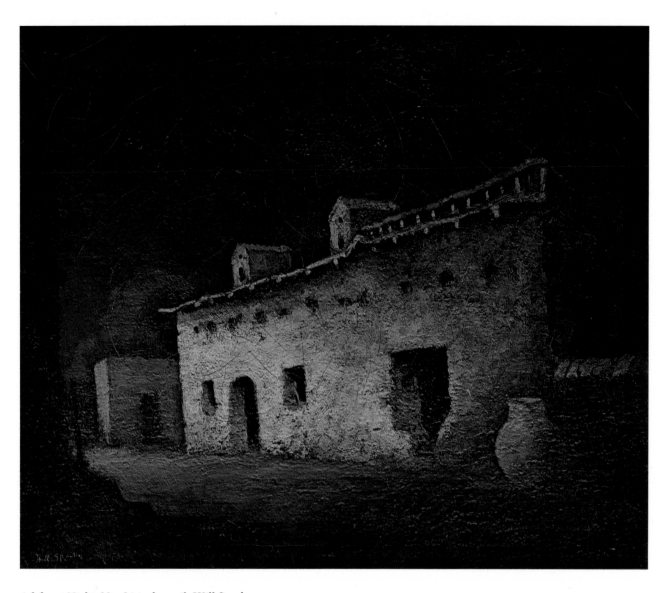

Adobe at Night. 20 x 24 inches, oil. Will Sparks.

Maurice Sterne NA

1878–1957

A MAJOR FIGURE IN AMERICAN ART, Maurice Sterne had a long and highly successful career as a painter, sculptor, graphic artist, teacher—and world traveler. A craftsman-like painter who possessed great charm, Maurice Sterne made a reputation throughout the world as an artist and adventurer.

Most of his paintings of the American Southwest were made in the late 1910s, during his marriage to heiress Mable Dodge. They made their home in Taos, New Mexico.

But Miss Dodge divorced Sterne in favor of a Taos Indian named Tony Luhan, explaining that the artist "seemed old and spent and tragic." Sterne, in his early forties, responded by marrying a seventeen-year-old dancer from Isadora Duncan's group, and they moved to a castle northeast of Rome, Italy. If Sterne's divorce from Miss Dodge was a setback, it was one of the few in his life.

Born in Libau, Russia, he immigrated to New York City with his widowed mother when he was nine years of age. He attended night school, joining a class at the National Academy of Design. To support himself he worked as a bartender. His first commissioned painting was of a foaming beer stein and was entitled "5 Cents."

He won many prizes and received critical acclaim for a series of etchings of Coney Island. He studied anatomy at the Academy under Thomas Eakins.

In 1904, Sterne won the Academy's traveling scholarship. He went to Europe, where he came under the influence of Manet and Cezanne; he then traveled to the Orient. In 1911 he visited Egypt and went to India, Burma, and Bali. In Bali, he painted a series of pictures that made him and the beautiful island famous.

He taught at the California School of Fine Arts in San Francisco and at the Art Students League of New York.

Despite his success, Sterne always tried to develop further. Writing to a friend in 1940, he stated: "I know only that painting being an expression of a point of view, there can't be just one right way, but innumerable ways."

In his latter years, Sterne settled on Cape Cod and painted seascapes. In 1944 he was elected a member of the National Academy of Design and, in 1945, appointed to the National Commission of Fine Arts.

Taos Indian Woman. Taos, New Mexico. Dated 1918.
20 x 13 inches, charcoal (detail). Maurice Sterne.

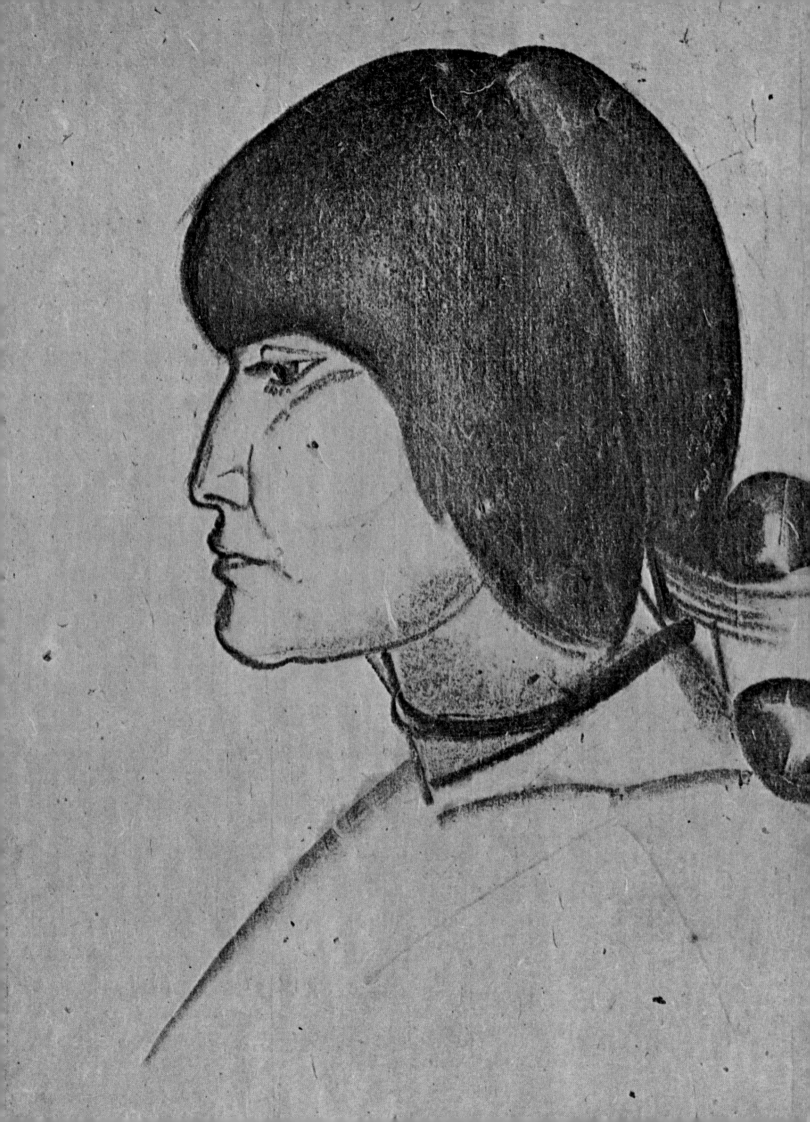

Vladan Stiha

b. 1908

A MAN SCHOLARLY IN MANNER AND APPEARANCE, with a foreign accent that makes his English unique, Vladan Stiha is today at the peak of his powers.

He was born in Yugoslavia, the youngest of eleven children. He drew and painted from his earliest years. Going to an art school in Belgrade, his training in both painting and sculpture was continued under Professor Karl Faringer at the Academie of Fine Arts in Vienna and under Professor Carlo Savierri in Rome.

After World War II he became one of Argentina's premier artists, holding more than twenty expositions and receiving awards for his stirring interpretations of Argentina's vast pampas, colorful gauchos, and the bashful, winsome children.

Stiha moved to Brazil with his wife Elena in 1958. There he found special inspiration in the tumultuous waterfront, markets, and the Carnival of Bahia. Ten very productive years resulted in more expositions, honors, and major commissions.

Stiha made his American debut in 1968 with a show at a gallery in Beverly Hills, California. Traveling through Arizona and New Mexico, the Stihas were in constant wonder and excitement at the endless supply of subject matter, expecially the Indians. Santa Fe, New Mexico, was the best artist's environment . . . they decided to settle there. In 1974 they became citizens of the United States.

Stiha paints his Indians and animals from life (even the buffalo which he sketches from a herd in Chama). "The Indian and the horse are one," he says, "but the Indian and the pick-up truck, no!"

Spending ten days each month out in the countryside, he paints landscapes which are almost finished before he returns to his studio to complete them. Leaving misery and violence for others, his paintings are action-filled western scenes of Indians, horses, cowboys, covered wagons, and landscapes. His canvases are rich tapestries of humanity.

His works were selected for the "Preview 73" show in Dallas, Texas, and the National Academy of Western Art's first annual exhibition at the National Cowboy Hall of Fame in Oklahoma City. They are included in major museums in Europe, South America, and the United States.

202

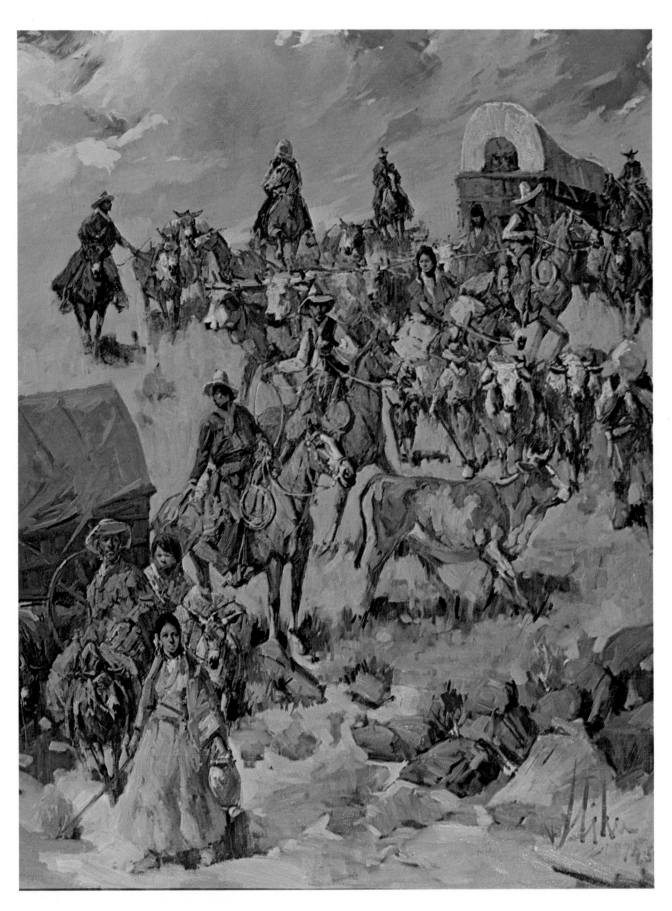

The Immigrants. Dated 1975. 40 x 30 inches, oil. Vladan Stiha.

Charles Stobie

1845–1931

THE ADVENTUROUS LIFE of Charles Stewart Stobie was just as colorful as his authentic paintings of the early West. In his day, "Mountain Charlie," as Stobie was called, was perhaps best known as an Indian fighter, scout, and buffalo hunter. In his record of "Crossing the Plains to Colorado in 1865," which was published in *The Colorado Magazine* in 1933, there was no mention of his artistic endeavors. But he was recognized locally as one of the best painters of the West.

Stobie was born in Baltimore, Maryland, and studied art for two years in St. Andrews, Scotland. He worked in an architect's office in the East before heading west in 1865 as a member of a wagon train.

The train was attacked three times by hostile Indians between Fort Kearny and Fort Sedgwick, and Stobie was credited with killing seven Indians. Before his arrival in Denver, the fete was noted in the city's daily newspaper, the *Rocky Mountain News*. "From that time forward, I never wanted for employment, friends, or money in Colorado," Stobie said.

Among his friends were such western characters as Buffalo Bill Cody, Kit Carson, Wild Bill Hickok, Jim Baker, and artist Frederic Remington. Stobie often took Remington on sketching trips to Ute Indian encampments.

"Preferring the Indians as companions," Stobie later said, "I gradually got into their ways, and on my hunting trips became more and more enamored of this kind of life."

He lived most of the time in Denver and in Grand Lake, Colorado, or among the Utes, who appropriately named him "Pagh-agh-et," which means "Long Hair." He also served as a scout for Major Jacob Downing, who fought the Arapahoe and Cheyenne along the South Platte River.

Stobie painted portraits of Buffalo Bill Cody, Kit Carson, and of many famous Indian chiefs, including Sitting Bull. Indian and cowboy life and battle scenes were other subjects for his brush. The first exhibit of the Omaha, Nebraska, Art Association in 1890 lists a number of Stobie works.

Thirty-two of his oil paintings and his collection of Indian clothing and equipment were donated to the Colorado State Historical Society. Many other of his paintings are in private collections. Stobie lived in Chicago for several years prior to his death there.

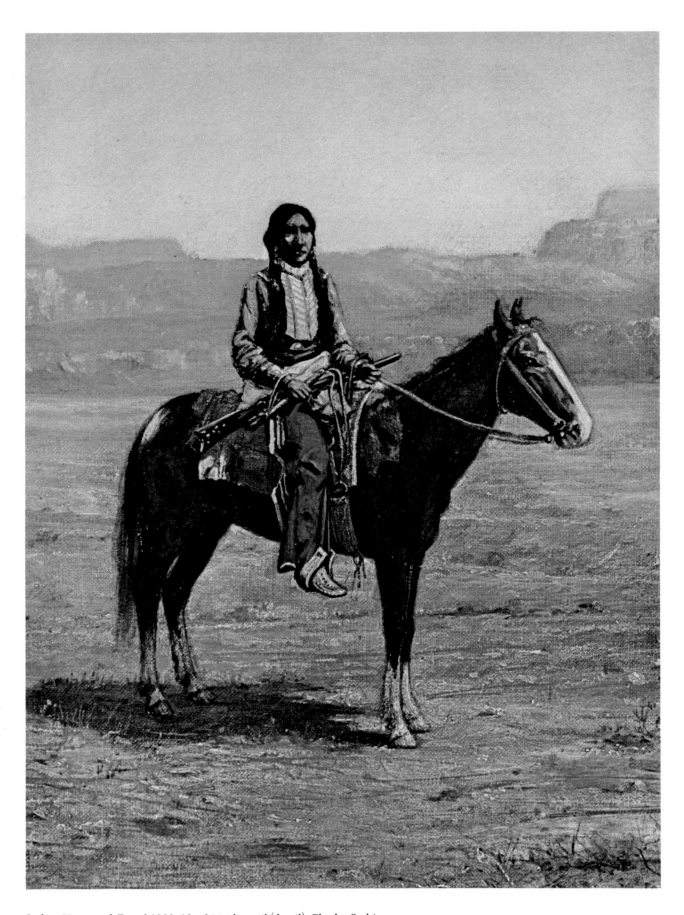

Indian Vanguard. Dated 1900. 18 x 24 inches, oil (detail). Charles Stobie.

Howard Streight

1836–1912

HOWARD A. STREIGHT ALWAYS MAINTAINED that his paint brush was guided by a supernatural power—the spirits of the great masters of art. The unschooled pioneer artist could make a good case for his claim, as he was a rapid painter, seemingly controlled by the disembodied spirits who used him to produce their effects upon the canvas.

Yet "Professor" Streight, as he was called, was considered an artistic, hard-working genius of his day, and his paintings were very desirable.

Born in Brown County, Ohio, Streight moved to Colorado in 1869 at the age of thirty-three, soon after his marriage to Marienne Ethridge. They lived in Denver for twenty years.

He painted both portraits and landscapes and was best known for his vivid portrayals of the mountains and his brilliant sunset scenes. As a painter of clouds he had few equals, and he mastered the blending of light and shadow. He executed his subjects with such realism that viewers said they could imagine themselves stepping through the picture frame and leaping among the rocks and trees.

In 1877, a reporter for the *Rocky Mountain News* visited Streight's studio. He wrote, "Mr. Streight commenced and finished a picture 20 x 24 inches in three sittings. His first effort lasted exactly seven minutes, the second, thirteen, and the third, fifteen minutes. He used tube colors, spreading and mixing them rapidly on his palette.

"Having set a large music box to playing," the article continued, "his brush at times moved in perfect accord with the music; meanwhile his left foot beat a lively tattoo upon the floor. His arm made all manner of gyrations, dashing from one end of the canvas to the other with lightning strokes. His eyes at times were entirely closed, at others nearly so. He seemed oblivious to everything around him. In the brief span of thirty-five minutes he produced clouds, a beautiful sky, mountains, valleys, a lake, and rocks, all blended into a harmonious picture."

He was a delight to the art circles—not only for his painting ability but his act of painting was an unforgettable performance.

In 1891, Streight moved to California where he continued to paint until his death in San Jose. He was survived by his widow and three children.

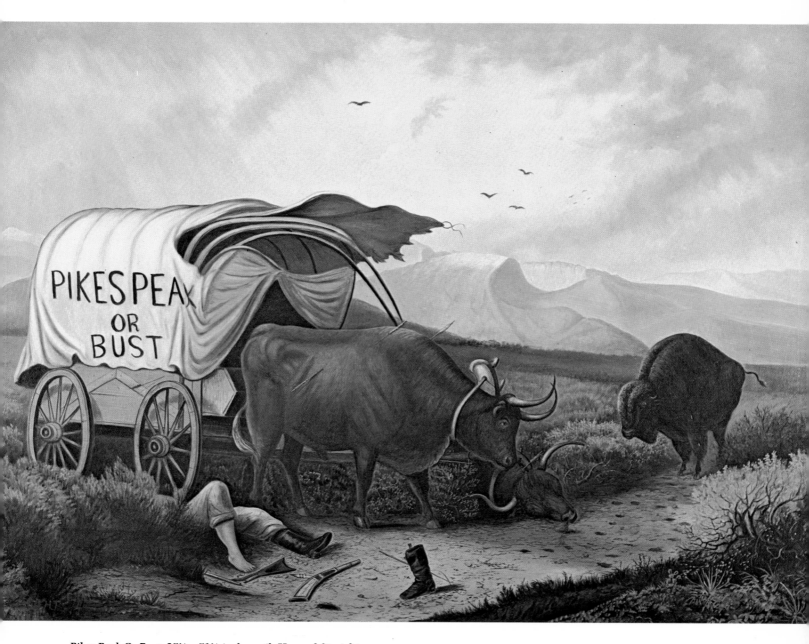

Pikes Peak Or Bust. 35½ x 51½ inches, oil. Howard Streight.

James E. Stuart

1852–1941

A PROLIFIC LANDSCAPE ARTIST, James Everett Stuart captured the beauty and grandeur of the early West in many of the nearly 5,000 paintings he created during his career.

Most of his life was spent in California, but he traveled throughout the United States, Alaska, and Mexico, sketching and painting the landscapes that became a legend to the art circles of early California. Although he was born in the East, Californians have always proudly looked upon him as a native son. Many of the traditional old homes are graced with a decorative James Stuart painting.

He developed a process for painting on aluminum where the pigments of the paint adhered to the metal, giving a permanence to the results. Some of his works using this technique sold for as much as $15,000.

Stuart was born in Dover, Maine, the son of Daniel and Lydia Stuart. At the age of eight, his parents took him to California, and the family settled in San Francisco. He attended the public schools there and first studied art in Sacramento, California, under Virgil Williams and Raymond Yelland.

He later studied at the San Francisco Studio of Design under Thomas Hill and William Keith.

His first paintings were of California scenes including views along the Sacramento and San Joaquin Rivers, the Sierras, Lake Tahoe, Yosemite, and Half Moon Bay.

He developed his own style of painting, but it showed the influence of the Barbizon School, moody and mysterious.

In 1881, Stuart opened a studio in San Francisco and began his extensive travels, which took him to all parts of North America. He lived in New York City for a time and painted in New England. He also spent fifteen years in Chicago and resided in Portland and Ashland, Oregon. In 1891 and 1907, he spent the summers in Alaska.

A bachelor all his life, Stuart returned to San Francisco in 1912, and he remained there until his death in 1941.

His paintings are in many public and private collections and in the state historical societies of Oregon, Washington, and Montana.

One of his paintings is in the White House, and others are owned by private collectors in both the United States and Europe.

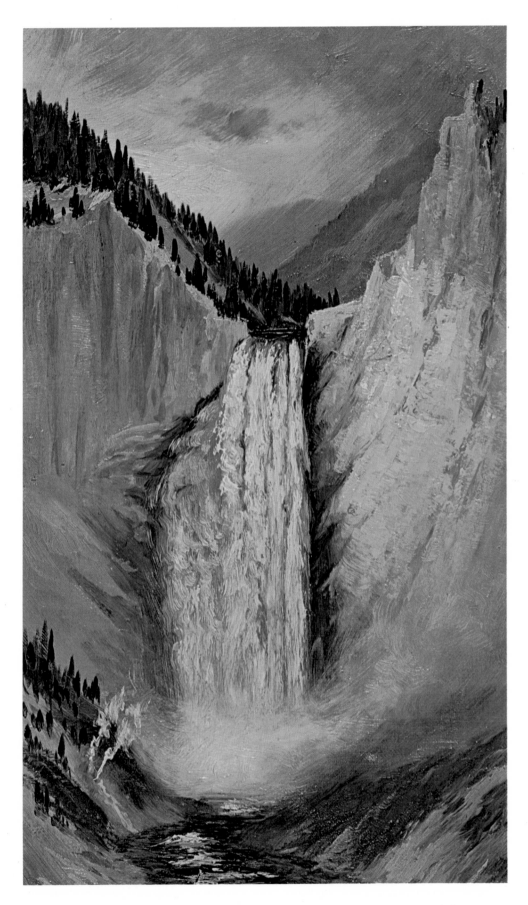

Great Falls of The Yellowstone From Red Rock. Dated 1887. 14 x 8 inches, oil. James E. Stuart.

Richard Tallant

1853–1934

RICHARD H. TALLANT SPENT MOST of his life in the American West; his paintings reflected its grandeur and beauty.

He visited and painted many important areas in the West, including Mt. Hood, the Tetons, the Grand Canyon, and the major peaks of Colorado. He captured on canvas both the majesty of the mountains and the witcheries of the desert. Of interest historically are Tallant's genre paintings—such as the Pueblo Indians of New Mexico, which he sketched in 1887 while visiting Santa Fe, and his Cripple Creek fire painting of 1896.

Reproductions of Tallant's oils have appeared on the covers of magazines and calendars and have hung in homes and galleries for nearly a century. An official of a railroad in New York once said that a painting by Tallant hanging in his office sold more tickets to Colorado than any energetic clerk in his organization.

He was born in Zanesville, Ohio, and came west as a young man, spending many years in Colorado mining camps and in Denver. His mind became a storehouse of memories of the adventures he had while ranging the West. His encounters in the Ute Indian country, about which he loved to reminisce in his later years, were the most vivid in his memory.

Following his marriage to Louise Bellamy Macdonald of Denver, the couple set up a homestead at Devil's Gulch, near Estes Park, Colorado. It was to remain their home for thirty-one years. He was loved and respected by the townspeople and served as a justice of the peace for many years. The service earned him the title "Judge Tallant." Many of Tallant's paintings were commissioned by F. O. Stanley, one of Estes Park's most prominent citizens and owner of the famous Stanley Hotel.

The tenderness and compassion Tallant showed for his friends, from the ordinary to the most eminent, also permeated his paintings. His very soul seemed to be revealed in everything he did. The smallest aspen grove, his largest canvas of the great mountains, the alluring purple canyons, or the wastelands of the desert—all radiate an exquisiteness that is lulling, tender, and gentle.

His wife died in 1914, but he continued to paint almost until his death at the age of eighty-one. He was survived by two sons, Leland and William.

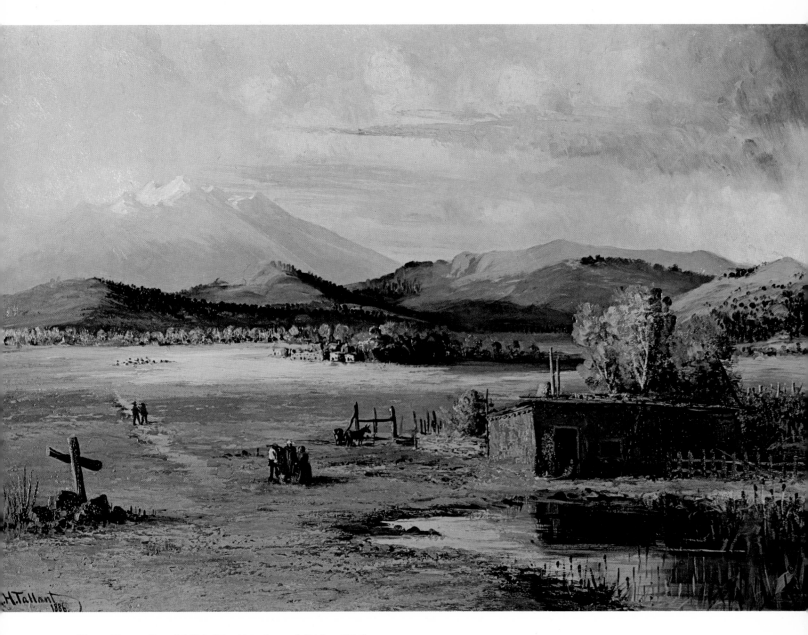

Sierra Blanca. Dated 1886. 27 x 40 inches, oil. Richard Tallant.

Jules Tavernier

1844–1889

ALTHOUGH A BRILLIANT ARTIST, French-born Jules Tavernier was best known during his lifetime as one of the most unpredictable characters of the San Francisco art colony. A Bohemian through and through, "the Crazy Frenchman" had little use for the wealthy patrons of the arts or the artists he felt were influenced by them.

He seldom cared about finishing paintings or exhibiting them. Even though his finances were usually at rock-bottom, Tavernier's philosophy—reinforced by his love for wine—was "never do today what you can put off until tomorrow."

Yet when the spirit moved him, he could paint with exceptional skill and rapidity, and he worked in many media. Much of his work highlighted the western frontier and the Indians who lived there.

He was born in Paris; Tavernier's parents were British subjects. He showed an early interest in art and was given the best training available. At sixteen, he became a pupil of Felix Barrias of the Ecole des Beaux Arts. He studied there four years and contributed works to the Paris Salon.

After serving in the Franco-Prussian War, Tavernier left France in 1871. He spent a year in London as a newspaper illustrator, then moved to New York City where he worked for the leading magazines.

In 1873, he and fellow artist Paul Frenzeny went west with an army unit assigned to control the Indians. His sketches were widely published, and he gathered material for many Indian paintings.

After several months on the plains, Tavernier arrived in San Francisco and decided to stay, renting a barren studio in a loft over a macaroni factory, where the beauty of the Monterey Peninsula inspired him to abandon his preference for drawing in black and white.

Tavernier was a member of the San Francisco Art Association, but after a dispute, he helped form the Palette Club. He also was a loyal Bohemian Club member.

His artist friends raised money to send him to Hawaii in 1884, and his paintings of the volcanoes did much to publicize the beauty of the Hawaiian islands. Unable to finance his return to the mainland, he died there of alcoholism in 1889 at the age of forty-five. His devoted San Francisco friends erected a monument over his grave in Honolulu.

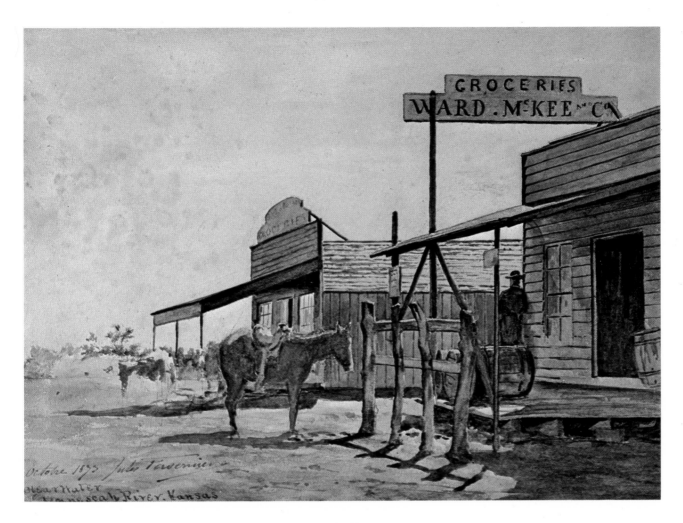

Clearwater, Kansas. Dated 1877. 8½ x 12 inches, watercolor. Jules Tavernier.

Donald Teague NA

b. 1897

ILLUSTRATOR DONALD TEAGUE IS highly respected by his fellow artists. His devotion to authenticity and exact detail is reflected in his paintings.

During the heyday of magazine illustrators, Teague was considered one of the best. He worked for *McCall's, Saturday Evening Post, Collier's,* and *Woman's Home Companion.* Because of the rivalry between the *Saturday Evening Post* and *Collier's,* his illustrations in *Collier's* were signed with a pseudonym, Edwin Dawes.

Teague's paintings are the result of painstaking preparation and research. He starts with black and white sketches and converts them to small full-color studies. After further sketching—always with models—the large final sketches are projected and traced on watercolor paper, ready to render in watercolor or gouache. He also works in oil.

In his earlier years in California, Teague lived near the motion picture studios in Hollywood and often used western props and movie sets as part of his subject matter. The quiet-spoken artist is now living in Carmel, California, surrounded by a private collection of his breath-takingly beautiful easel paintings, which compliments the tasteful decor of his home.

Born in Brooklyn, New York, Teague studied at the Art Students League in New York City under George Bridgman and Frank V. Du Mond. After serving in the United States Navy during World War I, he went to England to study under Norman Wilkinson. Back in the United States, he was tutored by Dean Cornwell while beginning his career in illustration.

Teague was married to Verna Timmins in 1938, and they have two daughters, Linda and Hilary.

The artist and his paintings have won numerous honors and awards. He was elected to the National Academy of Design in 1948. In 1962 he won the S.F.B. Morse Gold Medal from the National Academy of Design. In 1953 and 1964 he received the Grand Award and Gold Medal of Honor from the American Watercolor Society, the first artist to win it twice.

His western paintings have won similar acclaim. He took the Gold Medal for Watercolor from The Franklin Mint in 1973, 1974, and 1975, and he received the Gold Medal for Watercolor from the National Cowboy Hall of Fame in 1973 and 1975. His paintings are owned by many museums and private collectors.

214

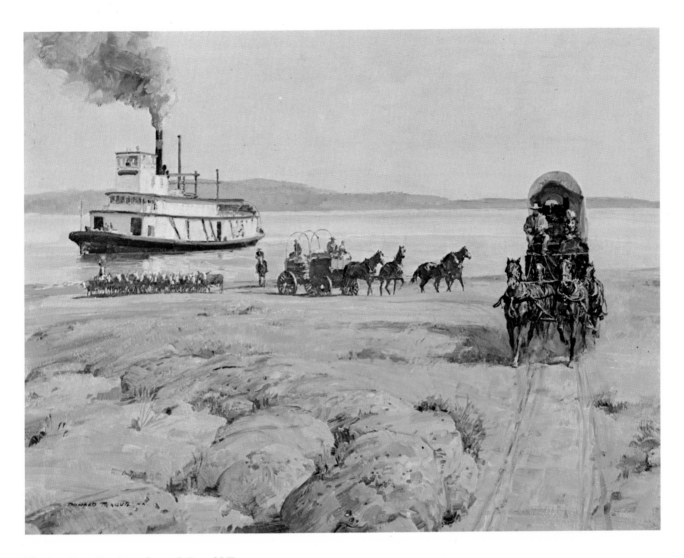

The Last Leg. 18 x 24 inches, oil. Donald Teague.

Paul Troubetzkoy

1866–1938

ALTHOUGH PAUL TROUBETZKOY spent only a few years in the United States, the people and animals of the American Southwest were the subjects of a good portion of his works.

Many of these action-filled bronze renderings of cowboys, Indians, horses, and cattle were created in his studio in Paris, France.

Troubetzkoy was born in the Italian village of Intra. His father was a Russian prince; his mother was American, which probably accounts for his fascination with the early West. From boyhood, his ambition was to be a sculptor. When he was seven years of age, he was making models out of soft bread. He next created likenesses of domestic household animals out of modeling wax.

His model of a horse's head made when he was ten was taken by his mother to Milan, home of famous sculptor Giuseppi Grandi, who said it was the work of a genius.

But despite the boy's obvious talent for art and his interest in it, his father wanted him to pursue a career in the military. At age seventeen, he was sent to live with relatives in Russia, but after a few months he returned to Italy and began serious art studies.

He studied in Milan, under Donato Bacaglia and Ernest Bazzaro. But Troubetzkoy preferred to work alone, and he soon opened his own studio where he developed an impressionistic style, influenced somewhat by Auguste Rodin. During this period, he also worked and studied in Russia and France. In 1894, he won the Gold Medal in the Rome Exposition for his work entitled "Indian Scout," which depicted an Indian in full headdress astride a horse.

Troubetzkoy made his first trip to America in 1911. He returned to the United States in 1914 and spent most of his time in California until 1920. But some of his best western works were created after his return to Europe, including "Roping Cattle," completed in 1927. He is also noted for his portrait statuettes of famous people in art, literature, and politics.

In the final years of his career, Troubetzkoy lived and worked both in Paris and on the shores of Lake Maggiore, Italy, but his memories of the American West were an inspirational force on his work. He died in Paris.

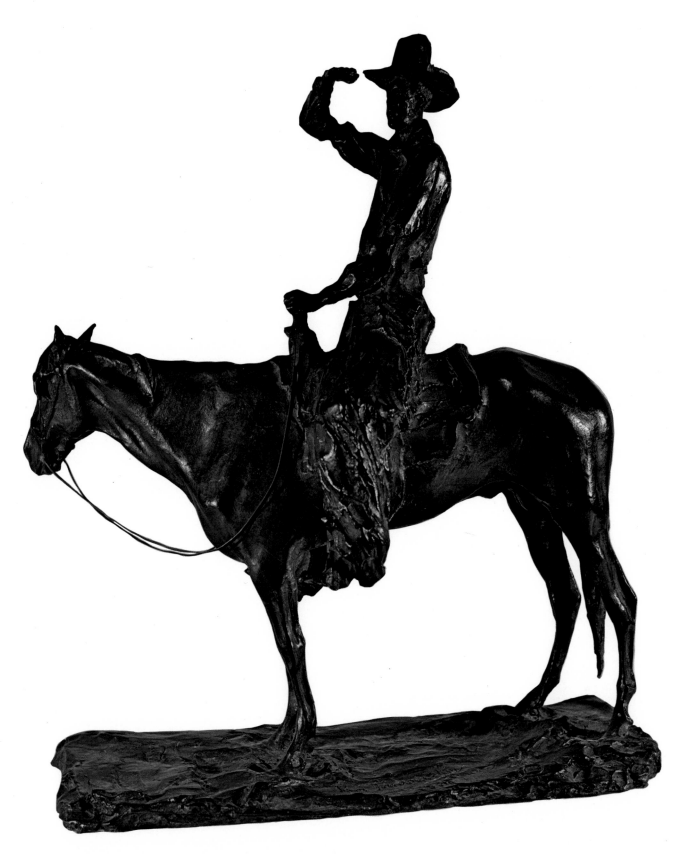

Cowboy On Horse. H. 18 inches L. 12 inches, bronze. Paul Troubetzkoy.

Allen True

1881–1955

BORN OF PIONEER PARENTS in Colorado Springs, Colorado, Allen Tupper True studied at the Corcoran School of Art in Washington, D.C., where his accomplishments earned him the attention of Howard Pyle and admission into that famous illustrator's elite group of proteges in 1902.

During the next six years his classmates in Wilmington, Delaware, included Frank Schoonover, Harvey Dunn, and N.C. Wyeth. With Pyle's help, True obtained assignments from *Outing, Collier's, Scribners,* and other popular magazines, often illustrating his own articles on western subjects. Much of his work during this period celebrated the man of action.

After an apprenticeship with the noted British muralist Frank Brangwyn, Allen True settled permanently in Denver and began to receive commissions for historical murals for the city's public buildings. His murals can be seen in the Brown Palace and Cosmopolitan hotels, the lobby of the telephone building, the Capitol rotunda, and the offices of the district and county courts. Notable murals with Indian themes were done for the Colorado National Bank and the Memorial Student Union Building at the University of Colorado in Boulder. Murals are also in the Wyoming and Missouri statehouses. True's finest mural painting is probably the "Commerce of the Prairies," which can be seen in the Warren Branch of the Denver Public Library.

He supervised the restoration of the original decor of the Central City Opera House and, as art consultant to the United States Reclamation Bureau, directed the color schemes at the Boulder, Hoover, and Grand Coulee Dam projects.

True painted many scenes of Indian life. He was fascinated by Indian decorative art, and he hoped that his own experimentation with their forms would provide the basis for fresh, authentically American trends in architectural decoration.

Having an abiding love for his native Colorado, True maintained a mountain retreat where he would often spend six months of the year fishing, hiking, and painting.

He was a member of the distinguished National Society of Mural Painters, whose members included John Singer Sargent and Edwin Abbey, and he was also a Fellow of the Royal Society of the Arts.

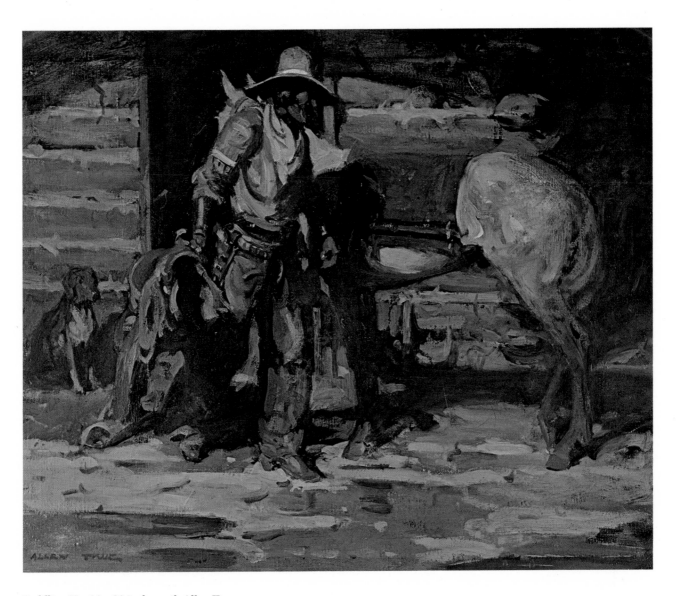

Saddling Up. 16 x 20 inches, oil. Allen True.

James Turpen, Jr.

b. 1930

HAVING LIVED ON and visited the Navajo Reservation for many years as a child, James Costello Turpen, who is part Cherokee, says of his work, "Due to my close association with the Indian people, it seemed natural to select their dances, ceremonies, and customs as the subjects of many of my bronzes."

Coming from a family of Indian traders, Turpen was born in Winslow, Arizona. Living and working in remote areas on the reservations, his family would be the only white people there for long periods of time. The Turpens lived at the Grand Canyon for several years, where the beauty of the changing moods of the canyon made a great impression on young Turpen.

Moving to Tucson, Arizona, he attended high school there and the University of Arizona while working during the summer at the Grand Canyon and the Grey Mountain Trading Post on the Navajo Reservation. In 1950 he married his wife, Robbie, and they have two children, Penny and John, and three grandchildren.

After serving with the Army in Germany, he returned to Tucson and finished his studies, graduating with a degree in wildlife management.

Colorado was the Turpens' next homesite; he continued his drawing and the study of western and Indian history. Visiting a foundry in Taos, New Mexico, he decided to try sculpture. His bronzes have been shown in galleries in Kansas City, Denver, and Santa Fe.

Since 1973, the Turpens have lived in Gallup, New Mexico, where he manages Tobe Turpen's Indian Trading Company and will on occasion design a handsome piece of turquoise jewelry to be handcrafted by the Navajo or Zuni Indians working at the trading post.

Presently he has turned to realistic easel painting, using the land and the people as his models. Turpen says, "I turned to painting as I became bored with the lack of color of bronze, and it is good to work with color for a stimulant. When I cannot obtain the dimension I desire in my painting, I go back to bronze for a greater feeling of depth. It is rewarding for me to work in both media."

Besides using a commercial foundry, James Turpen developed his own small foundry, where he will experiment with his works or will cast a one-of-a-kind model for a special commitment.

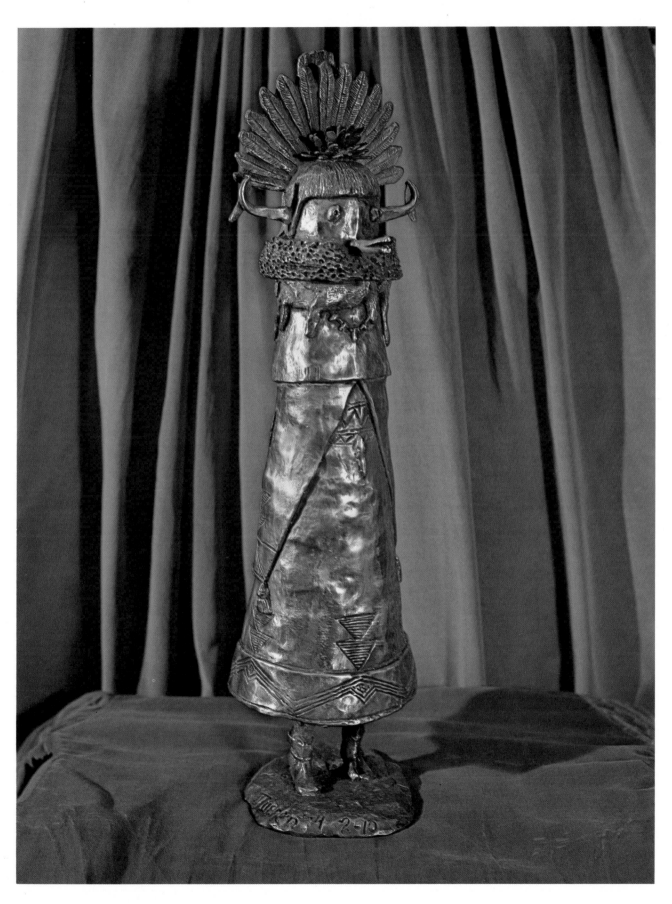

Shalako Dancer. H. 21 inches, solid sterling silver. James Turpen, Jr.

Manuel Valencia

1856–1935

A MEMBER OF ONE OF California's pioneer families, Manuel Valencia was a prolific painter of California landscapes and historical scenes.

Valencia was a descendent of General Gabriel Valencia, the first governor of the state of Sonora, Mexico, when it was under Spanish rule. In 1781, the residents of Alamos, the capital of Sonora, contributed eighty-five dollars toward the settlement of a new pueblo, Nuestra Sonora La Riena de Los Angeles de Porciuncula, which was to become the city of Los Angeles.

General Valencia went to California with the de Anza party and became the administrator of the San Francisco Presidio. Valencia Street in San Francisco is named for the family. Many Spanish grants were given to the Valencia family in the Bay Area.

The artist was born in the Valencia Hacienda, Rancho San Jose, in Marin County. His father, Manuel Valencia Senior, was also born there.

Valencia attended what is now Santa Clara University and studied art under the leading California painters of the day. Early in his career, he served as art editor of the *San Francisco Chronicle* under M. H. de Young, one of the city's leading art patrons. He also was the first illustrator on the *War Cry*, a Salvation Army newspaper published in the Bay Area.

With such an illustrious beginning, his future as an artist was almost assured, but acclaim and financial success came late in life for Valencia. In 1912, when he was fifty-six years of age, he took eighty of his paintings to a special sale in San Francisco to raise enough money to pay off the mortgage on his small home in Garden City, California. There had been little demand for his work, and he had a wife and nine children to support. However the subsequent years brought him the rewards he so richly deserved, and he was fortunate to live to enjoy the appreciation of his work during his lifetime.

Valencia spent his entire life in the San Francisco area. His paintings are in the collections of the Bohemian Club of San Francisco, in the State Capitol in Sacramento, and in many of the state's leading museums. His painting of the Yosemite Valley was purchased by President William McKinley.

He was an honorary member of Esquela de Bellas Artes of Mexico.

He died in Sacramento, following an operation, and was survived by his six sons and three daughters.

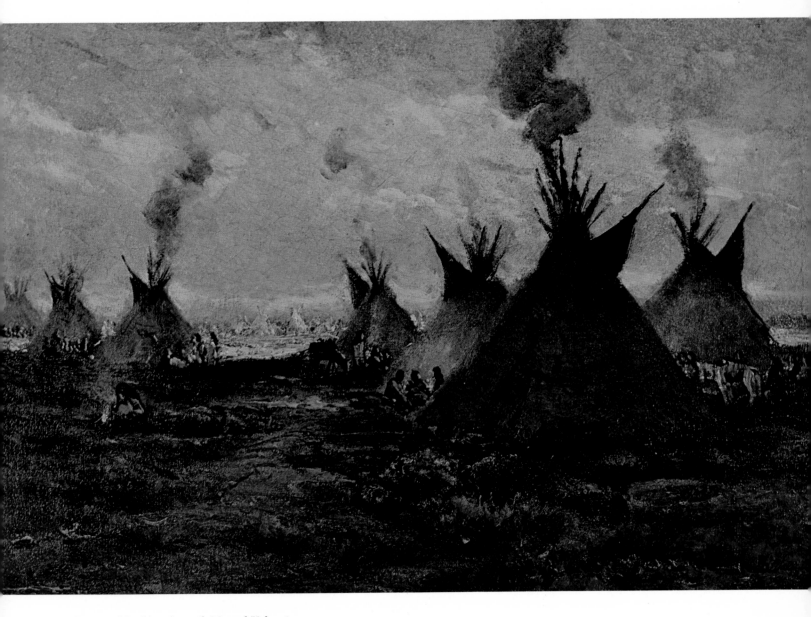

Teepees. 20 x 30 inches, oil. Manuel Valencia.

Dirk van Driest

b. 1889

HE HAS MADE HIS HOME in Taos, New Mexico, since 1957—a long way from his birthplace in Palembang, Sumatra, where his father was in the civil service for Holland. When he was eight years old, his parents sent him to The Hague, Holland, to live with his maternal grandfather. There, his parents felt, he could obtain a better academic education.

He became interested in photography and made his living with his camera, which was his first exposure to esthetic endeavor.

In 1919, after serving with the Dutch East Indian Army, he took up a career as an actor with a traveling theatrical company. He sometimes doubled as an opera singer, using more pantomime than song.

Dirk van Driest started painting seriously in 1927. This had always been his main interest, and in 1932 he complemented his painting with clay sculpture. Studying the works of the old masters, mostly in Holland, he says, "Rembrandt pushed me in the right direction. Never stop trying," he urges, "Look at the work of those who are better than you are and try to raise your standards higher."

When he was forty years old he attempted to enter art schools in Paris. He was refused because he was considered too old, and he also was not permitted to watch other students at work.

Leaving Holland in 1948 he went to Morocco, looking for a new artistic inspiration. He stayed for eight years. Being footloose and unmarried throughout his lifetime, his final environment was the United States, where in 1956 he traveled for a year. In 1957 he found just what he felt was the right climate for his work and his own comfort . . . in Taos, New Mexico.

Dirk van Driest is a tall man with a Yul Brynner haircut and a precise, telegraphic way of speaking. To him languages are communication tools, several of which he uses as naturally as his native Dutch. He willingly shares his vast knowledge and experience and is a gracious host with a continental flair in his studio-home.

Primarily a portrait painter, he does not paint likenesses—he captures people and their personalities in portraits. His paintings are in private collections in Europe and the United States. Geographically speaking, van Driest's art spans the globe.

224

Tellus Goodmorning. 24 x 20 inches, oil. Dirk van Driest.

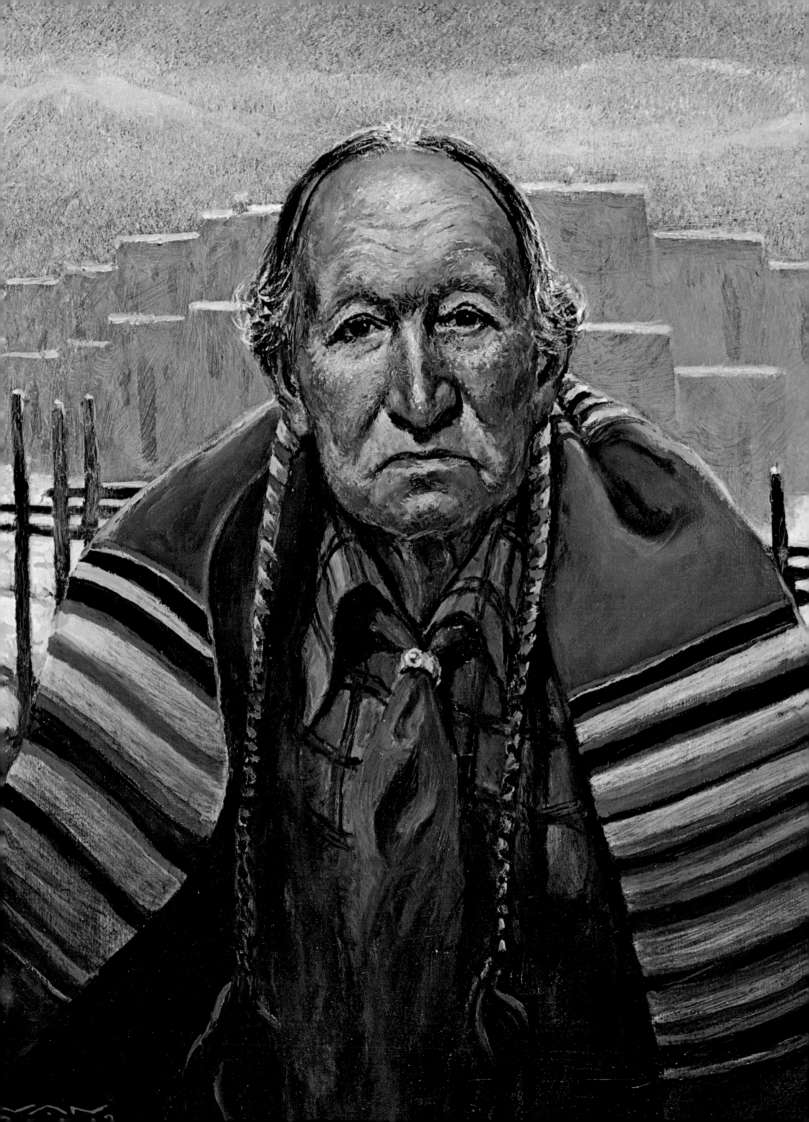

Theodore Van Soelen NA

1890–1964

LIKE SO MANY OTHER ARTISTS, scholars, and poets who made their home in the southwestern United States, it was tuberculosis that brought Theodore Van Soelen to New Mexico. Arriving there in 1916, he was a pioneer in the art colony and became one of the state's leading citizens. It has been said that Van Soelen was not just an artist in New Mexico, but a man who was deeply a New Mexico artist. He lived in the towns, at ranches, and trading posts throughout the state, painting the land and people—especially the Indians and the cattlemen—with keen insight. He was known for his portraits. His work in lithography also received recognition, and his murals can be seen in many public buildings.

Van Soelen was born in St. Paul, Minnesota, and studied art at the St. Paul Institute of Arts and Sciences. He made his first trip west to Utah and Nevada in 1910. The following year he entered the Pennsylvania Academy of Fine Arts in Philadelphia and in 1913 and 1914 studied in Europe on a Cresson Traveling Scholarship, obtained through the Academy.

He sold his first paintings in 1916. The following year he exhibited at the dedication exhibition of the Museum of New Mexico in Santa Fe.

Van Soelen subsequently lived and painted in many areas of the Southwest, including the Fernandez Company Ranch in San Mateo, New Mexico, and at a trading post at San Ysidro, New Mexico. He married Virginia Carr in 1921, and they made their home in Santa Fe.

Moving just north of Santa Fe to Tesuque, New Mexico, in 1926, he built a home and studio and painted many scenes of the Apache and Pueblo Indians. In 1934, he opened a studio in Cornwall, Connecticut, but also maintained his home in Tesuque.

Van Soelen was elected an associate member of the National Academy of Design in 1933 and was elected a National Academician in 1940.

He exhibited in many prestigious shows, including those at the National Academy and the Metropolitan Museum in New York City, the Chicago Art Institute, the Carnegie Institute, the Corcoran Gallery in Washington, D.C., and the Boston and Philadelphia Arts Clubs.

Van Soelen died in Santa Fe, New Mexico, and was survived by his wife and two sons, Theodore Jr. and Daniel. A daughter, Jay, preceded him in death; she was killed in an automobile accident in 1947.

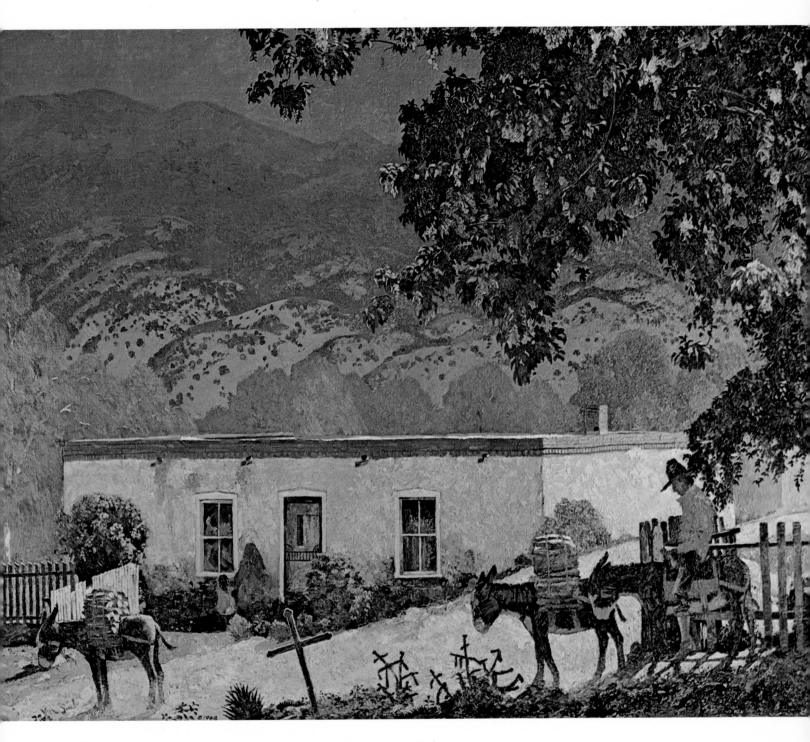

The Road to Santa Fe. Dated 1948. 38 x 48 inches, oil. Theodore Van Soelen.

Adrien Voisin

b. 1890

THE ARTIST WAS BORN in Islip, New York, to French parents. The family settled in Newport, Rhode Island where Adrien Alexander Voisin's father, who had been an officer in the French Army during the Franco-Prussian War, operated a riding academy.

Voisin wanted to become a naturalist, but lacking interest in the customary course of study, he dropped out of school to work with a taxidermist. For eight years he helped develop new mounting techniques. He worked the next four years as an apprentice for a French woodcarver and studied painting under Sargent Kendall of the Yale School of Fine Arts; Kendall encouraged him to seek more formal training abroad.

In 1912 Voisin went to Paris to study at the Academie Colarossi, then the Ecole National des Beaux Arts. He came to realize that sculpture, not painting, was his field and so began modeling the Indians who had intrigued him since his first contact with them at a Buffalo Bill Cody show in Paris.

He returned to the United States in 1916 and enlisted in the Army. After the war, he received many commissions for sculptures on public buildings, including the famed Hearst Castle, and memorial busts of public figures.

Financially successful, he was able to pursue his desire to portray the life of the Indian. In 1929, he and his wife Frances, the daughter of an Indian agent, moved to Browning, Montana. She served as interpreter, and both became honorary members of the local tribe.

After a year in Browning, they went to Paris, where his works were cast in bronze. His Indian collection was loaned to the United States government for its exhibition at the Exposition Coloniale in Paris. For this, the French government awarded him the Diplome d'Honneur. In 1932 he received a gold medal in the International Art Exhibition in Paris.

Returning to America, Voisin purchased the old Albion Brewery in San Francisco, which he spent twenty years restoring into a home and studio.

Interrupting his creative work, he served as a civilian employee for the Navy during World War II. At this time, Mrs. Voisin died. After the artist remarried, he and his new wife lived in the old brewery until his collection of Indian and animal sculptures could be moved to the Museum of Native American Cultures in Spokane, Washington, for permanent display. The Voisins now make their home in Southern California.

228

Happy Hunting Ground. Dated 1930.
H. 25½ inches L. 25 inches, bronze. Adrien Voisin.

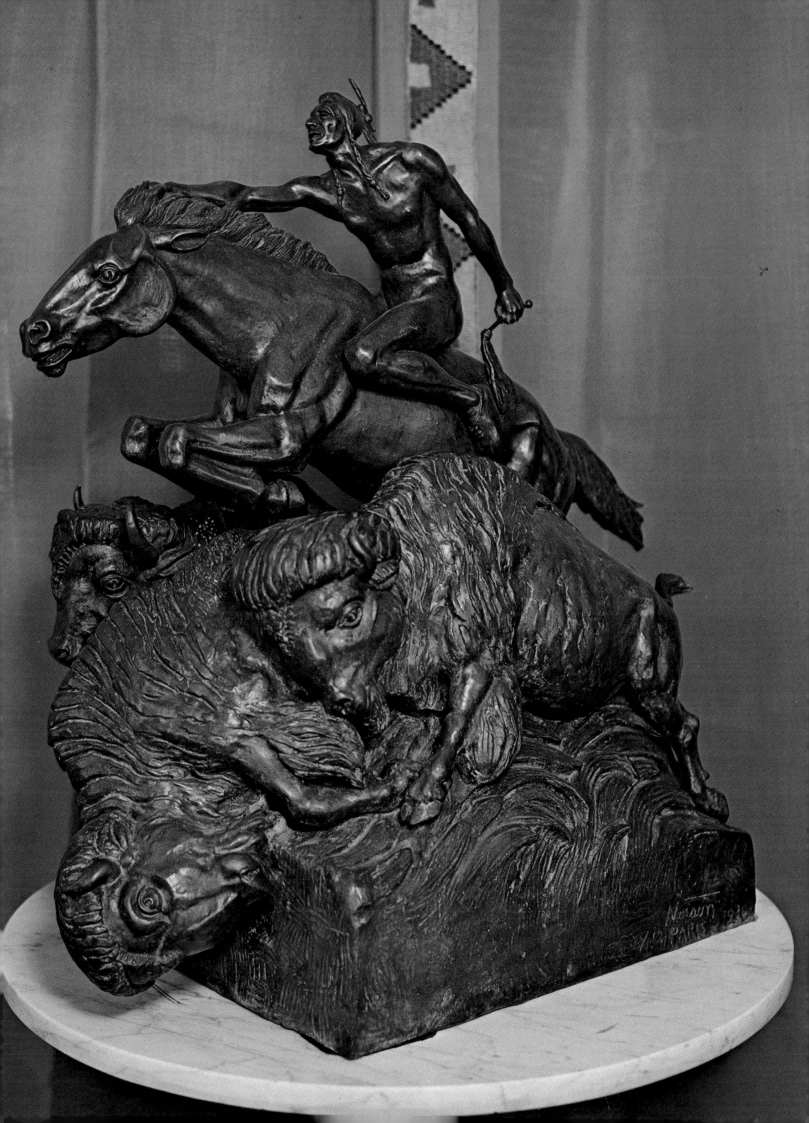

James Walker

1819–1889

JAMES WALKER IS historically important for both his paintings of famous battle scenes in American history and for his renderings of the Mexican culture of early California.

He spent the final years of his life in California painting the life of the vaqueros on the vast cattle ranches of the state. Walker deftly captured the action of galloping horses and accurately detailed the equipment and trappings of those early cowboys.

Born in Northamptonshire, England, Walker was brought to the United States at the age of six. The family settled on the scenic Hudson River near Albany, New York.

He left home in his early twenties, going to New Orleans, then to Tampico, Mexico, and Mexico City, where he developed his lifelong interest in the Spanish-Mexican history and culture. When the United States and Mexico went to war in 1846, Walker was imprisoned in Mexico City.

But he escaped to the United States and became an interpreter for General Winfield Scott and sketched many battlefield scenes of the war.

From 1857 to 1862 he stayed in Washington, D.C., to paint the "Battle of Chapultepec" on a commission from Congress. The painting eventually was placed over the west staircase in the Senate wing of the Capitol.

Although the work was considered mediocre and was reluctantly paid for by the lawmakers, it launched Walker on a successful career of painting battlefield panoramas, the most popular art-entertainment form of the day.

From 1862 through 1865, he sketched Civil War skirmishes, which he later converted into large panoramic canvases. Some of the most famous were "Battle of Lookout Mountain," commissioned by General "Fighting Joe" Hooker and "Third Day at Gettysburg," displayed in a building built for it at the site of the battlefield.

Walker made his first trip to California in 1877; he painted the life on the large ranches still Spanish in style and ownership. In 1884, with his twin brother Thomas, he made his residence there near Monterey.

His paintings are owned by the Denver Art Museum and the California Historical Society; twelve of his works hang in the United States Defense Department Building in Washington.

230   He died in Watsonville, California.

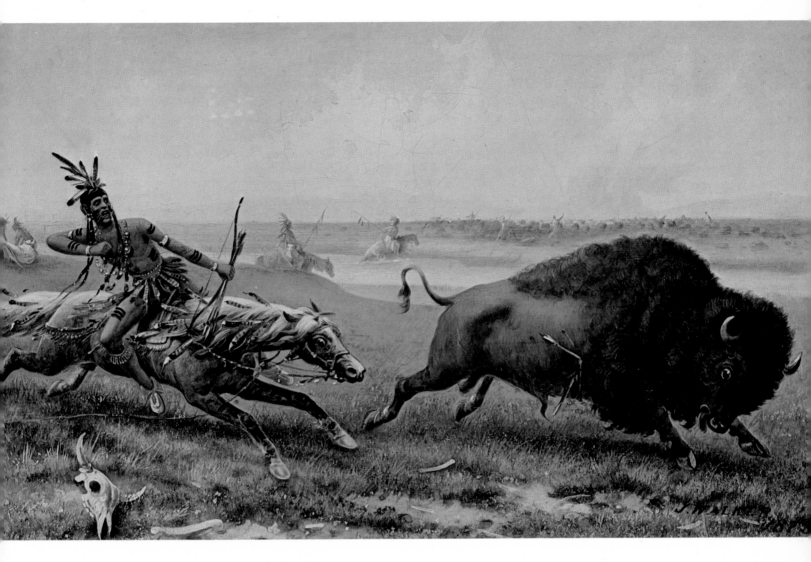

The Buffalo Hunt. 12 x 20 inches, oil. James Walker.

Thad Welch

1844–1919

THADDEUS WELCH WAS BORN in LaPorte, Indiana. When he was three years old the family made a perilous journey by prairie schooner to the Columbia River. There, they removed the wheels, mounted the schooner on a raft, and floated down the river to McMinnville, Oregon.

After a sparse education, Welch went to work when he was twenty at Wallings Printing office in Portland. He was exposed to a bundle of water-color sketches by Baron Von Toft, which inspired him to pursue an artistic career. The president of a steamship line recognized his talent and financed his trip to San Francisco. It was there he met his lifelong friend, James Everett Stuart, joined the San Francisco Art Club, and studied with Thomas Hill, William Keith, and H. R. Bloomer.

A patron of the arts sent him to Europe, where he attended school with Henry Raschen and Frank Duveneck at the Royal Academie of Munich, winning three bronze medals for his work. John Twachtman, the American impressionist, befriended Welch, and they traveled through Europe together, painting and studying.

In 1883 he married Ludmilla Pilat, who later became a recognized artist also. They lived in Boston where, through William Merritt Chase, Welch was able to work for lithographer Louis Prang, painting with Thomas Hill, George Inness, and Thomas Moran.

On a sketching expedition through the West, he painted the Spanish and Indian people in Santa Fe and also drew Colorado scenes.

The Welchs moved back to California in 1893, where they built a crude home in the Marin County Hills. They called it "Steep Ravine."

His poor health and their poverty had caused them many setbacks. They moved to Santa Barbara in 1905, but he still painted the Marin County Hills. His reputation was gradually building, and his paintings were beginning to command high prices.

When he was financially secure, he was able to develop his inventive nature, creating a rapid shutter for a camera and an electric dynamo. He also carved exquisite violins.

The work of this pioneer painter is in many private collections and museums throughout the world. He died in Santa Barbara, California.

232

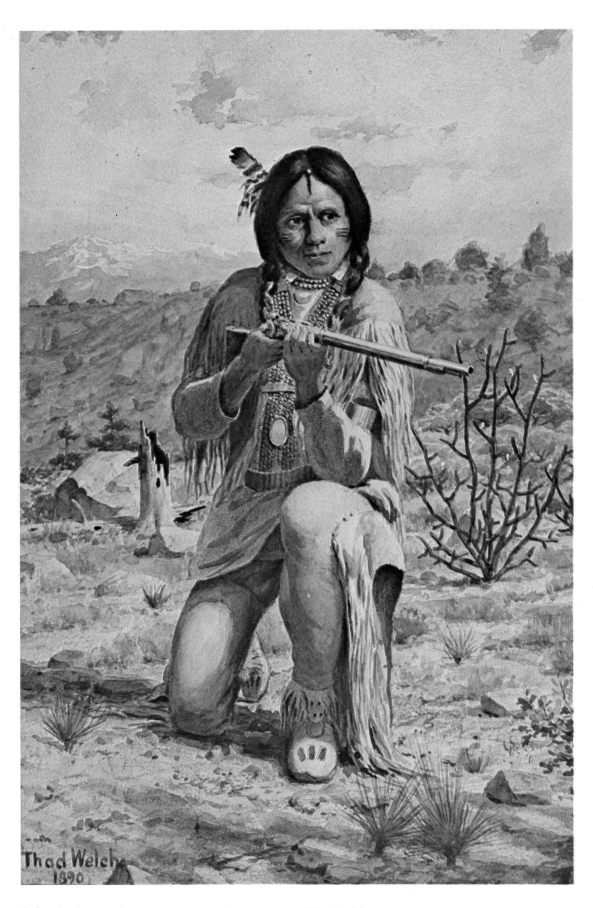

Indian Study. Dated 1890. 26½ x 19½ inches, watercolor. Thad Welch.

Cady Wells

1904–1954

HE WAS THE SON of an affluent eastern family and given all the educational and cultural advantages. But the creative talents of Cady Wells eventually were drawn to the bold, rugged landscape of New Mexico.

A brilliant, prolific watercolorist, Wells became one of the most individual, imaginative, and skillful artists in the state, and his semi-abstractions provided a personal vision of that region. He was concerned with the structural aspects of the bold, rugged landscape, rather than with the exotic qualities of its inhabitants.

Wells was born in Southbridge, Massachusetts, the son of Irene and Channing Wells, the president of American Optical Company. He first went west in 1922 at the age of eighteen, when he visited Yellowstone Park. That same year he entered Evans School in Tucson, Arizona. In 1925, he entered Harvard, but remained only one semester.

In 1932, he moved to Santa Fe and concentrated on painting. For two summers he studied under Andrew Dasburg in Taos and also worked with Tom Benrimo.

Restoring an old Spanish home in Jacona, New Mexico (north of Santa Fe), Wells made it his residence and became a popular figure within the art community and on the social scene. A friendly, generous man, he frequently gave anonymous financial aid to young artists who were less fortunate.

In 1940, he enlisted in the Army Engineers and served in Europe until the end of World War II. After the end of the hostilities, he returned to France to observe Rouault, Matisse, and Picasso, to visit the art museums, and to view the stained glass of the great cathedrals.

Back in New Mexico, he found it difficult to regain his long unused painting skills. But he developed new techniques, and his work took on new dimensions and popularity.

"The creative process in painting," he said, "is based on my needs and wishes to share with others what I cannot share in any other form."

Deeply disturbed by the atomic research that was going on at nearby Los Alamos, New Mexico, Wells moved to the Virgin Islands in 1950 where he painted for two years. He returned to Santa Fe, but died at the age of fifty following two heart attacks.

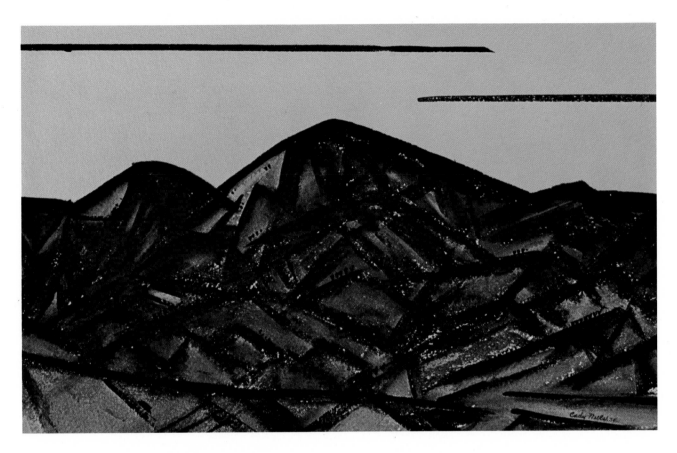

Mountains. 10 x 14 inches, watercolor. Cady Wells.

Frederick Weygold
1870–1941

AS A SMALL BOY, Frederick Weygold developed a keen interest in the American West, and as an artist he became known as a champion of the Indian. At a very early age, he was deeply moved by the plight of the red man and devoted his life and artistic abilities to help them in their degraded situation of reservation life.

He lived with many tribes, combining his artistic talent and cultural interest to perpetuate their heritage with a series of oil paintings that depicted their life.

Born and raised in St. Charles, Missouri, Weygold witnessed the covered wagon trains heading west over the Oregon Trail. In his sixth year he heard the excited talk about the great battle in Montana, in which General Custer and his regiment were destroyed by the Sioux. He saw soldiers returning with long strings of spotted Indian ponies, confiscated from Chief Red Cloud in South Dakota. He also heard other stories of Indian battles and pioneer life on the frontier.

After attending public schools in Missouri and Louisville, Kentucky, he was graduated from a European college and then studied modern languages and history at the University of Strasbourg in Alsace, France. Here he also began to learn the Indian language. Weygold studied art at European academies and at the Pennsylvania Academy of Fine Arts in Philadelphia.

In 1909 he was assigned by a European museum to live with the Sioux Indians in South Dakota, to study their language and lifestyle, and put together a museum collection of Indian artifacts. The records of his ethnological observations were of great importance to the expedition and were published in European scientific magazines.

Later he visited the Blackfeet in Montana and the Cheyenne, Arapahoe, Kiowa, and the Osage in Oklahoma.

While doing these studies, he also sketched the important scenes of Indian life, which were converted into oils. His narrative type of art portraying the religious ceremonies and superstitions of the Indian did much to promote more sympathetic understanding by the white man.

Frederick Weygold presented his private Indian collection to the J. B. Speed Art Museum in Louisville, Kentucky, where he died.

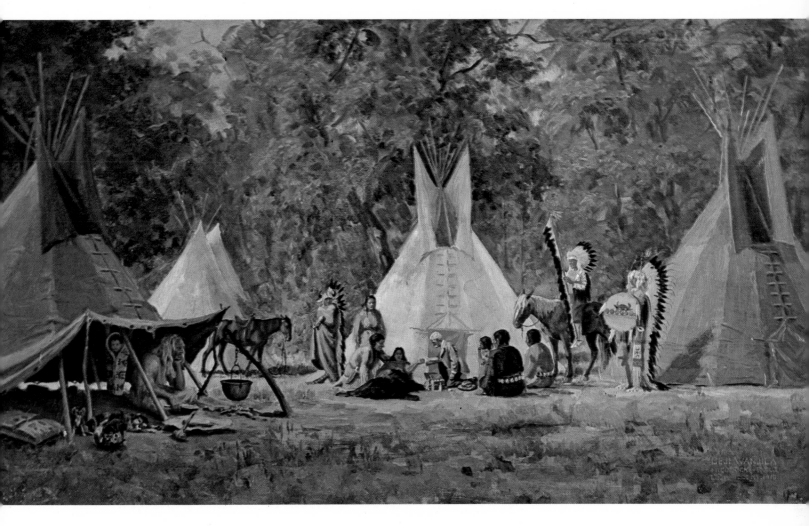

Ciji Wanjila (White Medicine Man). 30 x 40 inches, oil. Frederick Weygold.

Fritz White CA

b. 1930

HIS FIRST ATTEMPT AT A CAREER in art failed, but Fritz White went on to become a successful business man.

Born and raised in Ohio, he studied art in Cincinnati. Following three years in the Marine Corps, he opened a studio there. Moving west, by 1954, he had become the Rocky Mountain manager for an insurance publishing firm that served underwriters actuaries; he was traveling throughout eight states. "I did fantastically well," he recalls. "I made considerable money. But I messed up my first marriage." He quit. "I didn't quit the job to become a sculptor. I didn't know what a sculptor was."

White began a new life by making renderings for architects and gradually worked up a significant commercial art business. "I was making money again, but I was going all the time and working very hard, and not getting a chance to do my own art."

Then, with his second wife, Donna, he made a trip to Marble, Colorado, and loaded the backseat of his car with marble. Returning home, he carved the figure of a reclining male. He has been a sculptor ever since.

In 1973 he was elected to the prestigious Cowboy Artists Association and a year later won its Best of Show Award and a Gold Medal for Sculpture with his "And Finally Crockett Fell," at the Phoenix Art Museum. In 1975 he won a Silver Medal in the same show with "Beaver Thief." His bronze, "The Chisholm Trail Drover," received the purchase award at an Exhibition of Contemporary Western Art at the Missouri Athletic Club in St. Louis. This same piece was presented by the board of regents of Denver University to Chancellor Maurice Mitchell.

His work often finds a place before it has become a reality. He was one of only four "combat artists" selected by the United States Marine Corps to sculpt the American soldier engaged in battle in Vietnam.

Reflecting on his creations, White says, "My main desire through my work always has been to develop, in bronze, the character and the drives of the individual: to show him not just as a piece of art, but to bring to the viewer the emotion I felt as it was conceived." He has succeeded in both approaches to handling his creative ability.

Fritz White, his wife, and two children are living in Valley Mills, Texas. He has three other children by his first marriage.

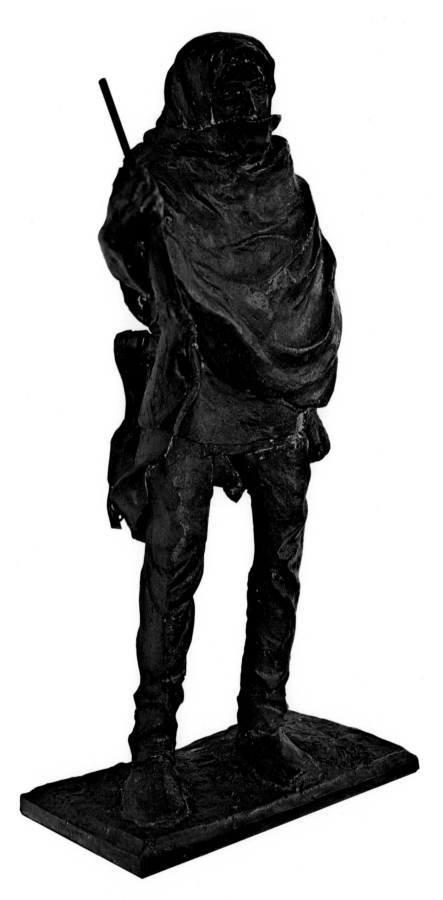

Taos Buck. H. 20 inches, bronze. Fritz White.

Frank Whiteside

1866–1929

HE MAGNIFICENTLY PAINTED the Indians of the Southwest for the people of the East. That was the highlight of Frank Reed Whiteside's career. A Philadelphian, Whiteside took every opportunity to escape the arduous training and somber atmosphere of that city, to travel to the Southwest and produce sun-filled canvases of Zuni Indian villages and New Mexico landscapes.

From the early 1890s through 1928, Whiteside made numerous trips from Philadelphia to New Mexico to live with and paint the Zunis. During his lifetime, his work was rarely exhibited in the West, although he was well known for his exhibits in his hometown and at the Worcester Art Museum, Massachusetts; Reading Art Museum, Pennsylvania; Corcoran Art Gallery, Washington, D.C.; and the Carnegie Institute, Pittsburgh, Pennsylvania.

Whiteside trained at the Philadelphia Academy from 1888 to 1892 under Thomas Anshutz and later at the Academie Julien in Paris, where he became established as a portrait painter.

Returning to Philadelphia, he took over the studio of Robert Henri and William Glackens and from 1902 through 1921 was an instructor at many art schools, including the Pennsylvania Academy in Philadelphia.

When not teaching, he was in New Mexico. He portrayed the Zunis in a number of ways, including their ceremonial dances and the more genre type of paintings in the pueblos. He drew wide acclaim for his ability to capture the complex light and subtle colors of the Southwest. In his impressionistic style, Whiteside also painted numerous landscapes and the adobe architecture of the Indians. He was always very sensitive to desert light, and his technique was toward the artistic, rather than the anthropological.

On September 19, 1929, as he stood on the doorstep of his home on Waverly Street in Philadelphia, a murderer's bullet ended his life. The gunman was never apprehended and the motive for the act (if indeed there was one) never explained or understood.

That year, the Pennsylvania Academy of Fine Arts held a memorial exhibition at the Academy. But in following years, his work seemed to be largely forgotten. In 1970, his efforts again became appreciated after the Academy presented two of his paintings to President and Mrs. Nixon, and, in 1971, a Whiteside exhibit was shown at the Phoenix Art Museum in Phoenix, Arizona.

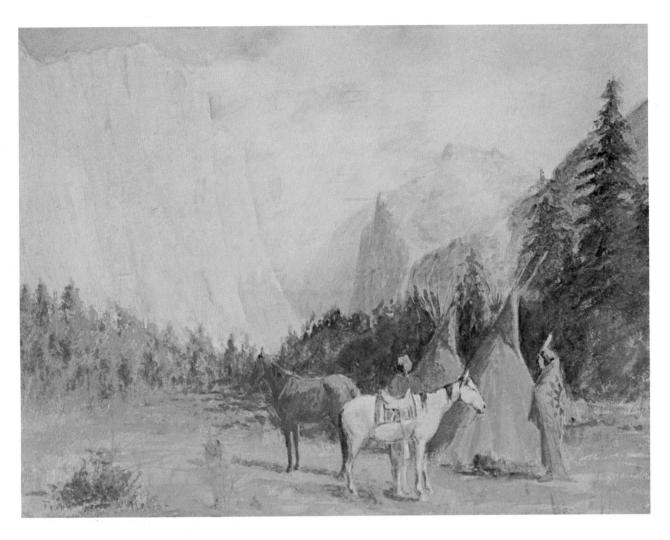

Encampment in Yosemite. 12 ½ x 17 inches, watercolor. Frank Whiteside.

Worthington Whittredge NA
1820–1910

REARED IN THE MIDWEST and trained in Europe, Thomas Worthington Whittredge was one of this country's most prominent Hudson River School landscape artists before turning his talents to the American West.

The artist was born in a log cabin near Springfield, Ohio, the son of a homesteading farmer. He left the farm at the age of seventeen to enter the Cincinnati Art School and financed his studies by working as an apprentice sign and house painter, commercial photographer, and portrait painter.

While in his early twenties, he saw his first Hudson River School painting at an exhibit in Cincinnati. Impressed, he decided to become a landscape artist and within a few years built a local reputation. During this period he lived in Richmond, Virginia, West Virginia, and back in Cincinnati, Ohio.

In 1849, a group of Ohio art patrons, headed by Nicholas Longworth, raised funds to send Whittredge to Europe. He went to Paris and London, before settling at the Royal Academie in Dusseldorf, Germany. He spent four years there and five more in Rome.

When he returned, he opened a studio in New York City and painted landscapes in the Catskill Mountains. His career took a new direction in 1865 when he joined a military expedition led by Major General John Pope. The unit made a 2,000-mile journey by horseback from Fort Leavenworth, Kansas, to Denver, Colorado, Albuquerque and Santa Fe, New Mexico; and back to Fort Riley, Kansas, via the Santa Fe and Cimarron Trails.

On this and subsequent trips west, Whittredge made sketches for paintings that were to become some of the classics of the vast western plains. Unlike most of the artists who concentrated on the majestic Rockies, he found more beauty in the plains and generally painted the mountains only as a background. On a later trip west in 1870, he was accompanied by two other Hudson River School artists, Sanford Gifford and John F. Kensett.

"I had never seen the plains or anything like them," Whittredge once said. "They impressed me deeply. Whoever crossed the plains at that period could hardly fail to be impressed with their vastness and silence and the appearance everywhere of an innocent primitive existence."

Whittredge was elected to the National Academy of Design in 1862. He died at the age of ninety at his home in Summit, New Jersey.

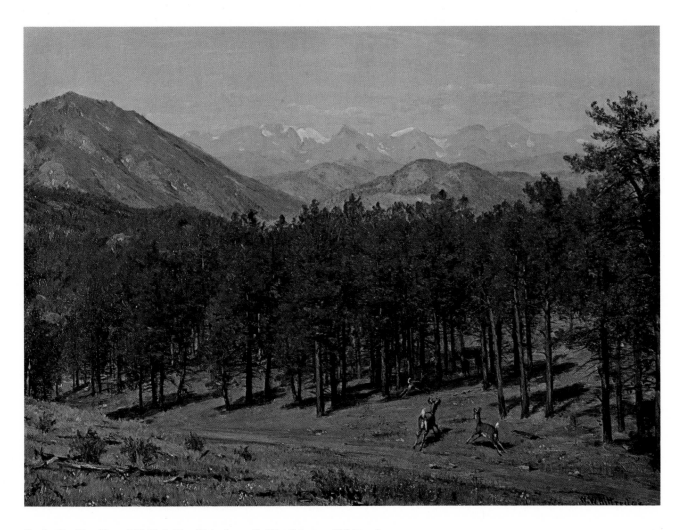

In the Rockies. Dated 1865. 14½ x 20 inches, oil. Worthington Whittredge.

Irving Wiles NA

1861–1948

A MEMBER OF ONE of America's distinguished artist families, Irving Ramsey Wiles is the father of Gladys Wiles, also a distinguished painter, and is the son of Lemuel Maynard Wiles, a noted painter of western America.

Born in Utica, New York, Wiles was raised in New York City. He was famous for his fluid, free way of painting, his bold, slashing techniques, and his use of large canvases. Yet his style also reflected the precise principles of draftsmanship he studied as a boy.

Critics admired his "honesty, sincerity, and devotion to his work," which helped his reputation grow through the years.

Wiles appeared to be headed for a career as a violinist. But he followed his father's footsteps and enrolled at the Art Students League in New York where he was taught by James Carroll Beckwith and William Merritt Chase, who became a lifelong friend.

His career was furthered in 1882 when he went to Paris to study under Carolus-Duran, who taught Wiles to "draw with a brush." A fellow student there was John Singer Sargent.

Returning to New York City, he opened the first of several studios and did magazine and book illustrations. In 1887, he was married to Mary Lee.

Wiles made numerous trips abroad to paint. Eventually, he moved into a New York studio across the hall from the famed Childe Hassam, and later lived year-round at Peronic, Long Island.

Although he painted figure scenes, interiors, landscapes, and still life, Wiles was most famous for his portraits. He painted many of the famous people of the day, including Theodore Roosevelt and actress Julia Marlow. The painting became as famous as the actress herself. His western paintings are few and were no doubt executed under the influence of his father.

He was a small, unassuming man, whose taste was eclectic, and who felt that all truly beautiful things were in harmony. His studios were memorable for their quiet richness throughout. Wiles loved the common people. His hobbies were sailing off Long Island and collecting model ships.

Wiles was elected to the National Academy of Design in 1897 and won numerous awards, including the Medal of Honor in 1943 from the American Artists Professional League.

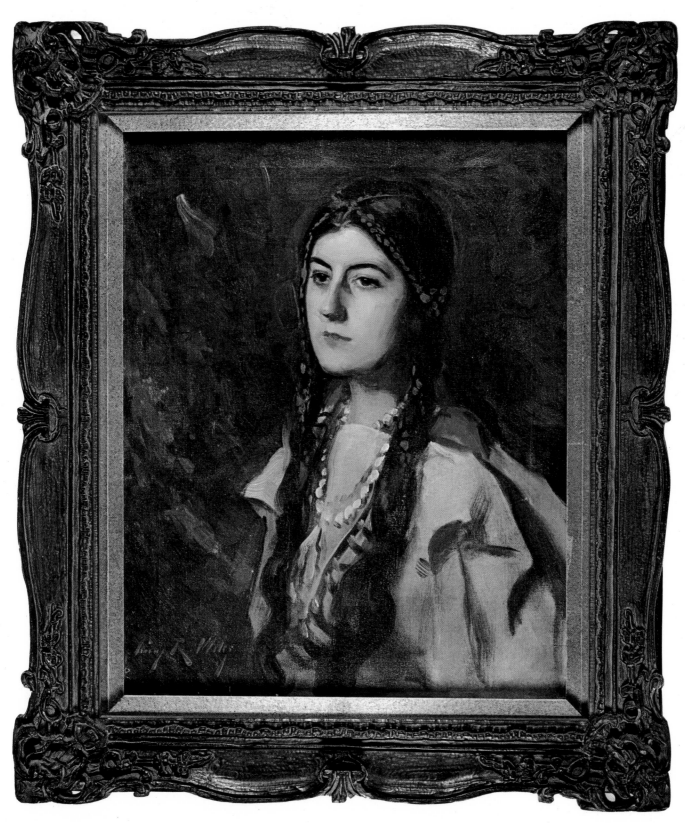

Indian Princess. 22 x 18 inches, oil. Irving Wiles.

Lemuel Wiles

1826–1905

THE FATHER OF Irving R. Wiles, the famed portrait painter, Lemuel Maynard Wiles was a noted artist in his own right and was also a respected teacher who spent many years painting in the West throughout his lifetime.

Wiles was born in Perry, New York, in the Mohawk Valley, the son of Daniel and Nancy Richards Wiles, and the grandson of George Wiles, who had come to the United States from Switzerland.

He was graduated from the New York State Normal School in 1847. For the next three years he studied art under William S. Hart in Albany, New York, and under Jasper F. Cropsey in New York City. During this period, he also taught art at the Albany Academy.

From 1850 through 1857, he concentrated on his painting and in 1854 wed Rachel Ramsey. Son Irving was their only child.

In 1857 Wiles became an art teacher in the Utica, New York, public school. He opened his own art studio in New York City in 1864. It was located in Washington Square, the same building in which painter-inventor Samuel F. B. Morse had a studio. Young Irving Wiles shared this studio with his father for a period of time. The two artists enjoyed a rewarding father-son relationship which was beneficial to both of their careers.

He developed into one of America's most successful landscape painters. In 1873 Wiles visited California and Colorado by way of Panama.

From his home base in New York, he traveled extensively throughout both the United States and Europe and painted many western landscapes.

He accumulated a large number of color studies, which he used for his studio works. The sketches also provided a valuable record of the old mission churches and cathedrals of the West. Some resulted in such paintings as "Ruins of the Cathedral of San Juan Capistrano," "Mount Jacinto," "Sentinel Rock, Yosemite," and "From Inspiration Point, Yosemite." He also did a view of Pikes Peak in Colorado.

Later in life, Wiles accepted more academic assignments. From 1876 to 1888, he was director of the College of Fine Arts at Ingham University at LeRoy, New York, and received a degree from that institution. In 1893, he organized the art department at Peabody College in Nashville, Tennessee.

246 Lemuel Wiles died in New York City.

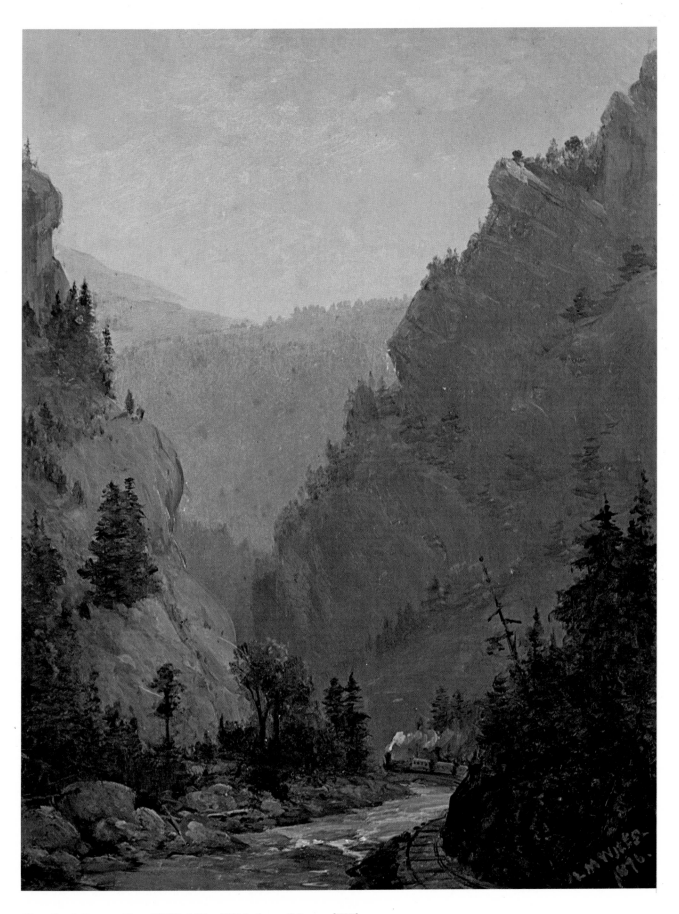

Clear Creek Canyon. Dated 1876. 13½ x 10½ inches, oil. Lemuel Wiles.

Harvey Young

1840–1901

IN HIS OBITUARY and through the years since his death, he has been referred to as Harvey B. Young. In a new book by Patricia Trenton, titled *Harvey Otis Young*, published in 1975, she gives the detailed facts concerning the inconsistency regarding his middle name, which was the result of a mix-up in the family records.

He was born in Lyndon, Vermont, son of Otis Jarvis Young. He graduated from St. Johnsbury Academy. In 1859 Harvey Young went to California to prospect for gold and continue his painting. He established a studio in San Francisco and became quite a reputable painter.

After returning east on the first transcontinental train from the Pacific Coast, he married Josephine Bowyer in 1870. They had a son and three daughters. Soon after they were married, they embarked on the first of six European trips, where he painted the Forest of Fontainbleau, and studied at the Academie Julien and with Dupin and Carolus-Duran in Paris.

In the 1880s, the Youngs moved to Denver, Colorado, to look after his mining interests. There he became involved with the prominent cultural people of the day. He was one of fourteen artists to form a new art society, The Artists Club of Denver, which evolved into the Denver Art Association, establishing its first permanent home in the Chappell House. This was the nucleus of the Denver Art Museum, which was incorporated in 1923.

After losing the bulk of his mining wealth, Young moved to Colorado Springs, Colorado, where he made his home until his death. There he gained recognition for his landscapes, using a new durable medium for painting that he had developed. It embraced the richness of an oil and the delicacy of a watercolor. He covered the completed work with a varnish that he had invented after twelve years of experimentation.

Harvey Young traveled several years in the Rockies with a burro, one of his favorite subjects. Later the Denver and Rio Grande Railroad furnished him with a private studio car, in which he traveled while he painted scenes for the company's advertising literature.

The paintings of Harvey Otis Young have hung in museums in Paris, Washington, D.C., New Orleans, San Francisco, and in Colorado, where he found both fame as an artist and wealth from his mining interests.

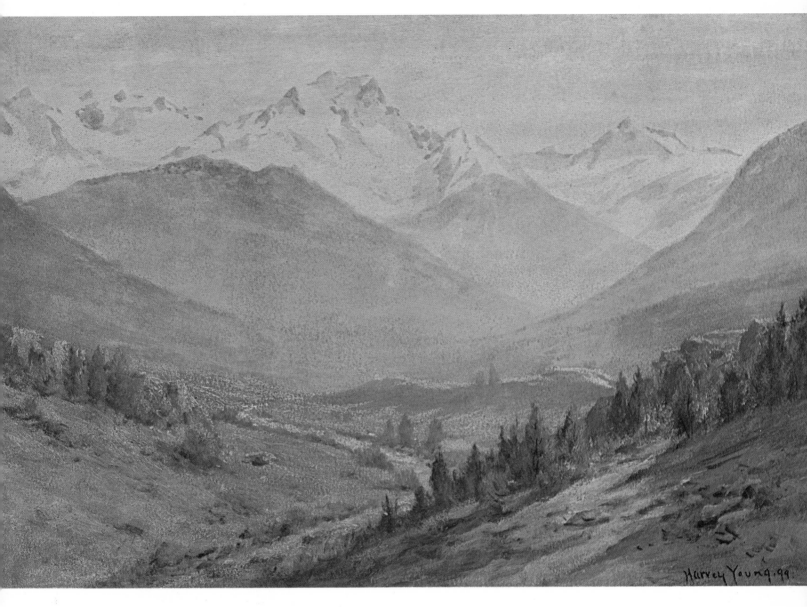

Sultan Mountain from Baker's Park, Colorado.
Dated 1899 22 x 32 inches, mixed media. Harvey Young.

Mahonri Young NA
1877–1957

THE GRANDSON OF BRIGHAM YOUNG, a pioneer leader of the Mormon immigration to Utah, Mahonri Mackintosh Young is best known for the historic works he was commissioned to create for the Church of Latter-Day Saints.

However, during his long and prolific career, he painted hundreds of scenes and subjects throughout the West, and his realistic style earned many outstanding awards. He was a member of the most prominent art societies of the day, including the National Academy of Design.

Young is represented in over fifty museums and galleries in the United States and Europe, and 800 of his sculptures, watercolors, oils, drawings, prints, and sketchbooks are in the Fine Arts Building at Brigham Young University in Provo, Utah.

He was born in Salt Lake City, the son of Mahonri and Agnes Mackintosh Young. As a boy, he molded clay taken from the canal banks near his home. He dropped out of school after the eighth grade to take a job in a stationery store and worked briefly as a newspaper artist for the *Salt Lake Tribune.*

In 1899, he enrolled at the Art Students League in New York City, then attended the Academies Julien, Colarossi, and Delecluse, all in Paris. He also traveled extensively throughout Europe.

Young spent most of his adult life in the East. He had an apartment in New York City and a country home in Ridgefield, Connecticut.

Despite the fact he strayed from the Church as a teenager, the Church commissioned him to do several major works. They included a life-size sculpture of Joseph Smith, church founder, now on Temple Square in Salt Lake City; the frieze design above the main entrance of the Latter-Day Saints Gymnasium; and the Seagull Monument in Temple Square which commemorates the birds that saved the crops of Brigham Young's followers from a grasshopper plague in 1848. His full-size statue of Brigham Young, done in Carrara marble, stands in the rotunda of the United States Capitol in Washington, D.C.

He was married twice, in 1907 to Cecilia Sharp in Salt Lake City, who died in 1917, and in 1931 to Dorothy Weir of New York City, daughter of artist J. Alden Weir. She died in 1947.

Young was survived by a son, Mahonri Sharp Young, who has gained fame as a writer, and a daughter, Mrs. Oliver Lay.

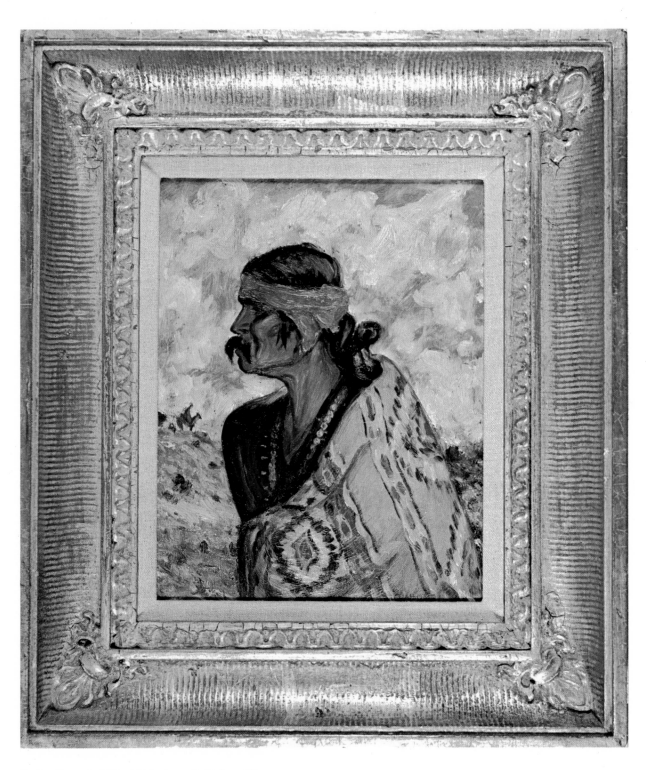

Indian Portrait. 10½ x 8½ inches, oil. Mahonri Young.

CHRONOLOGICAL LIST OF THE ARTISTS

1796–1872	George Catlin	1855–1933	Olaf Grafstrom
1811–1893	John Casilear, NA	1856–1935	Manuel Valencia
1813–1896	Thomas Hinckley	1857–1920	Mathias Sandor
1819–1889	James Walker	1857–1932	Fernand Lungren
1819–1895	Charles Lanman, ANA	1858–1930	Julius Rolshoven, ANA
1820–1910	Worthington Whittredge, NA	1859–1932	Elliott Daingerfield, NA
1822–1888	Felix Darley, NA	1860–1942	Edwin Deming
1826–1898	Ernest Narjot	1861–1909	Frederic Remington, ANA
1826–1905	Lemuel Wiles	1861–1912	Charles Schreyvogel, ANA
1830–1909	Victor Nehlig, NA	1861–1938	Charles Hittell
1832–1920	Samuel Colman, NA	1861–1944	Cyrus Dallin, NA
1835–Unknown	Theodore Baur	1861–1948	Irving Wiles, NA
1836–1899	Ransom Holdredge	1862–1917	Amedee Joullin
1836–1912	Howard Streight	1862–1937	Will Sparks
1838–1893	Joseph Hitchins	1865–1922	Karl Kauba
1840–1901	Harvey Young	1866–1929	Frank Whiteside
1840–1903	August Becker	1866–1938	Paul Troubetskoy
1840–1921	George Smillie, NA	1866–1943	Sheldon Parsons
1842–Unknown	Harry Learned	1866–1952	Albert Groll, NA
1843–1907	Edward Kemeys	1868–1913	Louis Akin
1843–1921	Cassilly Adams	1868–1947	Chauncey Ryder, NA
1844–1889	Jules Tavernier	1869–1949	Henry Keller, ANA
1844–1919	Thad Welch	1870–1941	Frederick Weygold
1845–1931	Charles Stobie	1871–1910	Frank Sauerwein
1846–1901	Julian Scott, ANA	1871–1951	John Sloan
1846–1933	William H. Holmes	1871–1955	Joseph Imhof
1847–1884	Henry Elkins	1874–1940	F. Luis Mora, NA
1847–1916	Henry Farny	1875–1934	Harrison Fisher, NA
1850–1903	Julian Rix	1876–1949	Paul Gregg
1852–1941	James E. Stuart	1877–1943	Marsden Hartley
1853–1934	Richard Tallant	1877–1943	William P. Henderson
1854–1940	Charles Fries	1877–1950	Stanley Arthurs
1855–1919	Gilbert Gaul, NA	1877–1957	Mahonri Young, NA

1877–1972	Frank Schoonover	1892–1960	Dean Cornwell, NA
1878–1938	W. H. D. Koerner	1892–1962	Leal Mack
1878–1955	B. J. O. Nordfeldt	b. 1893	Joseph Fleck
1878–1957	Maurice Sterne, NA	1894–1950	Harold Bryant
1879–1939	F. Grayson Sayre	1894–1963	Ward Lockwood
1879–1962	Charles S. Chapman, NA	1895–1976	Emil Bisttram
1881–1935	Philip Goodwin	1896–1969	A. L. Ripley
1881–1955	Allen True	b. 1897	Fremont Ellis
1881–1967	Waldo Love	b. 1897	Donald Teague, NA
1881–1971	Gustave Baumann	1898–1943	Willard Nash
1882–1956	Homer Boss	1899–1956	Leonard Reedy
1882–1963	Henry Balink	1900–1955	Russell V. Hunter
1882–1964	James Sessions	1901–1958	Alfred Morang
1883–1942	Walter Mruk	1901–1962	Herndon Davis
1884–1914	Donald Beauregard	b. 1902	Fred Harman
1885–1951	Gray Bartlett	b. 1902	Louis Ribak
1885–1961	Clarence Ellsworth	1904–1954	Cady Wells
1886–1969	Paul Burlin	b. 1908	Charles du Tant
1886–1972	Roy Mason, NA AWS	b. 1908	Vladan Stiha
1886–1975	Conrad Buff	1910–1941	Earle Heikka
1887–1958	Tom Benrimo	b. 1915	Marjorie Reed
1888–1977	Dan Muller	b. 1916	Conrad Schwiering
b. 1889	Dirk van Driest	b. 1923	Pawel Kontny
1890–1964	Theodore Van Soelen, NA	b. 1930	James Turpen, Jr.
b. 1890	Frances Greenman	b. 1930	Fritz White, CA
b. 1890	Adrien Voisin	b. 1934	Bill Sharer
1891–1955	Pruett Carter	b. 1936	Wolfgang Pogzeba
1891–1977	Jozef Bakos	b. 1938	Clarence McGrath
b. 1891	Raymond Jonson	b. 1939	Glenna Goodacre
1892–1942	Will James		

SELECTED BIBLIOGRAPHY

Ainsworth, Ed. *Painters of the Desert.* Palm Desert, Calif.: Desert Magazine Publishers, 1960.

Amaral, Anthony. *Will James, The Gilt Edged Cowboy.* Los Angeles: Westernlore Press, 1967.

The Art Students League of New York, 1875-1975. New York: The Adams Group, 1975.

Barker, Virgil. *American Painting: History and Interpretation.* New York: Macmillan Co., 1951.

Berger, John A. *Fernand Lungren.* Santa Barbara, Calif.: The Shauer Press, 1936.

Boswell, Peyton, Jr. *Modern American Painting.* New York: Dodd, Mead and Company, 1939.

The Britannica Encyclopedia of American Art. New York: Chanticleer Press, Inc.

Broder, Patricia Janis. *Bronzes of the American West.* New York: Harry N. Abrams.

Broekhoff, Helen V. *Thad Welch, Pioneer and Painter.* Oakland, Calif.: Oakland Art Museum, 1966.

Bryant, Lorinda Munson. *American Pictures and Their Painters.* New York: Press of J. J. Little and Ives and Company, 1917.

Canaday, John. *Mainstreams of Modern Art.* New York: Simon and Schuster, 1959.

————. *The Lives of the Painters.* New York: W. W. Norton & Co., Inc., 1969.

Carlson, Raymond. *Gallery of Western Paintings.* New York: McGraw Hill, 1951.

Chapman, Ada B. *Memoirs of Charles S. Chapman, NA.* Dumont, N. J.: Koval Press, 1964.

Cheney, Sheldon. *The Story of Modern Art.* New York: Viking Press, 1941.

————. *A Primer of Modern Art.* New York: Liveright, 1958.

Clark, Edna Maria. *Ohio Art and Artists.* Richmond, Va.: Garrett and Massie, 1932.

The Cleveland Museum of Art. *The Henry G. Keller Memorial Exhibition.* Cleveland: Artcraft Printing Company, 1950.

Coke, Van Deren. *Taos and Santa Fe: The Artist's Environment, 1882-1942.* Albuquerque: University of New Mexico Press, 1963.

————. *Nordfeldt The Painter.* Albuquerque: University of New Mexico Press, 1972.

Craven, Wayne. *Sculpture in America.* New York: Thomas Y. Crowell Company, 1968.

Dawdy, Doris Ostrander. *Artists of the American West.* Chicago: Swallow Press, 1974.

254

Earle, Helen L. *Biographical Sketches of American Artists*. Charleston, S.C.: Garnier and Company, 1972.

Eddy, Arthur Jerome. *Cubists and Post-Impressionism*. Chicago: A. C. McClurg and Co., 1914.

Eliot, Alexander. *Three Hundred Years of American Painting*. New York: Time Inc., 1957.

Ewers, John C. *Artists of the Old West*. Garden City, N.Y.: Doubleday and Co., 1965.

Fielding, Mantle. *Dictionary of American Painters, Sculptors and Engravers*. Lancaster, Pa.: Lancaster Press, 1926.

Flexner, James Thomas. *The Pocket History of American Painting*. New York: Washington Square Press, 1966.

Garman, Ed. *The Art of Raymond Jonson, Painter*. Albuquerque: University of New Mexico Press, 1976.

Getlein, Frank, and the Editors of Country Beautiful. *The Lure of the Great West*. Waukesha, Wis.: Country Beautiful Corporation.

Greenman, Frances Cranmer. *Higher Than The Sky*. New York: Harper and Brothers, 1954.

Groce, George C., David H. Wallace. *The New York Historical Society's Dictionary of Artists in America, 1564–1860*. New Haven, Conn.: Yale University Press, 1966.

Gussow, Allan. *A Sense of Place, Volume I*. New York: The Saturday Review Press.

Hamilton, Sinclair. *Early American Book Illustrators and Wood Engravers, 1670–1870, 2 vols*. Princeton, N.J.: Princeton University Press, 1968.

Haseltine, James L. *100 Years of Utah Painting*. Salt Lake City, Utah: Wheelwright Lithographing Company, 1965.

Hassrick, Royal B. *Western Painting Today*. New York: Watson-Guptill, 1975.

Hobbs, Robert. *Elliott Daingerfield*. Charlotte, N. C.: Associated Printing Company, 1971.

Hooper, Donelson. *The American Impressionists*. New York: Watson-Guptill, 1972.

Howat, John K. *The Hudson River and its Painters*. New York: Viking Press, 1972.

Kelley, James L., Lee S. Monroe. *Roy M. Mason*. San Diego, Calif.: Frye and Smith.

Look, Al. *Harold Bryant*. Denver, Colo.: Golden Bell Press, 1962.

Luhan, Mabel Dodge. *Taos and Its Artists*. New York: Duell, Sloan and Pearce, 1947.

Maher, Elaine. *Frank Paul Sauerwein, Panhandle-Plains Historical Review*. Canyon, Texas: Panhandle-Plains Historical Society, 1960.

McCracken, Harold. *Portrait of the Old West*. New York: McGraw-Hill Book Co., 1952.

255

_____. *The Frederick Remington Book.* Garden City, N.Y.: Doubleday & Company, Inc. 1966.

Moure, Nancy Dustin Wall. *Dictionary of Art and Artists in Southern California Before 1930.* Los Angeles: Dustin Publications, 1975.

Olson, Ernest W. *History of The Swedes of Illinois.* Chicago: The Engberg-Holmberg Publishing Company, 1908.

Pitz, Henry C. *The Brandywine Tradition.* Boston: Houghton, Mifflin Company, 1969.

Pourade, Richard F. *The Colorful Butterfield Overland Stage.* Palm Desert, Calif.: Best-West Publications, 1966.

Price, Vincent. *Treasury of American Art.* Waukesha, Wis.: Country Beautiful Corporation, 1972.

Reed, Walt. *The Illustrator in America: 1900–1960's.* New York: Reinhold Publishing Corp., 1966.

Reeves, James F. *Gilbert Gaul.* Huntsville, Ala.: Monroe Printing Company, 1975.

Robertson, Edna, and Sarah Nestor. *Artists of the Canyons and Caminos.* Salt Lake City, Utah: Peregrine Smith, Inc., 1976.

Samuels, Peggy and Harold. *The Illustrated Biographical Encyclopedia of Artists of the American West.* Garden City, N.Y.: Doubleday and Company, Inc., 1976.

Taft, Robert. *Artists and Illustrators of the Old West, 1850–1900.* New York: Charles Scribner's Sons, 1953.

Taylor, Francis Henry. *Fifty Centuries of Art.* New York: Harper and Bros., 1954.

Trenton, Patricia. *Harvey Otis Young.* Denver, Colo.: Denver Art Museum, 1975.

Tuckerman, Henry T. *Book of the Artists.* New York: James F. Carr, 1967.

Wakefield, Robert. *Schwiering and the West.* Aberdeen, S.D.: North Plains Press, 1973.

Wearin, Otha Donner. *Clarence Ellsworth, Artist of the Old West.* Shenandoah, Iowa. World Publishing Company, 1967.

Young, Mahonri Sharp. *The Eight.* New York: Watson-Guptill, 1973.